# The Woods and the Sea

# THE WOODS
# AND
# THE SEA

*Wilderness and Seacoast Adventures*

*in the State of Maine*

## DUDLEY CAMMETT LUNT

*Drawings by*

### HENRY B. KANE

1 9     6 5

*NEW YORK:* ALFRED·A·KNOPF

# ACKNOWLEDGMENTS

Some of the material used in this book has appeared in somewhat different form in the Wilmington (Delaware) *Morning News* and the *Portland* (Maine) *Evening Express*. The courtesy of their editors is hereby acknowledged. The passage describing Number Five Bog, quoted on page 201, is from the author's *Thousand Acre Marsh* (Macmillan, 1959), and the description of the seventeenth-century fishing station on Richmond Island, page 226, is from *The Maritime History of Maine* by William H. Rowe (Norton, 1948). Acknowledgment is hereby made to both publishers for permission to quote from these two works.

*L. C. catalog card number: 64–19098*

---

THIS IS A BORZOI BOOK,
PUBLISHED BY ALFRED A. KNOPF, INC.

---

FIRST EDITION

# Foreword

"WHAT A PLACE to live, what a place to die and be buried in! There certainly men would live forever, and laugh at death and the grave."

Thus did Thoreau, upon the conclusion of the account of his excursion to Mt. Ktaadn, apostrophize the Maine woods.

Maine has ever been a place apart. No man knows when its rugged fir-crowned coast was first used by white men. For a century and more it was our earliest and now forgotten frontier. To this day, more than any other area in the east, it has retained the primeval character of its woods and its waters. It is pre-eminently a place for a man to come from and a place for him to go.

The State of Maine. Why is it in popular parlance always so called? The reason, which takes its rise out of the root of things, was for generations obscured by a curious assertion of the first historian of Maine, James Sullivan. In April 1639 Charles the First in a grant to Sir Ferdinando Gorges proclaimed that this portion of the mainland should thereafter be called the Province of Maine. In 1795 Sullivan made a flat pronouncement that this name derived from that of the French province. This, he asserted, was in compliment to the royal consort, Henrietta Maria, whose family owned it.

The years passed. Then one day in the late nineteenth century an important document came to light. This was a grant by the Council of New England to Gorges and Mason of ". . . all that part of ye Maine land in New England lying upon ye Sea Coast betwixt ye rivers of Merrimack and Sagadahock . . . which said . . . lands [the grantees] intend to name ye province of Maine." Since this document was dated 1622, some three years prior to Charles's marriage, it knocked James Sullivan's theory galley west.

But why Maine? Today, when a fisherman on the island of Matinicus, at the entrance to Penobscot Bay, crosses over to Rockland to sell his lobsters, he speaks of going over "to the Main." In the early seventeenth century this usage was widely current. "This Maine," wrote the chronicler of Bartholomew Gosnold's voyage on the coast of Maine in 1602, "is the goodliest continent." And so you will find it in Rosier's *Relation*, where he speaks in 1605 of "trending alongst into the Maine," also in Captain John Smith's celebrated pamphlet on New England, in Purchas, and many another contemporary record.

This name—the Province of Maine—persisted long after Massachusetts acquired the Province in the late seventeenth century and it lasted until 1778. In that year the Continental Congress, in prophetic anticipation of the admiralty jurisdiction of the Federal courts, by a resolution assumed appellate jurisdiction of all admiralty causes. To this end Massachusetts was divided into three districts. The most easterly was that of Maine. And so, for a generation and more, down-east ships and men hailed from the District of Maine. Thus, when the separation from Massachusetts took place and Maine was admitted to the Union in 1820, what was more natural than that the phrase—the State of Maine —should attach by right of immemorial usage. There you have it in direct descent: The Province of Maine—the District of Maine—the State of Maine.

All of this is exemplified by the colloquial phrases that have grown with the years. Take, for example, the phrase "East of Boston." This derives from the old and familiar beckoning phrase—down east. To a State of Maine man this colloquialism has a tincture of Boston in it. He is right. Put yourself back into the eighteenth century. There are no railroads, no motors at all, and no roads to speak of. The sea, that is the broad highway. Now, when you cleared Boston

harbor for any port on the coast of Maine, how did you lay
your course? Due east, of course. And the chances are with
the prevailing winds you would be sailing downwind ahead
of a following sea. Thus, when a man headed from Boston
for the coast of Maine, he went down east. If he hailed from
there he was, in the eye of the Bostonian, a down-easter.
And that, by God, was—as they say in the Penobscot country—just exactly as it should be.

In a very real sense this book is an account of one man's
ecology. For it is a recording of the interaction from time to
time during six decades between myself and my environment along the coast and in the woods of Maine. Thus its
pattern is chronological.

I am one who likes links with the past. The continuity
they suggest goes a long way toward making a lifetime of
effort quite worth the doing, whether it be viewed in prospect
or in retrospect. They give point and validity to an old New
England motto that couched in seventeenth-century terms
and concepts tells us: Any man ought to serve God in such
a way whereto He hath best fitted him by nature, education,
or gifts, or by graces acquired. This, in modern parlance, is
very simply to say that the end of living is to function, and
that, to the utmost of a man's capacity.

This book, then, has its roots in the past. My exposure to
a habitat in the State of Maine was no accident. It was the
result of separate strains of inheritance, having their common source in the life of the settlements that here and there
were fringes between the dark forest and the coast of New
England in the seventeenth century. In that early day the
"Main," in addition to being the site of fishing stations of
West Country fishermen that were lively, going concerns
long before Plymouth became a landfall for the Pilgrims,
was destined to become the frontier of waves of migration
out of the scattered settlements along the shore of Massa-
chutts Bay.

*Foreword*

To this day, these diverse strains of inheritance are to be found in many of the inhabitants of the Province, the District, and the State of Maine.

Among my earliest recollections in this span of remembrance is an excursion up-country—as they still say in Maine —to the village of Limerick. Here on a farm there dwelt uncles, aunts, and cousins galore, the offshoots of a migration out of Newburyport in the early 1800's. Nestling amid the foothills of the White Mountains, Limerick lay beyond the range of modern transportation. The train from Portland took us only as far as Waterboro. Thence we went on an old crown road by stagecoach. This was sixty years ago.

It was a memorable journey. I remember the musty smell of the old damp mildewed leather, the deep dark interior, the ponderous swaying of the heavy coach, the dust, and the *clop clop* of the hooves of the horses. Later, when as a special favor I was passed up to sit beside the driver, there were the lunging backs of the four-horse team, the long reins, the whip that now and again circled out ahead and cracked, and the rough and hearty integrity of the ancient driver.

Not so long ago, while in flight over the Atlantic, as the jet plane I was in coursed westward along the coast of Maine, which in the light of the false dawn could be dimly seen far below, I listened spellbound to the broadcast report of the course of a man in orbit around the sphere. He and his ship had been thrust aloft as we had been passing the coast of Labrador. Before we reached our destination in Philadelphia, his excursion had been completed and he had pitched into the Caribbean. To have heard the account of this exploit in this manner was a considerable experience.

In the six decades that lie between that stagecoach and this jet plane, I have had many experiences in the State of Maine. A few of them are recorded in this account.

DUDLEY CAMMETT LUNT

# Contents

*The* Woods *and the* Sea

# Grayhurst

By the time the early days of the Civil War had rolled around, my grandfather's dry-goods business, which he had started a couple of decades before, having prospered, he decided that the time had come to establish himself in permanent residence. So in traditional American fashion he acquired in the west end of town what is now three quarters of a city block.

Something of the state of the economy of the time and of its social structure may be gleaned from two facts. Among the title papers that record this transaction there is one purchasing for small considerations the rights of several persons in the neighborhood to come on his land and draw their water from a well. Also, to the westward, where nowadays there range block after block of residences, extended open fields adjacent to an old farmhouse said to have been there since before the Revolution. It alone broke their contour on the western horizon.

My grandfather, whose property fronted the south on what was still referred to by the older inhabitants of the town as "the mast ro'd to Boston," proceeded to cut a street through from there, as his westerly bound. This he named for himself—Storer Street—and it ran the full length of the block up to his northerly bound along Spring Street, where there was a turntable for the horsecars.

How or from whence he acquired the name Grayhurst for his mansion is now lost in the dim recesses of the past. Whatever its origin, the name perfectly fitted the large square house of gray-painted brick that he built upon an eminence rising from the edge of a sheer bluff and overlooking the upper harbor. Out of the cupola standing at the center of the four slopes of slate that comprised the roof, the vistas carried the eye out across the blue sea in the east and away to the rugged contours of the White Mountains in the west.

The grounds were spacious. Between granite pillars on which there swung wide iron gates, a driveway entered from Danforth Street, and, curving on either hand, came full circle before wide granite steps that led to the tall front door on the columned portico. Within the oval thereby enclosed and in the corners thus cut off, there towered magnificent shade trees—beech, copper and silver-gray, several elms, a great wide-spreading linden, catalpa, cut-leaf birch, and a pair of Norway spruce. At regular intervals rosebushes spotted the sides of the circular drive.

This driveway likewise encircled the house. At the rear it led to the stable, the greenhouse, and the carriage house. In front of the stable, from a log slung high and connecting the yokes of two tall wine-cup elms, descended the ropes of a swing of Gargantuan proportions. Opposite the stable and facing on Storer Street stood my grandfather's hothouse, and here, too, there was an entrance for carriages that linked with the circular driveway.

Here lay the edge of his orchard, with its regular aisles of apple and pear trees, peach and plum. Through the center of it there led straight as a die toward Spring Street a gravel walk bordered by long narrow beds of begonias. Midway, with this path parting to surround it, stood a circular fountain. Then beyond, at the end, and shaded on either side by mountain ashes with their spectacular orange and red berries, was an ornate entrance, an arch, a wooden gate and latch.

There was another fountain, a smaller one, to the west of the house and between it and Storer Street. Here, enclasped within the points of two crescent-shaped beds of pale white tea roses, a naked urchin of Rubensian shape and proportions was to be seen struggling ceaselessly with a fat dolphin in his arms which spouted a triple column of spraying water. The sprays fell into three scalloped basins at the foot of the boy and from them overflowed into a large circular basin below. As the roses waned, their pink and white and red petals were scattered on the surface of the water, to be wafted to and fro by the cat's-paws like miniature argosies.

The fountains and the roses at Grayhurst were well known and have been long remembered.

Every month in the year had its own attribute; June was

the month of blossoms. Intimately is it associated in my mind with the roses of Grayhurst. I recall a particular bush, one of a multitude set out by my grandfather, who had thought himself a fancier and so became one. This bush grew with others arranged at regular intervals around the large circular driveway. As I write these lines on the thirteenth of June—my mother's birthday—I recall that this was the day that, year in and year out, this bush was the first to bloom. Always that single blossom was of a clear deep red. Pearled with dew its bud greeted the dawn, all day long its blossom was admired, and at nightfall it was plucked and transferred to a vase to stand as the harbinger of the beauty that was soon to come.

I no longer see rose gardens like those of my grandfather. Perhaps there is a different fashion as to how they should be constructed. I do not know. In addition to those roses that bloomed like gems set in the circle of the drive, I recall the two great oval, high-mounded beds that lay between the two branches of the driveway leading to and from the stable. These roses of Grayhurst had a local fame, and in this month of June people came from the neighborhood and up from the town to see the great nodding blossoms mounting in a gentle curve to the center of the beds.

I remember the end of a Memorial Day. I was seated in an upper window watching the long flag hanging aslant from its pole over the driveway, its bottom curling and uncurling in slight undulations stirred by the rise and fall of the breeze. The evening was dark and its silence was broken by the distant *clop clop* of a horse on a dirt road. An utterly peaceful moment, this was when time stood still and seemed to hang in the balance.

I remember, too, the ice storms, of all the sights of winter incomparably the most beautiful. Late in the winter they came. The night before when I went to bed, snow would be falling silently. The tone of the town bells was muted, and borne from afar came the monotonous *haarrunk* of the fog-horn. Then while I slept the miracle occurred. First rain, next a freeze, and finally the clearing before dawn.

Then, with the light of the rising sun streaming in my window, I looked out on a true and unforgettable fairyland. The trees were the sight of sights. There was the cut-leaf birch, a shimmering cluster of crystals in the early sunlight. There was the elm that towered, caparisoned in glistening ice through which the bark shone black. Here before me was a crystal world that tinkled faintly and creaked as a slight breeze swayed the ice-encased branches. Shafts of brilliant light gleamed from these bejeweled trees. And tragedy there was too—the frozen body of a sparrow at the end of its pitiful curved trail marking a half circle on the crust.

Then with the watching this magical world began to come apart. As the sun mounted, the ice started to melt, and I walked to school beneath shimmering arbors of ice-laden foliage amid a shower of falling crystals. By noon the miracle had ceased to exist. The world was a familiar one again. Only the memory remained.

Of the spring of the year, one of my earliest recollections is of a bird's nest—a beautiful pendent globule skillfully contrived of grasses which hung swaying from an outermost branch of the elm in front of the house. Here a pair of Baltimore orioles, known to my grandfather as golden robins, would foregather in May, mate, and rear their young. Particularly do I recall their liquidly whistled calls and their forays into the top of the nearby cherry tree. There, teetering on an upper branch, in a flashing of orange and black amid the green of leaf and the sparkle of the red, yellow, and black cherries, they would leave the gashes of their beaks in the ripest of the fruit.

My knowledge of my grandfather is a mixture of recollection and tradition so intertwined that it is hard to say where one ends and the other takes off. My earliest remembrance of the old gentleman is that he sported a large and luxuriant white beard. He was very proud of his collection of paintings, and in the course of a daily peregrination to look at them, on which I was borne in his arms, I used to plunge my small fists into the crisp recesses of this splendid hairy appendage, and clutch and pull. This was rare sport, fully enjoyed by both participants.

Among the legends that have descended to me is one that starts from the premise that in his boyhood Grandfather was inordinately fond of cucumbers. He was born in 1822, and in his boyhood, life on a York County farm in the State of Maine was a sparse and spartan affair.

Two causes, one universal and the other particular, underlay this state of affairs. The particular cause was my grandfather's father. He was the village banker. Again in the field of legend: it appears that at the Sunday night prayer meeting an old lady arose to descant in a wavering voice upon her vision of her home in heaven, whereupon from a back seat came: "You better not let John Storer hear of it. He'll git a mortgage on it."

Something further of the tincture of the life and times of my grandfather's boyhood may be glimpsed in the fact that his father bequeathed to his descendants life memberships in the American Abolitionist Society. *Clarum et venerabile nomen.*

Understandably, my grandfather's attitude toward things paternal and genealogical was a bit irreverent. Once his daughter, remarking upon the presence of coats-of-arms in the parlors of her contemporaries, commented on the absence of one in his household. My grandfather is reliably reported to have observed that while he had never heard of one in the family, he knew exactly what it ought to portray. My mother took hold of the butt end of this one and asked: "What?"

"The town pump and a barrel of rum," responded the old gentleman.

But there is nothing legendary about the universal cause of the sparse and spartan character of my grandfather's boyhood. This state of affairs lasted down into my own boyhood. Alas, I knew it well.

On the western coast of Maine in the early days of this century, just as in the 1830's, you never saw a green vegetable on the table from the middle of September to the middle of June. Nine months is a long time to go without even the sight of a green pea, or a crisp leaf of lettuce, or my grandfather's favorite vegetable, a fresh cucumber. The one substitute was that steaming mess of foul-smelling, nauseating greenness—spinach.

These then were the conditions that gave rise to my grandfather's hothouse. The reason for it, he is reported often to have remarked, was so he could have a "mess of fresh cukes" whenever he wanted them.

A laudable ambition this, and he achieved it.

The hothouse faced on Storer Street. Inside the door, the panes of which jangled when it was opened or shut, there was a chunk stove. Here in frames were nurtured by James Jennings, the English gardener, the cucumbers and tomatoes so relished by my grandfather. But overhead was the glory of glories. On a trellis of wood and wire just below the panes of glass, there stretched through the hothouse a canopy of green leaves. Half-hidden in the foliage, pendent in clustering bunches, were the grapes.

These are indeed well remembered—the deep dark purple of the black Hamburgs, the rich red of those known as West of England. And there was a green grape of the lushest hue, its name, alas, now lost. At table they overflowed the lattice-like china fruit dish; in cutting the stems my grandfather always used the grape scissors with his name engraved on them.

Well remembered, too, is the tale of an election night—of how a torchlight parade of stalwart Republicans filed up Storer Street past a greenhouse wherein lighted candles flickered amid the leaves and gleamed through the panes— and of how the marchers cheered this illumination in their honor.

There still exists a picture of those grapes—three great luscious bunches, one of each, hung by a scarlet cord against a palette of wood. These my grandfather had painted by an artist who came and lived at Grayhurst. In the lower part of the oval canvas there is caught in falling a single oval red grape—one of the West of England.

After his hothouse and his roses, the great love of my grandfather's later life was his orchard. In its time this orchard was not in any way unique. At the turn of the century almost every house in the neighborhood had its complement of fruit trees. They were set out in lines stretching from the rear of the house to the tall wooden fence that marked the bound of the back yard. Fruits, fresh and preserved, from one's own orchard—this was in the natural order of things.

There was another adjunct to the orchard at Grayhurst. This was the cold cellar, a hidden fastness deep within the bowels of the cavernous cellar. A small boy carrying a guttering candle through the murk would find his way to this mysterious dungeon through long, dark, drafty passages and around terrifying turns. If the candle went out, he would stand shivering with fright and cold until with shaking fingers he lit it again.

The cold cellar was near the center of the house and long wooden ducts carried the outside air into it and out again. Deliciously cool in the heat of summer, in the winter it was stone cold. All around the bricked-in enclosure, into which a single whitewashed door opened, were ranged wooden shelves. Here the apples and pears were stored, great care being taken that they did not touch one another. If they did, that was a certain cause of their rotting. I remember trips to this dark cold room in company with my father, who went down often to pick out his own Baldwins and Seckel pears.

In the latter days of my grandfather's life, the drivers and conductors of the horsecar line on Spring Street became the bane of his existence. It was their custom to take their nooning at the end of the line. After the car had been hauled onto the turntable, they would unhitch the horse and turn her out to pasture in the neighboring fields. Next, with both of them heaving on the bar, the car was swung on the turntable until its empty shafts pointed downtown. Then the driver would seat himself on the front and the conductor on the rear steps, and they would eat their sandwiches.

From this vantage they enjoyed a fine view of Grandfather's orchard with its orderly rows of apple and pear, peach and plum trees, and amid them, scatterings of quince and crab apple and cherry trees. In the wine-like air of late May, the aisles of the orchard were green canopies burgeoning with pink and white blossoms. Then, as summer wore away into autumn, their fruits would come on to ripen.

The cherries were the first—in the late days of June— little round globes of yellow and orange, of red and dark purple. Grandfather had two superb cherry trees. One was safe from the depredations of the horsecar men; it stood hard by the southeast corner of the house. The other my grandfather secured against their raids in characteristic fashion by wrapping the trunk to a considerable height with barbed wire.

This did not, however, deter the urchins of the town, and for them my grandfather applied another remedy then in vogue for all manner of juvenile delinquency. It was a sight to be seen—a tearful youth descending gingerly over the encircling barbed wire with a backside well exposed to the by-no-means-tender applications of a stout switch in the hands of my irate grandfather. In my own latter days I have encountered certain of the sober citizenry of the town, male and female, who confessed to a keen recollection of my grandfather's switch. And their recollections invariably included the excellence of his cherries.

Albeit he forebore actually to apply this form of deterrent to the horsecar men, he was wont to appear in his orchard around midday for a short walk, and curiously enough, it would appear that he had just come in from exercising his Morgans, for he always had his horsewhip in his hand. This to my grandmother seemed a bit unseemly, so there was also a generous gesture. A bushel basket of windfalls was set out conspicuously handy to the turntable.

But when the basket disappeared and it was reliably reported by the grapevine that a certain family down on Center Street was preserving peaches—MY peaches, quoth Grandfather—he resorted to sterner tactics. Another bushel basket of windfalls was set out, but this time a watch was set, from a window in the carriage house.

In the upshot, when two stout forms were seen in the upper branches of an apple tree, a constable in the company of my grandfather made the arrests. And in the ensuing litigation, damages were assessed for the trespass, for the basket, and for the apples. Thereafter, so the tale ran, the streetcar men were content to help themselves from the basket of windfalls.

Of all the trees in the orchard I particularly remember the crab-apple tree. There are two reasons for this, the one related to the other. Since I was inordinately fond of crabapple jelly, it always fell to my lot to pick the crab apples. The tree was a tall one and the apples were small, the size of oversized marbles, and golden yellow in color. But, oh, the profusion of their growth! They so weighted down the limbs that they would break if great care was not taken in the harvesting.

My method was simplicity itself. I would spread several old sheets on the ground around the tree, and then gently shake the lower branches, one after another, with a long pole. Later, when the risk of splintering the limbs had been diminished, I would shinny up the trunk and climb into the topmost branches. Then, with recurrent shakings, a veritable torrent of crab apples would descend, and woe betide any luckless wight who stood beneath. At the end of the operation, the apples were rolled into the center of the sheets and then scooped up into bushel baskets.

The pay-off was the jelly—great trays of glasses through which the afternoon sun, slightly filtered, made of the jelly luminous molds of translucent amber. The sight has not lost its charm to the present day, for a glass of clear jelly standing in the sunlight still arrests my eye, and carries my mind back to my grandfather's crab-apple tree.

And when I was but a sprout the two great cherry trees had grown to what is now recalled to be stupendous heights. In one of them my interest was slight for the festooned rounds of barbed wire precluded my ascent. But that other tree stood near the house and it sheltered one of those old-fashioned summerhouses—a structure that I once heard a visting lady from Boston call "the gazebo."

Therein lay the trick. Perched on the rail of the gazebo, and between its sculptured uprights, a small boy gifted with a certain dexterity would catch his breath and then leap forth to grab "a holt" with both hands on an outspreading limb of the cherry tree. Then I swung my short legs up and cocked them around a branch. A heave and a grunt and there I was, up on the limb.

Slowly I crept in toward the trunk. It was an enormous trunk, not for circling by the legs of a small boy, and it required skillful maneuvering to climb, hoisting my belly over the protruding bumps and squirming up over the stout limbs. I remember the congealed sap, how it stuck out in yellow globules like bits of translucent amber against the black bark. Finally I edged myself aloft. The ground was hidden below and I was hidden from the sight of all and sundry amid the green leaves.

Here in the top grew the ripest cherries—yellow, red, and black orbs of burnished brilliance gleaming in the green and exuding a faint exotic odor. I had but to reach out and pluck and spit out the seed, and then pluck again. For company there were the noisy robins and the glorious orange and black Baltimore orioles. They perched hard by on a shaking branch and gashed the ripest cherries with their sharp beaks. After a bit, when I had eaten all the fruit within reach, I hitched myself on over to another perch and commenced anew. All the while, my small belly was rounding out into a little round dome.

Ah, those were the days, the salad days when school was out and life was a vast bowl of cherries in the top of Grandfather's cherry tree.

Today not a single tree remains of my grandfather's orchard. He and they were of another era, and I count myself fortunate that I lived in it.

Down near the waterfront in a house that overlooked the harbor and the islands there dwelt another grandparent. This grandmother was a link with another past in the State of Maine, that of the waterfront and the sea. Her father had been a pump and block maker in the days of wooden ships, and in the early days of my boyhood the old shop down on one of the wharves was still in operation under the skilled guidance of her brother, John Cammett.

Midway between the two high bluffs marking the Eastern and the Western Promenades of the old waterfront town, and athwart the Neck, as old-timers once called it, there ran a street, straight, spaciously wide, and arched over by towering wine-cup elms.

I remember this street, this State Street, well—how in midwinter the bare limbs of the elms formed a fretwork against the sky and a mountain of snow on the wide grass plot bordering the brick sidewalk towered above my head; how in summer a great span of green arched overhead, hiding the sky from my sight and framing in the perspective of distance a view of the harbor—a span of blue where fillets of sunlight glanced and white sails were in slow motion.

At the foot of this street I would mount a long flight of wooden steps, then pause at the top to give a pull at the bell. There was nothing electric about this contraption. My pull at the polished knob activated a wire leading to a bell somewhere deep within, and before its jangle had ceased, I was on my way in. My path was always the same—down the narrow hall, through a door at the left into a dark pair of steep stairs, and down into the basement, where lay the heart of the household—its kitchen, dining room, closets, cupboards, larder, and cold cellar.

By this time my grandmother would be on her way, running down two flights of stairs, as was ever her wont, not to supervise but to admire this raid upon her larder which with her hands on her hips she would view over the tops of a pair of rectangular steel-rimmed spectacles. There was always another participant in these rites; and so soon as I entered the closet in the dark narrow hallway, I would feel his stiff upright tail as he wove in and out between my legs. This was my grandmother's long lean yellow tomcat—Julius Caesar.

On the second shelf over to the left in the dim dark stood a tin. Herein, always in long supply, reposed what in the vernacular of the family were known as "seeds"—square, almost wafer-thin, sweet, and deliciously crisp sugar cookies—"seeds" so-called because they had once been seasoned with caraway seeds. I always started my crunching on these. To the right there was another tin. Here were the molasses cookies—round, mounding, and of a mouth-filling consistence. One of those would be next. In between were the pie tins. Here I would knife out a generous quarter section of molasses apple pie that when eaten in the hand dripped rich brown molasses in generous measure to be licked from the fingers. Sweet apple there was, and pumpkin too.

At the head of the hall and the foot of the stairs a door opened into the cold cellar directly below where I had stood to ring the bell. This was the next port of call. Here stood the crock, and therein were the pickles—Grandma's pickles, crisp, sharp, and utterly delectable.

The ritual of their preparation has been faithfully followed over the years. Every summer the same recipe is dredged up. In the holograph of the distaff side of my household this recipe has been embellished somewhat by the kind of comment that speaks for itself. The caption reads: "Grandma's Pickles—an old, old Lunt treat."

On the table in an earthenware crock—and mark you, today these are by way of becoming museum pieces—submerged in a small sea of gray brine that just covers their corrugated green skins, there float the pickling cucumbers, "or cukes, as they so quaintly put it." That's right, a peck of "cukes" in the half-grown stage that is known as "pickling." They have been soaking for two whole days. The pungent and, alas, to my companion the somewhat disagreeable odor of the brine is now permeating the kitchen, and it becomes my task to remove the cucumbers, dump the brine, wash out the crock, and fill it again with the "cukes."

Meanwhile the pickle is in course of preparation—a cup of sugar, a cup of salt, a cup of mustard, and a gallon of cider vinegar—mixed with the aid of a judicious and businesslike footnote that reads: "N.B. Make paste of dry ingredients & a little hot vinegar." Now into the crock this goes, again my task.

There is more—a quart of "pickling onions"—the little white round-button ones—and again in quotes in the recipe, a "couple pieces of horse-radish." Finally, if you are able to get it, a horse-radish leaf is now reverently draped over the top. Presto—the recipe has been followed; the pickles are made.

But the ritual calls for more, a small and unrecorded mystery handed down by word of mouth and performed in the secrecy of the cellar. A plate of a proper size to fit snugly within the crock is procured perchance by stealth. This is inserted and now submerged by the weight of a brick it presses beneath the surface of the pickle, the "cukes," onions, and horse-radish. Now time and the cool calm air of the cold cellar will do the magical rest.

There are two schools of taste as regards Grandma's pickles. There are those whose mouths water at the mere mention of them, and there are those who think that they stink. The former are of a special tribe. In the alongshore parlance of my grandmother Cammett, they are the salt of the earth, but in the York County idiom of my grandfather Storer, they are the white hen's chickens.

# The Old Town by the Sea

THE HEADLAND that fronts on Casco Bay is for me a kind of magnet. I can never long resist the vistas stretching away from its bluff-sided crest eastward toward the sea. Here on a late winter afternoon across the wide expanse of gray-blue water the islands stand in sharp outline. So clear is the air that the slender stems of the birches are seen as etched white lines traced against the dark ridges.

In the foreground, built into two islands, are ancient forts. Their sally ports are empty and their great granite walls are monuments to the forgotten fears of another age. From these ramparts a cross fire of cannonade could have annihilated any man-of-war of the nonexistent Confederate Navy that might ever have sought to run the Ship Channel.

The Ship Channel, a path of deep blue, lies between the islands to the eastward and the shore on the west, known always as the Cape Shore. Beyond lies the broad reach of the Atlantic, broken by a small vessel from which at recurrent intervals there comes a dim yellow flash. This is the lightship—on the mariner's chart, Cape Elizabeth Lightship. In the distance two freighters are on converging courses that will lead them into the Ship Channel and so to harbor by nightfall.

Time was, from this headland, on the clearing day after a northeast storm, men watched five hundred sail beating their way out through the Ship Channel to the open sea. In my own time I have seen from this same bluff six six-masted schooners and a seven-master at anchor. But today all the seagoing traffic consists of trawlers, tankers, and freighters. Still, there is that day in late summer, the day of the local yacht club's race around Monhegan, when the Cape Shore is lined with those whose delight is in the days of sail, and who watch the white wings as they sweep seaward.

This Ship Channel does not lack for lights and beacons. As the mariner approaches from the sea, in addition to the lightship there is on his port bow Two Lights and then Portland Head, and on the starboard hand there lies Ram Island Light, Half Way Light, and down east off the mouth of the Kennebec, Seguin. As the blue-water man comes on up the Ship Channel, there is still another light that marks for him the presence of Spring Point Ledge. And then, as if to welcome him in his turn to port into the harbor, there stands at the end of a long breakwater of great granite blocks the squat little lighthouse that was long known as Bug Light.

This afternoon its little fat form is the backdrop for the passage of a small ferry bearing the grandiloquent name of *Berkeley*. Nowadays Bug Light no longer shines, but when I was a youngster in these parts it gave off throughout the dark nights a warm, fixed red light.

And never do I see Bug Light but it puts me in mind of a sunny Sunday in the middle of May I once spent with another lad on one of these islands. His father was all morning in his garden bent over a hoe—a little potato bug of a man, with black galluses stretched across a red flannel shirt. Come noon, when we were ready to set down to table I went to fetch my coat. Then I got my orders:

"Take off thet co't, young man, an' set to yer vittles. They's no Sundays east o' Bug Light."

This favorite headland of mine was in former days a fortified spot. Today a couple of pieces of antique artillery mark the forgotten fact of its construction during the Revolution after Captain Mowatt of the British navy, in a fit of wanton destruction, had fired the little town of Falmouth and reduced it to ashes.

There is another lookout from this eminence, and now at sundown on this gray winter day I swing around to the western bastion of this hill. As I traverse the broad esplanade that runs in a curve around the crest of that hill, I travel between lines of towering elms that merge in an arch overhead. From here the broad waters of the bay stretch forth, carrying the eye to the islands.

Now in an open space beside an old schoolhouse I look out over the top of the town far away to the mountains that stand shoulder to shoulder on the western skyline. These are the White Mountains.

There is a red fire above the purple hills, the dying glow of a winter sunset. Here, too, there is water where a bay cuts around in back of the neck of land on which the town stands, and now headlights are winking along the curving drive that encompasses Back Bay.

A parcel of gulls float overhead, silent and on still wings, heading into the wind. The houses of the town stand out through the limbs of the trees. Far over to the left I catch the gleaming gold of a small dome. This is the Portland Observatory, where in the long lost days of sail a man on watch 227 feet above the level of the sea would report to the shipowners and merchants of the town, by the setting of the appropriate house flag, the sighting of their ships, brigs, and schooners when they appeared in the offing.

Once in the late afternoon of a long-ago June day I stood on that tower as a thunder gust came out of the west and passed over the town. I watched the vast white cumuli sailing in a brilliantly blue sky come together, broaden at the base, and darkening, assume the awesome proportions of thunderheads. Then there commenced the procession to the sea down the watershed of the Presumpscot, with the rain drumming the pace, the lightning lighting the path, and the clap and peal of thunder celebrating this air-clearing occasion.

Once upon a blue and golden September day during the War of 1812 tradition has it that Captain Lemuel Moody watched from this same tower and reported to the citizenry below the progress of the fight in which the American brig *Enterprise* whipped the *Boxer*, a British brig, off the island of Seguin twenty miles to the eastward. The *Boxer*, Captain Blyth, was shepherding a smuggler up the Kennebec, when the *Enterprise*, Captain Burrows, crowded with sixteen guns and a hundred men, came upon her and fired the traditional challenging shot across her bow.

For a while the two vessels maneuvered, each endeavoring to gain the weather gauge of the other. Then the wind died and they lay becalmed in the waters between the mouth of the Kennebec and the island of Seguin.

"At half past 11"—so runs the contemporary account of the action—"a breeze sprang up from the southwest which gave us [the *Enterprise*] the weather gauge. We maneuvered to the windward until 2 p.m. to try our sailing with the enemy and ascertain his force."

The end came quickly. Sailing on the same tack, the two brigs slowly converged until they were broadside to each other and but a stone's throw separated their bulwarks. Then came the exchange of broadsides and when the smoke cleared both youthful captains lay on their quarterdecks, Blyth shot through by an eighteen-pound ball, and Burrows mortally wounded by canister. A quarter of an hour later it was all over.

"She [the *Boxer*] ceased firing and called for quarter, saying that as their colors were nailed, they could not haul them down."


"LOOK!"

The shout echoed through the shipyard. Heads rose and faces turned. Atop of a shanty at the end of Union Wharf, a man stood with his left leg twisted around the flagpole. His right arm pointed out toward the harbor.

Past the end of the wharf a jibboom came into view and a brig under full sail swept slowly across the foot of the shipyard. Astern of her there came on another. The splintered stump of her main topmast stuck up above her after rigging. Midway from her forepeak there floated the Union Jack. Just above it were the red and white bars with the familiar seventeen stars in a blue field.

This was the brig *Enterprise*, with His Majesty's ship *Boxer* in tow.

A clamor arose. Why were the colors at half mast? Then

the word passed along the waterfront. On their quarterdecks, each wrapped in the flag of his country, lay the bodies of the two youthful captains. Blyth of the *Boxer* was but twenty-nine; Burrows of the *Enterprise*, his junior by a year.

For a time this melancholy news dampened a vociferous welcome. But as the *Boxer* came slowly on, curiosity broke the spell.

"God! Look at them shot holes. Right between wind and water!"

"They're lucky to get her in here without she foundered."

"Her starboard bow's all stove."

This was no exaggeration. Wherever a man might stand alongside the *Boxer* and raise his hands on her side, he could reach and touch at least two gaping holes. And here and there round shot were still stuck in her planking.

"That'll do fer the *Chesapeake*," shouted a sailmaker.

A cheer rose from the end of Union Wharf. Up and down the waterfront it ran, rising to a roar. The men working the *Enterprise* answered in their turn.

The next day they would bury the dead captains.

In the forest of masts out in the harbor, on the wharves, and on top of the buildings of the little town, flags fluttered at half mast. Early in the morning Fore Street and the wharves were thronged with people. Work was suspended. School was out. In the calm cool air of early September the inhabitants of Portland watched and waited in silence for the obsequies to begin.

Among them was a small boy of the town, one Longfellow by name, who nearly half a century later would write:

> *I remember the sea fight far away,*
> *How it thundered o'er the tide!*
> *And the dead captains, as they lay*
> *In their graves o'erlooking the tranquil bay*
> *Where they in battle died.*

BOOM!

It was a gun from the *Enterprise*. Simultaneously two barges, each propelled by the single stroke of a bank of twelve oars, left the *Enterprise* and the *Boxer*. Slower and slower they came on until they floated motionless on the calm water, the poised blades of the oars dripping. In sharp contrast to the white blouses of the sailors were the rich colors of the shot-torn flags draped over a coffin in the stern of each barge. The crowd ashore was tense and silent. A full minute elapsed.

BOOM!

A gun from the *Boxer*. The blades of the oars dropped into the water. Both barges surged ahead and again came slowly to a stop to await the next gun. Thus, with minute guns, the two dead captains were rowed to the shore.

Then the cobblestones of Fore Street resounded with the slow tramp of feet in time to a solemn dirge. A rifle company was in the van. Then came the coffin of Captain Burrows borne aloft on the shoulders of his crew. At either side, grasping the black tasseled cords of the pall, walked his fellow officers. Next came a portly figure in a blue uniform with his fore and aft hat cocked toward the end of his nose. A murmur arose.

"That's Isaac Hull!"

"Him that sunk the *Guerrière*."

People craned their heads. Children were lifted aloft for a look. They saw the coffin of Captain Blyth passing before them, similarly borne, similarly attended. Trailing the funeral band with its drums muffled with black cloth, came the clergy, the judiciary, and the minor dignitaries of the town. As the procession left Union Wharf, the onlookers tailed on.

The bell in the First Parish Church was tolling. The elms lining the streets formed a green arch for the passage of the funeral procession. Past the market with its empty stalls, in front of the vacant courthouse, on between the frame houses and their gardens the procession wound, mounting toward the town burying ground on the side of the hill below the Observatory. Here the headstones rose, row upon row, facing the harbor and the open sea.

The ranks of the riflemen parted. Facing the two graves that lay side by side, they stood with their arms reversed. The coffins came on. The crowd formed a silent circle. The deep voice of the Reverend Mr. Tappen boomed forth the burial service. The two torn flags were removed from the coffins. They sank from sight.

A sharp word of command. The rifles of the men beside the grave of Burrows rose toward the sky. A volley rang out, then another and a third. A pause, and then the rifles by the grave of Blyth resounded.

As the echoes died away, the riflemen fell in. Their colors were unfurled, the muffling was removed from the drums, and with the fifers piping a lively tune they marched smartly back to the courthouse and were there disbanded.

Soon the ring of mauls and the chunk of broadaxes were resounding in the shipyards. A schooner with its white sails close-hauled beat back and forth in the ship channel toward the open sea. The waterfront had returned to work.

The first account of the dramatic action between the *Boxer* and the *Enterprise* appeared in the *Portland Gazette and Maine Advertiser* on September 13, 1813. Three weeks later it carried the report of Oliver Hazard Perry's famous dispatch:

"We have met the enemy and they are ours—2 ships, 2 brigs, 1 schooner, and 1 sloop."

Despite these, and many another signal victory, American commerce was well-nigh driven from the high seas. Hence, in consequence of what the Federalists called Mr. Madison's War, a vast amount of coastwise trade was conducted in wagons on the meager highways of that day. Being of the

Federalist persuasion, the *Gazette* took occasion to lampoon this slow-moving traffic. When my eye caught the caption HORSE MARINE NEWS, followed by the slogan "Free Trade and Wagoners' Rights," I began to read the faded print with care.

The entries, in part, follow. It is the humor of that day, and they are the earliest examples I have encountered of the craft of the columnist in the American press.

### PORT OF BOSTON

Last evening arrived the tandem Philadelphia pilot-boat-built gig, *Scramble*, Captain Splash, from a three weeks cruise in Rhode Island and Connecticut. She came to about 5 P.M. at Spurd's Cove, Trasks Light bearing South ½ east. We extract the following from her log book:

"On the 2nd instant Pawtucket Bridge dead to windward saw 2 four horse wagons standing abreast, upon their larboard tacks, head toward us, upon a quick trot; hove about immediately but owing to our leader missing stays, fell afoul of the starboard forewheel and carried away our step.

"Sunday, 17th instant at 11 A.M. Weathersfield Meeting House bearing West, northerly 20 rods, the *Graves* just under our lee, was boarded from a government cutter called 'Tything Man,' who put a prize master on board and ordered us for the first tavern there, notwithstanding the known law that 'Free Gigs make Free Passengers'; was detained till midnight, when upon paying innkeepers fees, was released.

"Monday, 18th, 2 P.M. spoke a drunken soldier laying to under the lee of a board fence—wind blowing fresh could not take him in tow—from his rolling judged him deficient in ballast, with too much heavy stowage between decks . . .

"On Tuesday bore away for *Clapboardtrees*—came to the sign of the Horseshoe at 11 A.M. Sold three boxes of 'Curative Unctious Liniment,' which, applied to the broken leg of the landloard's horse effected an immediate cure."

## PORT OF PORTLAND

Thursday, October 21, 1813. Arrived, four ox wagon *La Hogue O'Leary*, 3 days from Limerick with potatoes, murphies & dungarvins—put into Saccarrappa in great distress of whiskey.

Same day. 1 horse team *Tickler*, cargo pumpkins from Gray. The captain states that the people were in distress whiskey being scarce and sold only by the gill, they wished for a change of *measures*. Saw near Black Strap a two ox cutter, bottom up. One hogshead was picked up marked *Gerrymander*.

I made other finds of like import. Some of the finest English prose has been written in the ordinary course of a day's work by an untutored man intent only on making an accurate record of a sequence of events. It has every virtue—simplicity, sparseness, terseness. It is utterly to the point. Witness this from the log of the privateer schooner *Teazer*, on the sixteenth day of July 1812.

At 8 P.M. a man by the name of Hewes White was at the main peake clearing our ensign which had got foul of the topping lift and gaff topsail halyards. A sudden lee lurch threw him from the gaff. Luffed to and hoisted out boat. Darkness coming on, the men in the boat could not see him. Hearing his voice, we tacked about and at 8½ picked him up.

This has all the austere verity of Oriental art, where the mere line of a single wave suggests the turbulence of the ocean, or a white-capped cone the majesty of a mountain. This swift, short account of the salient detail of that awful half hour in the life of Hewes White stirs the mind, and in his imagination the reader lives again with the participants now long since dead.

He sees White, a lithe young hand in ready response to the shout and upraised arm of the mate, running up the ratlines of the mainmast. At the crosstrees, wrapping his legs around the topmast, he starts shinning. Now he is poised on the gaff in the angle between it and the topmast, right hand grasping the halyards, left hand free and reaching aloft for the fouled ensign. He rises on tiptoe.

"A sudden lee lurch."

My God! He pitches out to leeward. Down he comes head first. There is a splash on the lee quarter. He disappears. His hat comes fluttering down and settles in the water, to be overturned by the crest of the following wave.

Man overboard!

The *Teazer* comes swiftly to the wind, her foretopsail aback and flapping. Now you hear the creaking of sheaves, and a slap as the boat hits the water. Two hands tumble in. They rig out the oars—start rowing. A tense silence ensues. Then a call comes out of the darkness. They cannot see him.

The mate cups his hands about his bearded mouth:

"Hewes!"

"Aye, sir."

The response is faint—from away and off the port bow. The *Teazer* falls off, her mainsail fills, and she bears away on the port tack. Now the silence is broken by the mate's calls and the answering hails. On the second tack a hand is seen to rise from the crest of a wave.

In jig time he is treading water under the lee quarter. Willing hands haul him aboard.

The *Teazer* comes to the wind to pick up her boat, and her mate goes below to write up the log:

At 8 P.M. a man by the name of Hewes White. . . .

Here is another instance of stark simplicity and clarity from the log of the *Dash*.

September 7, 1812. Commences with pleasant weather. At 1 P.M., sent up the royal yard and set the sail. At 3 P.M. saw a sail to the south and west. At 4 she had got nearly in our wake. At 5 P.M. she bore down before the wind and gave chase with a press of sail. She proved to be a schooner.

In that day a schooner was a topsail schooner, which is to say that she was a two-masted vessel schooner-rigged save for her foretopsail and whatever square sails she carried on her mainmast above the mainsail. What is today known as a schooner was then called a fore-and-after. A topsail schooner was light, handy, and when well handled extremely fast. "A press of sail"—in all probability this was common usage in the waterfront of that day. Can you not see her?

> Still kept on our course, all hands to quarters. At 8 P.M. lost sight of her. At 9 P.M. jibed ship and shifted studding sails.
>
> At 2 A.M. heard a gun fired on the larboard quarter and directly after a false fire and blue lights were shown astern. At 5 A.M. discovered three men-of-war in chase of us, one on the larboard quarter and two on the starboard, about three miles distant. Made all sail before the wind.
>
> At 9 had seen one of them out of sight. At 11 the second one gave up the chase being about eight miles distant. Weather very squally and variable accompanied with rain. At half-past 11 A.M. hove over the spare topmast, gaff and jib-boom and made and shortened sail occasionally.
>
> September 8, 1813. Begins with strong breezes from the north and west. Found we left the chase very fast. At 4 observed her take in her light sails, reef her topsails and haul on a wind. At 5 P.M. lost sight of her . . .

Again the *Dash* had won. She was a Letter of Marque—a private, armed brig. Her home port was Freeport in the District of Maine. Rigged first as a topsail schooner and later as an hermaphrodite brig—that is, square-rigged forward and schooner-rigged aft—she sent in fifteen prizes, never took a shot, and ran away from all pursuers. On her last cruise, running before the wind in a northeast snowstorm, she is believed to have foundered on George's Bank. All hands were lost.

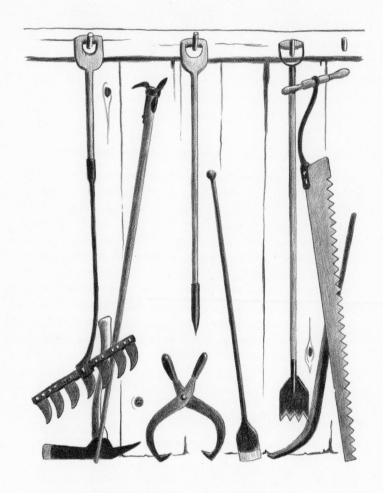

# Red-Letter Days

UNLIKE THE PHRASE making hay, which has survived in the American language with a slang connotation, its wintry counterpart—making ice—has entirely disappeared from the contemporary scene. Yet in the setting of the eighteenth and nineteenth centuries in rural America, each was a phrase of harvest time. In July, barebacked and sweating in the fields, a man got in his crop of hay; in December, bundled to the ears and crowned with a black fur cap, the same man went to work on his pond and got in his crop of ice. And in the course of it he often raised a considerable sweat.

I well remember on one particularly cold December afternoon a long trek out from the town over to Redwater, with the parental injunction "Keep off the black ice" ringing in our ears, and the sad fate of Jimmy Redlon imprinted on our young minds. Jimmy, said my father, had gone through the black ice there just about this time of the year, and they never found him until spring. On this trek we had to cross the railroad trestle over Fore River; that foot-wide catwalk with the green water below filled with chunk ice left an indelible memory. Once ashore, we soon came to the earthen breastwork that impounded the wide waters of a small stream. This was Redwater.

Here on the west bank, like a great weatherbeaten gray box, loomed the enormous icehouse of the American Ice Company. In those days, making ice was the foundation of a great American industry in which fortunes were still being made—and later lost.

On that December day in 1906, what a sight there was from the top of that dam! The wide expanse of open water completely frozen in from willowed shore to willowed shore.

Making ice made a scene of colorful activity on a freezing December afternoon. The cold red sky of a winter sunset back of the willows formed a backdrop against which the forms of men and horses moved slowly to and fro out on the ice, with their deep-drawn breaths coming out like jets of steam. On the cold air there came the shouting of men hallooing to their teams and the clanking of the chain of the endless belt punctuated by snorts from the old donkey engine that operated it. The ice glinted with the special shades of green and blue that come only at the time of winter twilight.

And there was a camaraderie that went with making ice just as there was with making hay.

The general scheme of the operation was this: A team of horses would drag an implement akin to a plough, scoring a great long gash in the ice. Counter-scores were gashed, and this resulted in a pattern of potential ice cakes like a great frozen checkerboard. Meanwhile the great saws were at work, the backs of two men, one on each side, bending to the task. When a slab, say fifty feet long and three feet wide, was cut loose, it would be poled by men with pickpoles down through the black open water to where the icehouse stood.

Here an endless conveyor ran up over a long trestle at a 45-degree angle. At its foot on a platform stood a powerful man armed with a great iron tool like a long spade. With unerring aim he would drive this into the cross gash, thus cutting off the great block, which would then rise majestically, caught by the next bar on the conveyor.

As the massive blocks of ice mounting on the conveyor reached the tier that was being filled, each one would disappear inside the cavernous icehouse as if it were being swallowed. In the open doorway stood a stout lad armed with an implement like a large baggage hook with which he guided and shunted the heavy, moving block onto an inclined sluice, and away she went, on to the next turn, where another fellow would give her another shunt.

Thus, on a series of inclined planes and by the prods of men strategically stationed, the great blocks slid on to their resting place on a bed of sawdust. Here men with wooden scoops, working feverishly, filled the crevices between the cakes and lay the bed for the oncoming cubes. As the tiers were filled, the sluices had to be relocated, and here inside the icehouse the work was really dangerous, particularly when some ill-formed block, some malevolent maverick, would go off on a frolic of its own, mount the side of the sluice, and come crashing down, out of control. Then it was a case of Jack be nimble, Jack be quick.

A great deal more than a colorful calling was lost when making ice was relegated to the past. For the best of refrigeration died with it. As every housewife worth her salt once knew, the cold of melting ice is the best preservative, not the cold of freezing ice with its dehydrating effect, as in the modern mechanical contrivances. And Americans, who pride themselves on their practicality, are so bemused with gadgets and machines that today there cannot be had anywhere, at any price, a good old-fashioned icebox where a man can go and chip the ice as he needs it, and never have to monkey with those accursed trays and cubes.

I remember the summer a few years later when the old icehouse of the American Ice Company at Redwater burned to the ground. It made a glorious blaze against the sky and that night you could see the glow of it in the water of the pond. But it was not until the heat of the second summer had passed into memory that the great mound of ice under the damp sawdust melted away and ran down into the ground.

The other summer, I took a trip in to find Redwater, and what did I find? A tank farm on the site and the old pond all filled in. I was warned off the place by some minion of the now—alas—American Oil Company.

In the winter half a century ago in this old New England town by the sea, another red-letter day was the twenty-second of February. For the youngsters George Washington's birthday was the winter counterpart of the Fourth of July. It had its quaint special customs, the sources of which were completely unknown to the vociferous celebrants.

First of all, you got off from school. This in itself was an extraordinary event. Generally at this time of the year the back of the winter was not yet broken, and a cold clear day would dawn with the sun shining down upon all the accumulated snow and ice of the season. Then at a quarter past eight, just as you were finishing breakfast, all the bells in the town would begin to toll. Each peal would be followed by a deep-throated *harumph* from an old wheezing whistle that somehow functioned down at the powerhouse. This was the town's fire-alarm system, in the days of a volunteer fire department, and albeit you knew what was coming, you waited and you counted breathlessly—for you never could be dead sure, it might be a fire after all—until, through the reverberating tolls and resultant howls, there came the magic number.

THIRTY-THREE! *Yippee!* No school!

Then you burst out into the street, horn in hand. Just why the nativity of George Washington—or G. Wash, as he was locally known—a full century and three quarters before, should be proclaimed by blasts from a fishhorn, remains a minor problem for the social historian. But what a noise a pair of youthful lungs could make with those long, tin horns. The streets of the old town sounded and resounded far and near with those dreadful blasts. Occasionally today one again hears them. Fishermen use them and small boats running in a fog, as also the fast-dying race of street vendors.

This horn blowing would go on until the young lungs of the town were exhausted or until the next part of the traditional celebration took over. This is betokened by the other name often given to G. Wash's birthday—tar-barrel night. For weeks now every neighborhood gang in the town had been gathering and caching stray lumber and raiding each other's caches. Abandoned boxes and barrels, rubbish of all kinds, and especially old Christmas trees and empty tar buckets were sought with assiduity. Come the late afternoon —and dusk descended early in this latitude—the gang was hard at work stacking, buttressing, and building as high a pile as possible.

Then after supper the black elms lining the streets of the old town would be outlined against the blue-black sky by the glow of a bonfire in every other block. And when the roaring flames rushing aloft in the still night air touched off the dried balsams stuffed into the tar barrel atop the pile, then came a mighty chorus of blasting fishhorns from the rows of shining and excited faces rimming the blaze.

Hurray for G. Wash!

I remember, too, the early spring day when the handcuff king came to town. Harry Houdini was the name, and half a century ago his was a name to conjure with. The great escape artist he was—out of iron chests, safes, sealed milk cans filled with water, blocks of ice, a huge firkin of cheese, and God knows what all. He got out of every one of them in jig time, dripping with water or spread with cheese, as the case might be, and with the trusty handcuffs dangling in one hand. The handcuff business was assumed to be bona fide, but there were skeptics when it came to the containers. These doubters muttered in their beards about mirrors and such like.

The day this great handcuff artist was billed at the local vaudeville house of the Keith circuit, the posters blazoned the announcement all over the town and added that the Great Houdini, manacled both hand-and-foot and hand-to-foot, would jump from the drawbridge over to the Cape Shore. This latter was for the youngsters. And they were there in the noon recess—in force, all the schoolchildren in town.

Atop the span was the Great Houdini, his long hair streaming in the wind and his bathrobe flapping around his hairy legs. It was a raw March day with a chill west wind blowing, and every now and again a chunk of rotten ice would bump against the pilings and go rumbling through the draw.

Harry looked down at the water and, no mistake about it, that water had a sullen look. From the sea of upturned faces there rose a chorus of yells and cheers for the great man. The great man wearily waved his hand and snuggled his robe around him. Again he looked down into the channel. Another ice floe was flowing slowly through. This went on for a considerable spell.

There is one lad standing on the rail. Suddenly he points. Then all the eyes in the crowd as suddenly shift to follow the line of his outstretched arm.

On a spar standing well out from a coastwise schooner and high over the water, the upturned eyes glimpse the frame of a huge black man. Slowly, slowly he is disrobing and now his shirt and pants come floating down to the deck.

Then he stands there, clad only in a clout, his great black body outlined against the sky, his muscles rippling beneath his ebony skin. The crowd is silent. Slowly his arms rise over his head, his body leans out into the air, then falls in a soaring arc and pitches with a great splash into the ice-cold waters of Casco Bay. Full-throated is the yell. Now he has come to the surface and, arms folded across his chest, he treads water so powerfully that his full chest rises up above the surface. A bit more, it seemed, and he would have walked.

This was the show for the day. I forget about Houdini. Some say he jumped, but for my money this magnificent man of ebony—the cook on that coaster—had completely stolen his show.

Later in the spring of every year there was an annual ritual known among its initiates as a sulphur stink. "Sulphur stinks" came to pass because somewhere down along the waterfront there was an old match factory. The way of it was this. Sulphur matches were half again as long as the ordinary safety match is today and they came in cards or sheets with the upper ends split so you could break off a match whenever you wanted one. Well, the women and children who worked in the match factory would dip the cards first in hot sulphur—the fumes were terrible—and then they stuck the tips in fuming phosphorus.

I have not seen any of these matches for a generation and more. Some say the manufacturers were run out of business by the law, and this may well be, considering the awful stories we used to hear about what happened to the women and children that handled that live phosphorus—their eyes all eaten out and great burns on their hands and arms and faces.

Well, these matches—the Portland Star Matches—were in everybody's pockets when I was a little shaver. People used to keep them in the kitchen in a tin box handy to a square of sandpaper for striking. It never would do to strike them on the woodwork or along the wall. Every strike left a great long brown scar that you never could get out. You see, they were friction matches. You gave them a good long stroke and that would heat up the phosphorus so it would smoke and this in its own good time would set the sulphur going. Then after a bit the wood of the match would catch afire and there you would be, with a live match in your hand. A man had to be patient, though. If he was a little too hasty in lighting his pipe, he would get a snootful of phosphorus and sulphur. Phew! "Eight-day stinkers" is what some people called them.

But there was one thing about these old friction matches that beat all matches before and since, and that was this. If a man should go overboard and get them wet, all he had to do when he came out of the water was to set them up on a rock in the sun until they dried out. Then they were just as good as new. They were dangerous, though. The mice used to nibble at them, and many a fire got started that way. I once heard a tale about a man who had some in his coat pocket one day when he was playing with his youngsters. They started climbing up on him and the friction set his card of matches afire. In less than no time, he was all ablaze and they had to get the town fire department to put him out.

They were always handy in a wind. Once you got the phosphorus smoking and it set the sulphur going, there was no wind in Christendom that could put it out, so a man had plenty of time to cup his hands and protect the little yellow blaze when it commenced to eat along the clear wood.

The sulphur used to come all the way from Sicily. The arrival of the sulphur schooner was infrequent, but she usually came to her berth off the end of the wharf of the Pocahontas Coal Company in the early spring. And just as soon as she tied up, the kids that lived on the south side of town, on the height of land there overlooking the upper harbor, would see her unloading. This way word that a sulphur ship was in would pass through the town on the wings of the wind, and the next day, come the recess at noontime, Fore Street would be full of kids watching her unload.

This was a pretty sight on a clear day—really colorful. The old wharf carpeted thick with black coal dust was dotted here and there by the white piles of the last snowfall. The sulphur that got swung ashore in cargo nets was gleaming yellow. Pretty soon the black coal dust and the white snow were spotted with yellow chunks of sulphur like nuggets of gold. With the green harbor on each side of the wharf and out beyond, and a clear blue sky overhead, there was all the color a man could ever want.

Just as soon as school was out in the late afternoon, you could see the kids going down the long steps that led down to Commercial Street, and then across the cobblestones, dodging through the jiggers and the drays and out on the Pocahontas coal wharf. Every last one of them was packing a gunnysack. Directly they took to scurrying around, pitching chunks of sulphur into their sacks. Nobody gave a tinker's damn about the old loose sulphur, but the youngsters figured they were swiping something, and that tickled them. Then every once in a while old Daddy Look, the watchman, would come out of his shack and chase them off the dock, and this would help keep up the illusion. So everybody had a fine time, and after a while they would all climb up the long steps again, loaded with sulphur. The sacks were heavy, and they were puffing.

But the sulphur stink was still a long way off. What was wanted was a clear blue spring day when the apple trees were beginning to blossom out, when the sun would warm your back, and a fellow could lie down in the long grass and watch the white clouds go sailing by without getting all damp from the wet ground. Then, too, it would have to be a day off from school. It was too risky to play hookey to have a sulphur stink.

So the kids hoarded up their stores of sulphur and laid their plans—when they would have the stink, who was to be in the party, and the all-important question, where. The safest place was way out on Brown's Island, a triangular plot of wasteland enclosed by the railroad tracks to the west of the town. Others were in favor of the field down back of the Western Promenade, where there was a frog pond. But the best place of all was in the old Western Cemetery.

Memorial Day was always a holiday. But it was more than that. In retrospect, it was a day of color. There was the fading blue of the uniforms that marched up Congress Street in a wavering curve stretching from curb to curb. There was the purple and the white of the lilacs that always bloomed for that day. It was a day, too, of other blossoms—of apple and pear and plum and peach in the orchards. On those long-ago Memorial Days the white clouds sailed across the blue sky, steadily coursing before a fresh westerly breeze.

The sun was out. It was warm. And it was good to be alive in the spring of the year.

On this particular Memorial Day, before the break of day, two small boys were to be seen hauling a small express wagon piled high with a couple of gunnysacks down Spring Street to where, at its dead end, it debouched into the old Western Cemetery. Here, on a descending slope from high on the bluff above the blue water encircling the town, the dreamless dead slept in ordered ranks and the grass grew tall to wave above their rounded graves.

Crouching, the boys crawled beneath the heavy chain that barred the roadway into the cemetery, and then they hauled their little wagon inside. It was still dark and just a mite scary, with the white gravestones staring at them in the dim light. But they kept on at a steady pace until they were almost across the cemetery, at its western edge. Here they came to a stop.

This was the rendezvous. By now other small dark forms were appearing out of the darkness from this direction and that. All hands were laden with sacks, bags, baskets, and some even lugged heavy firkins between them. In short order these receptacles were emptied in an open space where soon there was a considerable pile of sulphur. In the dim light it was a ghastly yellow.

Newspaper, dried leaves, sticks, and dry grass were gathered. Then the match—one of the eight-day stinkers—was applied. It took a while for the sulphur to catch, but when it did—oh boy! It bubbled and melted and ran fuming in long rivulets. The stench was immense. Aside from the general excitement, the idea was to stand to leeward of the mess and see who could stand there the longest. You held on as long as you could, and then you stepped out of the fumes with your eyes streaming and you were choking and gasping for breath.

There was another curious aspect of a sulphur stink. It

seemed to exercise a baleful influence on the wildlife in the cemetery. All manner of insects and frogs and snakes especially seemed to be impelled toward the fuming flames. They came flying and leaping and coiling toward the boiling mass of burning sulphur. Into the holocaust they plunged. It was a sort of natural suttee. You would find their skeletons afterwards.

By now the thick acrid smoke and fumes had been carried across the cemetery and on down into the town. Men sniffed the spring air and grinned. They knew what was up. And the womenfolk, they leaned on their brooms and sniffed too. They knew now that it was useless to call that dratted boy to breakfast. He was out there burning his sulphur at that sulphur stink.

Given a westerly breeze that was freshening with the sun, a crowd of small boys, and the stinking sulphur fuming and smoking and blazing out there in the early morning, it was inevitable: they set the grass afire. Then it wasn't long before the old whistle in the powerhouse down back of Deerings Oaks would begin honking like a wild goose:

*Aa—umph!*

*Aa—umph!*

And all the bells in the town kept company with it.

Fire! Fire!

In those days you never heard sirens roaring to a fire like nowadays—only the church bells all over town and that steam whistle honking. The firemen were all volunteers. Men dropped their tools where they stood, and came on the run.

Out on the Western Promenade old Tom Ball was standing by the police box with the receiver to his ear. He was calling the desk in the City Hall to report the end of his duty. Then he heard the bells and the whistle and he saw the white smoke billowing up above the trees down in the Cemetery. He knew what it was, and leaving the receiver dangling, he set off. Tom was on the stout side and the wrong side of fifty, and he was still chewing the doughnut that came with a mug of coffee in Kate Flaherty's kitchen, where he'd been just before he called the chief.

"Runnin' warn't easy," he would complain " 'twas like milkin' a moose."

Down in the Cemetery, by now a widening crescent of flames was going great guns, eating up the tall grass and roaring through the dried bushes. The kids were chasing the flames, beating at them with their coats and shirts. They could not get out in front of the fire because of the fumes of the sulphur; what they were really doing was fanning the flames. And they were so busy they failed to see old Tom Ball bearing down on them from the rear. Leastways, two of them didn't, and he collared Punkadoo and Bottle-ass.

Then the fire engine came down Spring Street, with the horses galloping and the stack trailing black smoke and cinders. The firemen came running, and directly there was a considerable commotion. Hydrants were tapped and great long lines of hose run out. There was a hell of a lot of hollering and men with black helmets went rushing around, struggling into black rubber coats and getting in each other's way. Then, when everything was all set up, it was discovered that there wasn't any pressure.

Just about this time the old Black Maria came galloping up and lugged off Punkadoo and Bottle-ass. They were bawling and the tears made little runs of white down their sooted cheeks. When they got down to the station, the Chief turned them loose, but they were thoroughly scared. And out in the Cemetery the fire swept everything off, neat and clean, leaving the headstones sticking up like scattered teeth. People used to say they knew it was a cemetery again after a real good grass fire in the spring of the year.

And later that day, after the Memorial Day parade, when

the Civil War veterans came by and stuck little flags in the holders by the graves of their comrades, the bright spots of red and white and blue fluttered against the blackened ash of the grass.

# Over on the Cape Shore

"IF YOU WANT to get lost," my grandfather used to say, "just go over on the Cape Shore."

But whenever I got lost over there I always found something worthwhile—the best place in the county for arbutus;

the Great Pond, where there was a common right of wild-fowling so nobody could run me off; an alder swamp filled with woodcock that whistled up from underfoot; and the beechnut ridge, where partridge could always be found in the fall of the year.

Then there was the cunner hunt. This was an annual excursion in the spring of the year under the skilled guidance of a favorite uncle. Uncle Jim was a small man. He was kind of short and kind of square, a circumstance that was somehow tied up in my young mind with the legend that in the days of his youth he had punched cows out on the plains of Montana. He wore great round gold-rimmed spectacles behind which his blue-gray eyes were always twinkling, and he could make a small boy laugh just by the way he said things.

These excursions after cunners took place long before the days of scouts and scoutmasters. They almost antedated the automobile, though the one or two that had been taken out of the winter's mothballs in the stable were occasionally to be met wheezing painfully and fitfully along a dirt road, and were always greeted with the derisive injunction that the occupants had best get a horse. Such is the lot of the pioneer.

The occasion was always a surprise. My uncle would appear without warning at breakfast time and squeeze his portly form into a chair at the table. In reply to an invitation to partake, the stock response was that he had had his oats and backed out of his stall an hour ago. Generally this would be a Saturday, but there was one memorable time when Uncle Jim mixed up the days of the week. And two small boys wisely kept their mouths shut and got off from school.

First came the trolley ride that started in the main square and went on, it seemed, forever. How that old creaking crate would yaw from side to side as she careened downhill with the motorman stomp—stomp—stomping on the clanging bell! The motorman had a marvelous pair of handlebar mustaches, was a prodigious consumer of cut plug, and endowed with unerring accuracy in the art of expectoration. It was reliably reported by that unimpeachable source, my uncle, that at ten paces he never failed to drown a fly asleep on a sun-warmed board. Uncle Jim knew. He and Charley Ross had gone to school together in the days of the horsecar.

After an eon of time—it might perhaps have been three quarters of an hour—this single-truck trolley came to the end of the line, where it just played out on the side of the road.

Here was a country store. Here purchases were to be made. Within its dark recesses, a generous quarter of country cheese was carved out, a hunk off a flitch of bacon procured, a packet of tea, and bread in a long loaf.

Here, too—up against the roof of the porch—one selected, after considerable handling and pondering, one's choice from a thicket of long bamboo poles. The lines and hooks were attached.

At the end the sad-eyed cadaverous grocer, who looked as if he had never once emerged from his store into the open sunlight all winter long, would plumb the depths of a big glass jar with a long wooden ladle, and present at the side, in the murky liquid, for the observance and approval of the prospective purchaser, a round green pickle-lime.

"The pucker," said my uncle, "will make them cunners taste sweet."

And so, leaving Charley Ross seated in the open door of his trolleycar, expertly rolling up balls of dust with contemplative spurts of ejaculated tobacco juice, we would set off down the road, sucking our pickle-limes—the rotund and somewhat truncated form of my uncle flanked by two small boys, and the three bamboo poles pointing back toward the town.

A warming sun, a cooling breeze off the ocean, the song sparrows bursting with their streams of song, soft white clouds hanging in the sky, and the three of us gone afishing —this was of the essence of the spring of the year.

Pretty soon we climbed a fence and took out through a pasture, its green spotted with the gold of buttercups and the brown of cowflaps. Then followed the traverse of a cool grove of cat spruce, where, out of a dark recess, a brace of woodcock would flutter aloft, dodging through the thick branches and uttering frightened cries. Then Trundy's Reef —a great backbone of land studded with outcroppings of gray ledge and covered with bayberry bushes and juniper —stretched ahead out into the blue Atlantic.

By that time we were on the run, in complete disregard of the avuncular injunction to take it easy, and in jig time everyone was fishing.

Bait? You used cockles, tearing them from the rocks under the rockweed and demolishing the shell with a stone till you got to the wet brown morsel of meat and stabbed your hook through its outer protective cover. These excursions were expertly timed by my uncle, and by now the tide was on the make and the cunners were biting. Great hands they are at taking your bait, so there was always an opportunity for an uncle to show you how to do the trick. We always let him catch the first one.

I can see him now, his sombrero—a relic of those early days punching cows on the plains of Montana—pushed back on the crown of his head, his moon-round face, his gold-rimmed spectacles, also round, all intent on the tip of that bamboo pole. He'd give it little jerks and swings, and you could see where the cunner was nibbling.

"You always want to let 'em get a little greedy," he would say.

Of a sudden, there came the sharp snap up, and a wiggling cunner would come flapping through the air to be caught in his outstretched hand. Then he would let you take over, cock himself on top of a rock, and holler advice.

At the nooning, a little fire of driftwood would give off a pungent smoke and pretty soon the little slabs of cunner, tom-cod, and pollock were sizzling and spitting in the hot bacon fat, the tea was boiling, and the bacon drying out on brown paper. And, as predicted, the pucker of the pickle-limes made the cunners taste sweet. Now there was the silence, a deep, votive silence, for the eating.

Soon the rotund form of an uncle was recumbent, the sombrero hiding his face, and a slight rasping sound would bespeak his deep enjoyment of a snooze in the sun. Then the green water of the cove would be cleaved by dive after dive after dive of two youngsters gone swimming.

The Cape shore is rugged—a shore of ledges and cliffs and reefs with here and there a small cove making up to a little sloping shingle beach at its head. On one of the boldest and baldest of its headlands there stands a white lighthouse that was built in the first days of the Republic. It still towers, its powerful beam at once a warning to mariners and an early monument to the mercantile strength of the new nation in 1790.

The last time I saw Portland Head Light was on a gorgeous August day when all things shone in a brilliant clarity—the blue blossoms of the chicory that grew so thick in the field by the side of the cliff, the white of the gulls floating ceaselessly on arched and outstretched wings heading into the steady sou'west breeze, the gray of the ledges descending to the sea, the creaming of the seas that smote them, and then the far stretch of blue water carrying the eye to another shade of blue at the fine taut line of the horizon.

Across this scene came a trawler trundling in leisurely fashion up the ship channel toward the harbor with a medley of gulls in its train, circling, wheeling, and now and again diving.

In this setting on the edge of the cliff far above the endlessly heaving sea there is a cluster of structures. First, in-shore, there is a many-gabled house, its white-painted sides, its deep green trim, and its bright red roof all agleam in the sunlight. A low, covered catwalk runs out from this house and it too is sparkling white.

Here the tower commences abruptly—a round tower that tapers slowly as it goes up and up and up, the simplicity of its shining white wall enhanced by the shattering effect of a single small window. Then it is capped by the black cage of the lamps, and this in turn is surrounded by a black railed catwalk and surmounted by a black ball. Then at its foot again, hard by the edge of the cliff, there thrust forth from a low squat housing of gleaming white the bell-like mouths of the foghorns.

This ensemble—the lightkeeper's gabled house, the tow-ering light tower, the foghorn, all in white save where the whiteness is set off by green and red and black—this en-semble by the side of the sea, seen in outline against the bluest of skies, is the classic lighthouse scene.

IN MEMORY OF THE SHIP
ANNA C. MCGUIRE
WRECKED HERE
DECEMBER 24, 1886

As I stood at the foot of the tall conical tower and looked out across the Gulf of Maine, there before me, painted against a background of black on the side of the ledge, was this legend lettered in white.

I have seen a remarkable photograph of another vessel, a schooner, taken at night by the light of the beam shining out across the dark water. There, foundered on a submerged ledge, is a schooner. The tops of her two masts, the forestay and topping lift, and the tops of her three sails—jib, fore-sail, and mainsail—gleam white against the dark water. You can see in the picture where the waterline is mounting.

It has risen a couple of feet on the canvas sails. Within minutes of the clicking of the shutter of the camera, she had gone down on the reef that can be seen awash in the corner of the photograph.

This remarkable picture appeared on October 7, 1932, in the New York *Herald Tribune*, with this caption:

> The light of Portland Head, Maine, caught this view of the masts and sails of the *Lochinvar* as she sank on a reef on October 4. The captain and crew took to lifeboats when she struck and got ashore safely.

There are other mementos of the sea over on the Cape shore. Out near Kettle Cove in an open field there is a small graveyard, where the following epitaph may be seen:

SACRED

TO THE MEMORY OF

MISS LYDIA CARVER

daughter of Mr. Amos Carver of Freeport, Aet 24, who with fifteen other unfortunate passengers, male and female, perished in the merciless waves by the shipwreck of the Schooner Charles, Capt. Jacob Adams, bound from Boston to Portland, on a reef of rocks near the shore of Richmond's Island on Sunday night, July 12, 1807

> The sweet companion and the friend sincere
> Need no mechanic help to force the tear.
> 'Twill flow eternal o'er a hearse like thine
> 'Twill flow while gentle goodness has a friend
> Or kindred tempers have a tear to lend.

A white picket fence surrounds this sequestered spot— this quarter acre given over to a record of life now long since gone. The stone before which I knelt to copy this epitaph is of ancient gray slate, rounded in a perfect semicircle at the top, where traced in fading outline are the traditional tresses of the weeping willow.

Alas for Miss Lydia Carver! On either hand, seven on the

left and eight on the right, in a regular pattern, are the un-marked stones that mark the moldered remains of the "fif-teen other unfortunate passengers, male and female, per-ished in the merciless waves . . ."

The graveyard stands on a slight height of land in the midst of open meadow where the long grass waves gently before the light southwest breeze. Hard by is a clump of white oak. This small eminence runs in a slow descent to the sea. There is the cove, Kettle Cove by name, and a beach most appropriately called Crescent. In the offing across the cove rises the brown rounding mass of Richmond Island, its contour broken by a copse of black pine and a single frame house.

Here it was that a century and a half ago "on a reef of rocks" the "Schooner Charles, Capt. Jacob Adams," had come ashore and had broken up.

This Island has other memories for the reflective Ameri-can. For before Plymouth and the Pilgrims it was a fishing station and had been a landfall for the West Country fisher-men who for untold years had been fishing off the Maine coast and drying their cod on the shores of what they called "the Main."

The contemporary scene is in alien contrast to that of former days. On the highway at the edge of the meadow cars go zipping past, bound for the beaches, the golf links, the swimming pools, the lobster pounds, and the country clubs. The cove is dotted with the white sails of pleasure craft, and overhead in the clear blue sky there is a great long fishhook of white vapor—the trail of a passing jet.

As I leave this small country graveyard—there are no more than thirty graves within the confine of the white picket fence—my eye is caught once again by a reminder of things past. Three flags mark three graves. They had been soldiers of the Revolution, and I note their names—as Ameri-can as apple pie—Dyer, Ramsbottom, and Solomon Jordan, the latter a scion of a family that still dwells on this Cape Shore.

Not far from this graveyard the tip of Cape Elizabeth juts out into the sea. This has long been known as Two Lights, for since time immemorial there have been two lighthouses on this cape, one of them now long in disuse. It is a spot for those who love the sea and find their solace in watching the white surf beating endlessly upon the rocky shore.

I was there once in the wake of a three-day northeaster, and when I stepped out on the ledge I could taste the brine in the fog that came stalking in great gray wraiths before a light easterly across the greasy surface of the sea.

*A-a-a-r-r—U-u-m-m-ph!*

That first blast always makes the wayfarer jump, particularly when he is out beyond the bell-like mouths of the double horns that stretch seaward from under the eaves of the "Whistle House." Then comes the blast again. It is a series of three, and their combined blasts take eight seconds out of each minute.

When they are over, the silence is filled once again with the rote of the sea, punctured by the occasional shriek of a gull. And also in the lull there comes ever so faintly to ear, borne by the easterly, the low muttered tone of the foghorn at Half Way Light, so-called because it lies halfway to the light on Seguin off the mouth of the Kennebec.

I take a look around the horizon. All that is to be seen is grayed by the fog. High up on the bluff and some distance inshore is the deserted column of the old lighthouse, and then to the east'ard and handier to the sea there rises the white tapering tower of the one now in use, its top sheathed in glass. On the grassy edge of the ledge a deserted frame house fronts the sea. Its gray contour is decorated, as if in a motif, by regularly spaced white gulls, all facing east, snuffing the salt breeze.

Out over the water the mains'l of a sloop barely emerges

from the fog. Hard by at my feet there is a cove where the seas are rolling ashore in slow undulation until they rasp up on a steep, shingle beach. Here a small boat bobs, laden with five figures shrouded in sou'westers, fishing. A lobsterman's bluff-bowed boat emerges from and then disappears again into the fog. I see on a black can buoy a single white gull facing seaward, riding its tossing top. Then, as I sweep the horizon, I come to the westerly shore, with its row of cottages built into the bluff and fronting the sea. In a hollow hard by is the little settlement. Here a single chimney sends up a column of gray smoke to merge with the gray fog.

I speak to no one in the short space I am there, and this is well. There are times when a man wants solitude, and particularly is this so when he is watching the endless undulation of the sea.

# Summers at Pine Point

FOR A SMALL BOY, the days of June were long, long days. This was the month when school would let out and then these long days would stretch ahead in an endless procession. There was the anticipation of the shore, of the broad flat beach at low tide and the rolling breakers when it would come to the flood.

Pine Point was a great spit of sand out of which there towered a grove of tall pines—a place of dunes and marshes and a wide beach on which in those long lazy days of June little waves fell with little rasps. Here the air was all that nostalgia can ever claim for it—fresh, crisp, invigorating, and scented with salt.

Along this point a path led wandering through the pines. This was the common way for all the inhabitants. By it you went to the store, or perchance to visit a neighbor, or again for a cooling swim in the creek. But my keenest recollection is of the open spots where, out of the warm mixture of black earth and white sand, there rose great thick rounding bushes studded with the buds and wide pink blossoms of the wild rose. The first sight of these in a season would be long remembered.

Often we plucked them and set them in a bowl. A single blossom would scent the whole room.

But before this there was the annual excursion that consumed the whole day in traversing a distance now encompassed in a short half hour. On a warm day, with the sun sailing across a cloudless sky, there was that long slow ride in the carryall through the fresh June countryside, behind an endlessly trotting mare with the sand rising in little columns behind the slowly revolving wheels.

The cottage was of a weather-beaten red, and it faced the sea. When the front door was opened, the air would be musty and dead. My first task always would be to run upstairs and throw open the windows that looked out over the sea. Then the gentle sea breeze, a soft southerly, would catch and raise the curtains into curves that would rise and fall in undulations as the old cottage filled with fresh salt air.

Andrew Wyeth has painted a picture that always recalls this moment to me—a pair of muslin curtains bellying in from an open window as they are lifted by a salt sea breeze.

Once the sea breeze was blowing through the cottage I would head for the beach—over the front lawn, across the dirt road, down the plank walk through the stretch of sand that was grown over with salt grass, and at the end of the walk I would kick off my shoes for the rest of the summer and, standing one-legged, rip off each stocking. Then I stepped off into the warm sand to feel for the first time its soft texture between my bare toes. There I would stand for a long time, clutching my toes in the sand, sniffing the salt air and looking out across the wide beach and the blue sea to where the sky and the sea met in a fine line.

In those early days of June the beach peas would be blossoming in profusions of red, white, and blue—in anticipation, I always thought, of the great day to come. Trudging through the salt grass, I would pick a bunch of them and set them off with sprigs of the gray pearly everlasting.

Then a voice from the house would be calling. I was wanted—to fetch a bucket of water for the pump. In those days you had to give a pump a drink to get it going, and it gave off deep cavernous throaty gasps before it began coughing up its own supply out of the well.

Next would come a trip through the pine woods that gave the place its name of Pine Point, to the old corner store for a load of groceries.

And so began the summer . . .

Associated with the Fourth of July was the fire balloon. This called for light offshore airs. If there was any appreciable amount of wind, or if it was onshore, the event would have to be postponed. But always, sometime in the early days of July, there would come a twilight when the sea was a broad flat span of blue, when the little waves lapped in recurrent raspings on the sand, and the long shadows of the tall pines ran out across the beach. Then the cry would go up:

"Let's send up the fire balloon."

Fire balloons came packed in a long wooden box and their handling called for circumspection and care. A small procession would form—the elders in front, the small fry bringing up the rear—down across the stretch of beach grass, which was still spotted with the red, white, and blue blossoms of the beach pea. At the edge of the beach we would find a shallow depression in the lee of a low dune. Here, carefully, the balloon was unpacked and laid lengthwise on the sand. Whoever was tallest clambered on top of a box. The top of the balloon was passed up to him and he held it as high as he could reach. Others plucked at the paper sides, pulling them out until at last there was the semblance of a pear-shaped balloon. At its foot, attached by wires to the open mouth of the bag and suspended well below it, was a round box-like contrivance. Within this, packed tight, were foldings of excelsior.

Now the match is applied. The excelsior burns and the hot air rises, flowing into the open maw of the balloon. Soon its flat sides begin to fill out. Then the one on the box lets go and jumps down. The big paper bag is now nearly distended. The word is given:

"Let go!"

Slowly the balloon rises. The wired excelsior is burning fiercely. Slowly she mounts into the air. A murmur of approving "Ohs" and "Ahs" is heard as the clustered circle, faces upraised, watch the now filled balloon ascending. Above the beach it encounters a small eddy of air. It spins slowly, its red, white, and blue panels revolving. Up-up-up—and up she goes.

Up the beach there is another just ascending, and beyond it another. Our neighbors are sending up their fire balloons. Then catastrophe strikes one of them. A shred of the burning excelsior is carried aloft. There is a small puff of smoke at the bottom of the bag; an enveloping flame creeps and then flares up the paper side. All ablaze now, it descends and falls into the sea.

High in the upper air and oscillating gently so that the little yellow fire below swings to and fro, our fire balloon mounts and mounts. Darkness is gathering and the balloon comes on to glow, with the light of the flame reflected from below, its red and white and blue panels gleaming. So it must have been, now upwards of two centuries ago, when the brothers Montgolfier made man's first ascent into the air in a hot-air balloon.

For a long time we would stand in our small circle on the sand and, with craned necks, watch our fire balloon trending out high over the calm sea until it was a mere speck of light against the darkening blue of the evening sky.

Do you remember that morning after the Fourth? How your ears rang! And that lazy lassitude when you first awoke after a few short hours of sleep on top of eighteen hours of tightly packed excitement. Ouch!—that burn on your thumb that you got when a split firecracker backfired, you just rubbed it raw against the sheet. So you lay there for a bit and wondered how that guy was, up at Grand Beach. He had a six-inch salute go off alongside his ear when he was trying to chuck it up in the air. Some said he'd lost half his right ear. Be no loss to him. They stuck out like stun'sails anyhow.

Better get up now: there was always some salvaging to do. That was the fun, the day after the Fourth. First thing, right alongside the path to the front door you found a bag full of torpedoes. And what did a small boy do with an unexploded torpedo when he found one? Right—he exploded it. And so the sleep of the neighborhood was once again shattered by a succession of staccato reports.

Down on the beach, that was where you could pick up the best relics of the Fourth. In front of every cottage a clapboard trough still stood in the sand, pointing out over the water. Here the night before the rockets had roared, soared, and flared to explode into clusters of colored balls of fire that exploded in their turn and then dropped away, fading, toward the black surface of the sea. Pretty soon someone found an old pinwheel with a single unexploded fuse. So you set that off. It spun crazily, giving off a blast with every fourth turn and sometimes missing its trick, sounding for all the world like one of those one-lung gasoline engines. Hey, there's a Roman candle stuffed into the sand. That must have been the one that hit the little Rogers girl right smack in the belly and never hurt her a mite. You set it off and it gave off a dim and pale light in the early morning air.

At length you exhausted all the unexploded fireworks, including a couple of packs of firecrackers that you touched off in a chain, creating a dandy racket—just like the Fourth again. So you set to work collecting all the burnt rocket sticks, the mine cases, Roman candleholders, and pinwheel frames. The acrid smell of stale burnt black powder, like the open ends of the twelve-gauge shells that gunners cast on the beach—that was a pleasurable aftermath of the Fourth.

Today these delights of the Fourth of July exist only as bits of remembrance in the minds of those who are known as old-timers. Nowadays the Fourth of July is safe and sane, and God knows, with the power of modern explosives, this is a good thing. In those old days it was anything but safe— that added the spice—and definitely it was insane. But it was one hell of a lot of fun.

The next heyday of summer was the birthday of a younger brother. Always at sundown, I now recall it, with the golden sunlight filtering down through the long needles of the tall pines into the grove beside the cottage. Against the soft soughing of the breeze in their tops, there arose from down there in the grove a chorus of thin, high-pitched voices— the little girls in starched dresses, the little boys uncomfortably encased once again in shoes and the blue Sunday suit. Candles there were everywhere, and bowls filled with wild roses and a picnic table fluttering with red, white, and blue paper napkins and favors galore. And ice cream in all the fancy shapes and in every color. And a cake that gleamed alight with the right number of candles. Everybody would read the legend traced across the top in red peppermint:

HAPPY BIRTHDAY
1904

In those long-ago halcyon days, there were times when the two small boys became possessed of a special kind of madness. The spring of the year was one of them, and many a mysterious grass fire could be laid to this source. In midsummer there would be another. I have in mind the limp and long days of breathless quiet in late July or early August when the leaves of the trees hung lifeless, when the sea was an unblemished platter of blue, and when from somewhere out in the pine grove a cicada from time to time gave off a high keening like a sharp line suddenly etched against the silence.

Such a day was a do-nothing day. It was one to be spent in the shade, in a sitting posture, soaking up in contemplative mood the pleasant warmth, the stillness, and the absence of strain. But this is the mood of maturity. It does not comport with the mood of two small boys.

For small boys are active. They must be up and doing. This is the law of their nature. Otherwise, for them time is a-wasting. Still, the externals of so placid a morning do have their subtle effect. There does not seem to be anything in particular to do.

I have in my mind's eye a picture of them. They are seated in the shade of the veranda; their chores are long since done. It is too hot to play on the beach. To go swimming in the creek is impossible because of the vicious greenhead flies. For one reason or another, all their usual activities seem to be proscribed. So there they sit, with their bare feet hauled up so that their heels are hugging their hams. They have reached the dead end of existence. There is nothing to do.

Then suddenly there is action. One of them can be seen at the foot of the pine tree that rises up through a circular extension of the veranda. He starts shinnying up the rough bark, soon reaches the roof and steps off. Meanwhile the other lad has disappeared inside the house and now reappears with a length of line. This he coils and pitches up to his brother.

Now the operation commences. The lad below makes the dangling end of the line fast to the top of a small rocker and gives the signal. Up she goes, to be set on the roof, where she rocks for a bit. Then follows another chair, then a table, and next a bench, until the roof of the veranda is covered with all the porch furniture, save for a single heavy chair. The boy below now shinnies up the tree trunk; this calls for the strength of both of them. Now they seat themselves in two rockers for a bit of a rest.

Just about this time of the morning, Bert Skillins would come driving by in his surrey with the fringe on top, on his way to the depot to pick up the passengers on the noon train out of Portland. He would start to laugh as he reined in his horse, and then he would sit there and laugh and laugh until all the neighbors would come to their doors to see what was up. And in his telling of the tale, Bert would always claim that the horse laughed too.

This operation was known quite simply as fishing, and every summer for quite a spell it would while away the hours of a hot drowsy do-nothing day.

Then there was the celebrated annual affair known to all denizens of Pine Point as Uncle Ira's clambake.

A clambake is an American inheritance from the Indian.

On the shores of the little salt rivers in New England you can still find, at a turn here and in a cove there, vast mounds of ancient clamshells. These are the kitchen middens of the aborigines, the sites of a thousand and one of their succulent clambakes.

I can claim a kind of kinship with those aboriginal fetes; for to the first one I ever attended I was taken as a passenger in another aboriginal relic—a birchbark canoe. In the early days of the century everyone who took pride in the possession of a canoe owned what was known as a "birch." They were made on the Indian Island above Oldtown on the Penobscot River by the tribe that to this day has a reservation there.

My family had one, and that almost legendary character known to all as Uncle Ira had one too, a big, twenty-footer. Well do I remember trudging one sunny August afternoon in the sandy dust by his side as he plodded toward the creek with the mid-thwart of his birch resting on the nape of his neck. In the distance it looked as if he were wearing a vast and grotesque fore-and-aft hat. His voice, when he spoke, reverberated as in a cavern.

By the edge of the creek, with a deft turn of his shoulders and a pair of ready hands he caught the mid-thwart crosswise as it slid down off his neck, and lowered the birch slowly to set it gently in the water. There it floated lightly as if it were merely kissing the surface. There never was a craft of lighter draft than a birchbark canoe.

Then came my task. This was long before the time of Boy Scouts and boys' camps and in those days a small boy was supposed to know how to "bear a hand." So, while Uncle Ira returned to his woodshed for the great square basket of clams and the gunnysack full of lobsters—birds, he always called them—it was up to me to see to it that his birch did not float off on the rising tide. Also I was enjoined, under penalty of being "skinned," to keep out of her, and to this injunction I gave ample heed.

Pretty soon he was back and then off again for another load, which consisted of the most enormous camp coffeepot in my remembrance and a capacious bag of doughnuts—"sinkers," he called them. This time he was accompanied by his wife, who, beloved by all, was known as Aunt Emily. Then he loaded the birch—a nice operation in which passengers and duffle were expertly distributed so as to ballast and balance her properly.

In the bow was Aunt Emily, a small spry woman wearing a sunbonnet. She had charge of the lantern. This she was to keep upright at all cost. "It only takes one drop of oil to spoil a mess of beans" was her husband's warning. Just forward of amidships he stowed the clams, the lobsters, and the coffeepot. Then, in charge of the doughnuts, came myself. And finally there was Uncle Ira.

As we left the beach, he rose to his feet. He was a tall man, rising six feet, and had a nose like a fish hawk's bill which came down and threatened his chin. This he kept covered by a short, pointed beard. But it was his paddle that took your eye. It was taller than he was.

Propelled by great wide broad sweeps as his back and shoulders swung to the task, the birch slid swiftly out into the creek.

Threading a zigzag path swiftly through the tangle of dories, clam-boats, pleasure craft, and lobstermen's boats that lay tugging at their moorings at the mouth of the creek, we soon swung close by a high brown mudbank, atop of which grew the coarse green marsh grass, and out into the little salt river. Here, at half tide, the current was racing upstream. Uncle Ira now seated himself on the bias across the rear thwart. He started paddling with the slow sustained ease of sweep and the twist of the wrist inboard at the end of each stroke that marks the woodsman and true canoe-man.

From my vantage point at the water level in the bottom of the birch I could watch the tide creeping swiftly over the bare flats. This put up successive flights of feeding plover and the air was filled with whistling yellowleg, golden plover, beetlehead, ruddy turnstones, and myriads of smaller shore-birds winging downriver to alight on the outer foreshore to feed again as the tide pushed the seaweed up in windrows. In those days there were even a few jack curlew.

On either hand extended the Scarborough Marshes, their flat course running to meet a fir-covered ridge here and the rising slope of an open field there, with the square frame of a little saltbox house occasionally fitting into the scene. Only two things broke the monotonous level of the marsh: here and there the square frame of a gunner's shanty, and in aimless profusion—a sight never seen nowadays—the coni-cal shapes of the haycocks of marsh hay that had been cut and piled on the circular pilings called staddles sunk all over the marshes for that purpose.

As the birch sped swiftly, borne along by the rising tide, we passed the mouths of little creeks that wound on into the marsh, each one opening an enticing vista for the mo-ment of our passage. There are several small salt rivers that drain into and through these marshes like the fingers of an outstretched hand, and they finally join in a single stream that bears the generic title "the River." Then there are a myriad small tributaries of each, winding in tortuous blue curvings through the marsh.

*Hoo-roo! Hoo-roo!*

I looked for the familiar sight. Across the wide spread of the marsh and the blue river ahead, on a low trestle, a passenger train was running with a long plume of white smoke trailing out over the grass. In the distance it was like a toy train. And after traversing the marsh, it came to a stop by the side of the box-like toy station. Soon a buckboard of passengers would be seen trundling along the causeway over the marsh, bound as were we for the clambake.

Then we passed beneath the railroad trestle, sliding quickly between the barnacle-lined pilings. Around the next bend the stream, with the wide marsh on one side, would make in toward a high shore. There, shouldered against the sky, were the black plumes of a grove of matchless white pine. That was our destination: Eagle's Nest.

Now the birch nudged its nose into the soft gray clay that formed the bank of the creek. Instantly a kingfisher launched from an overhanging birch stub and, sounding his warning rattle, swung in a long curving bow of flight upstream. In the unloading and lugging a small boy again bore a hand, and in jig time the birch was pulled out of the river and placed overturned at a safe distance above the tide line. Then came the hard climb up the steep bank, and the toting of the gear and supplies.

Eagle's Nest, I like to think, was a stand of virgin timber. There was no underbrush. You walked with elastic step on a bed of yielding brown needles. This was the accumulation of generations. Overhead was the dark tapestry of the plumes of the pines. There was no sunlight, hardly a chink through which to see the sky. The light came in from the low sides of the grove, and now, as always, it was a dim, filtered light. From far up aloft came the soft sound of arboreal music as the air soughed in the thick tops of the trees. And they were legion—tall and majestic, their limbs intertwining and bare, until away up above they formed a dark canopy.

This stand of white pine, this Eagle's Nest, had been a picnic grove for so long that the mind of man runneth not to the contrary thereof. In the middle, near to and facing the steep bank of the stream, were the weather-beaten tables and benches that over the years had served for many a clambake. Midway in this long line of benches and tables, and overlooking the stream, was a flat cairn of stones about three foot high.

Now the work began, and a small boy had his share in it. With the stub of an old broom, the litter of dried-out rock-weed, old clamshells, and weather-stained lobster shells was swept to the edge and down over the bank. Meanwhile, Uncle Ira's axe was flashing in the dim light by the wood-pile and the still air rang with its *chunks* and his grunts, the one punctuating the other. Aunt Emily was setting up the tables and carefully mixing the eggs and the grounds that go to make up the woodsman's coffee.

Soon the cairn had been swept clean, the missing stones replaced, and Uncle Ira was building his fire of birch and maple stubs stacked crib-fashion on top of the cairn. Down into the center of the pile he thrust several rolls of birchbark. Then he struck a match—one of those long, sulphur, and phosphorous-tipped matches that he broke off a card; a whiff of its fumes coming downwind always reminded me of a sulphur stink. Shreds of black smoke curled aloft, to be dissipated by the hot flames mounting up through the birch and maple. In short order, a blazing fire was roaring up from the cairn.

Now we had time for a little ease. Uncle Ira lit his pipe, a long curving calabash. Aunt Emily sat on a stump and looked out over the marsh, where the afternoon sun was lighting the grass with a golden fire. As for me, I would sneak down over the bank into the bushes and strip for a swim in the creek. And when I was out in the stream, between ducking my head underwater to keep clear of the greenheads, I could hear voices of welcome and cheer. The buckboard had arrived. The clan was gathering.

As the sun fell toward the skyline and the shadows of the tall pines commenced to creep out over the marsh on the other side of the river, the moment approached. The fire was now burning low. Every now and again Uncle Ira would manhandle a long rake and haul a still-burning stick back and forth over the glowing coals. Soon he had the fire burned down to a level bed of embers that was alive with little dancing blue flames.

"Bear a hand now, men, lively!" sung out Uncle Ira.

This was it. All hands worked fast. Each had his appointed task. Two long-handled rakes operating from each side of the cairn raked the coals off the white-hot stones. Those in charge of the rockweed flung off the tarpaulin that had covered the glistening mound, and came forward with great armfuls to toss on the hot stones. A loud hissing arose as great clouds of salty steam ascended in puffs. The rakes leveled the bed. Then the clams were flung on the steaming rockweed. Next came more seaweed, burying the clams.

"Lively there, boys, lively."

Now the lobsters—Uncle Ira's "birds"—their dark bodies and claws barely distinguishable against the green-brown weed, were tossed on. Feelers waved agonizingly and claws gesticulated in the split instant before they, too, were buried beneath more rockweed.

"Bear a hand there with that tarpaulin."

In jig time it was flung over and covered the entire mass, and men were laying stones along the selvage to secure it on the ground.

Now all hands stepped back to survey the scene. Where three minutes before there had been a bed of blazing coals there now rose in a rounding mound a bulging mass of rockweed covered in close by a huge tarpaulin. Not a breath of steam was escaping anywhere.

There was the trick. Underneath the tarpaulin and nestled amid the rockweed, the "birds" and clams would steam and steam. How long? That was a matter of judgment, Uncle Ira's, that is, and he had a reputation for good judgment in a fog, in those parts the highest encomium one man can pay another.

For the moment he had turned his attention to a smaller fire, where the ritual of boiled coffee was performed. First the water was brought to a furious boil. Then in went the congealed mass of coffee mixed with a couple of eggs. This was stirred vigorously. The pot would then be lowered into the flames and allowed to come to the boil again. At the moment of boiling over, it was withdrawn. This magic rite was performed once—twice—three times. Then away with her, and the cold eggshells would be plunged down to "settle her." The result: the finest drinking coffee in the world, sir, bar none.

Here, too, in an old washbasin another mess of clams was steaming. This was for the hot clam broth, into the salty essence of which the clams would be plunged before being devoured.

Now Uncle Ira is at the cairn, deftly rolling the stone off the corner of the tarpaulin with a moccasined foot. He lifts the corner for a short inspection, and then:

COME AND GET IT!

For a space there is bustle and confusion. Plates piled high with brick-red lobsters and shells yawning wide open, disclosing the succulent clams, pass from hand to hand down the long picnic tables. All hands fall to. Ah, the remembered taste of those clams and lobsters, permeated with the salt and the smoke and the steam. At the end, generous quarters of sweet apple pie are dished out, the great copper pot full of woodsman's coffee comes by, and there are doughnuts for dunking.

At length the moon rises out of the black tops of the pines on the opposite ridge. As it climbs and shines down on the wide marsh, its pale light mingles with the ruddy glow from the fire and from the candles that, mounted in empty bottles on the table, are flickering and guttering.

On the way home I would watch the shores of the dark marsh slipping past and listen to the soft sweeping drip of the paddle as it swung forward. And this would be punctuated now and again by the startled *frawnk* of a night heron flushed into flight by our alien course downstream.

# Crossing Moosehead Lake

In the Maine Woods Thoreau has given us his account of crossing Moosehead Lake in a birchbark canoe in July 1857. There were three of them—Thoreau, his friend Edward Hoar, and their guide, the Penobscot Indian Joe Polis. The canoe—a birch, as it was called, measuring "18¼ feet long by 2 feet 6½ inches wide in the middle and one foot deep within"—was a new one, recently made by the Indian.

"Our little canoe, so neat and strong," says Thoreau, "drew a favorable criticism from all the wiseacres."

How three grown men, with all their gear and supplies, could get into this craft and paddle the length of Moosehead Lake, a distance of nearly forty miles, without being swamped will ever remain a mystery. The time of their passage was unusual. They left the foot of the lake at four in the morning and followed its westerly shore past the mouth of the Moose River, where they crossed its narrowest strait, and arrived at Mt. Kineo near noon.

This was a swift passage, the distance run being a good twenty miles. The wind must have been both light and favorable, and Thoreau tells us that it was "at first southwesterly"—a favorable wind.

The first night they camped just north of Mt. Kineo. During the afternoon they had ascended the peak and enjoyed the remarkable prospect of the Maine woods and streams and lakes from its summit. The next day, again aided by a favorable southwest wind, they made a long traverse of the arm of the lake that lies northwest of Mt. Kineo. They lugged across Northeast Carry twice and arrived at the West Branch of the Penobscot with their birch, stores, and gear at about four o'clock in the afternoon of the second day.

This was a remarkable passage, and as soon as I had read Thoreau's account of it I was possessed of a strong desire to do the same.

In early September of 1923, in company with Baptiste Roncourt, a French-Canadian guide, I left the foot of the lake at dawn. That first day we made the head of Deer Island. There we remained in camp for two days—windbound. In the twilight of the second day, the smoky southwester that had been blowing having dropped to a whisper, we made a quick short passage to Hogback Island. There we camped and the next day with a good southwest breeze astern we paddled around Mt. Kineo and across North Bay to Northeast Carry.

Daybreak this September morning had seen a southeast wind driving tumbling clouds overhead and covering the surface of Moosehead Lake with long rolling swells. Along the skyline to the eastward there lay furled a low bank of fog and cloud. Over this the wind swept, catching at its edge, tearing off large masses, and rolling them, tumbling, across the lowering sky. These reached to the far skyline and spread over forest and lake a low panoply of dirty gray, its curving contours swiftly scudding.

In the west the dark shoulders of Squaw mountain thrust aloft and arrested the clouds in their flight. A thick mantle of mist and fog and cloud covered its dark wooded sides. Here the wind again caught at the edges, tearing off great strips that stalked away down wind until they were lost in the gray distance. It was a wild, cold, foreboding scene.

At the foot of the lake lies the town of Greenville, a hamlet of squat frame houses at the edge of the forest. From its scattered chimneys no smoke emerged. The nearby woods rose dank and dark—forests of dripping pine and evergreen. In the heavy silence of early morning the weather conspired with the night to prolong its spell.

On a point of land that, jutting, makes an arm of West Cove stood the form of a man. Motionless and silent, he gazed out over the broad rolling expanse of Moosehead Lake. An old conical black felt hat of the type long affected by lumbermen was canted over his face, hiding it. A lumberman's shirt of checkered green and black and a pair of khaki trousers, their legs cut off halfway between ankle and knee, blended with the rocks and trees. He stood on a rock as if he had always stood there, studying the turbulent surface of Moosehead Lake. Suddenly he turned and was off down the path to the shore in a curious lope, swift and light-footed as a cat. By the side of the path, overturned in the grass, lay two canoes.

Leaning over, he seized the middle thwart of his broad-beamed twenty-footer with his right hand at the near gunwhale and his left hand at the far one. He raised the near side onto his right knee, and with a quick heave and a powerful assist from his right knee under the bottom, he lifted the canoe shoulder high and then, with a quick turn to the left, slid its middle thwart across his shoulder and neck.

Thereupon he walked away with her, bottom side up. At the water's edge this swift evolution was reversed; she now floated ever so lightly on the waters of Moosehead Lake, and my sixteen-footer joined her.

The two canoes now stood away from the shore. Each carried a small cargo of boxes, firkins, gunnysacks, tents, bedding, and the like, carefully stowed with an eye to the balancing of the craft and secured against the spray and the weather by a heavy tarpaulin. The larger canoe was in the van. In French-Canadian style she bore her name, *White Water,* on her port bow, and that of her owner, Baptiste Roncourt, on her starboard bow. Roncourt sat quietly in the stern, his paddle resting across his knees, gazing down the lake while waiting for me to join him.

The sixteen-footer slid alongside and we started off in company, with slow and easy strokes of the paddle and a fair wind astern. The dark shores of Moosehead Lake slipped past. Soon the Frenchman's cabin, where I had spent the night, grew indistinct in the mist, and at length it merged with the hillside. Squaw Point ran out ahead to the left. Beyond it, with the force of the wind sweeping out from the length of Sandy Bay, the surface of the lake was etched in fine white lines, which appeared and disappeared in an uneasy offbeat rhythm. The Frenchman's eyes were fixed on them, his thin lips compressed.

"Hummm! I tink as how maybe we better hug de shore roun' Squaw Point."

The prow of his canoe turned in response to the quick twist he gave to his paddle as he lifted it from the water to swing it forward. I followed suit and we bore down on Squaw Point, a low straggling sandy bar with scattered rocks, sparse brush, and scrubby trees that became distinct as we approached. Near the shore the waves were rolling and they swept up over the gravel and sand with resounding rasps. The Frenchman turned:

"Young feller, you watch Baptiste, how he take de wave."

Hitching himself sidewise in his seat, he dragged his long paddle astern so as to bring the course of the canoe at a 45-degree angle with the waves. A wave rode under her stern. She rose and then, as the wave rolled under her, she sank. When it reached amidships, he buried his paddle in a short, sharp stroke, and the canoe surged ahead. The wave, still rolling, was under her bow. With his supple body rolling with the roll of the canoe, there came another short swift stroke before the next comber slid under her stern.

This difficult bit of balancing, timing, and paddling I had to learn. The sixteen-footer tossed like a clamshell in a tempest. The waves were greedy. As they rolled under her rounding bottom, they slapped salaciously at her sides. Now the crest of one wave slatted aboard, clearing the gunwale and dousing the tarpaulin.

"Keep her out o' de trough!"

I edged forward and down from my seat to my knees. Here I concentrated on keeping the canoe at the proper angle to the rolling waves. Once we were clear of the chop occasioned by the backwash from the bar, the rolling became steadier and I was able to make better progress. But when Squaw

Point was at long last weathered, and the canoe was sliding through the quieter water in its lee, my arms and chest were aching. I christened a bright new red bandana on a dripping brow.

Squaw Point had now been left astern and the two canoes were passing in the lee of Moose Island, with a fair wind on the port quarter. The surface in the lee of this shore was deceptively calm. On the ridge that rose on the island to our left the tops of the trees were twisting and lashing, and to the right, far out in the full force of the wind, the lake presented a vista of rolling whitecaps.

The water shoaled; great boulders stood out. The passage of the canoes scared up three gulls and, from their comfortable perches on the rocks, they lurched into ungainly flight and mounted unsteadily into the air. The wind hauled over to the south of west and rifts of blue began to appear between the swiftly scudding clouds. Perhaps it would clear. But the guide shook his head. This meant more wind —a good old-fashioned smoky sou'wester, this time of the year.

"Hey you! Read me what she say on dat *affiche!*"

He pointed to a yellow tin sign nailed to a tall birch on the bank. It indicated the location of a spring hard by, and I conveyed this intelligence. Whereupon:

"Dis be a carker lunch groun'. We lunch right here, young feller."

A word is in order as to this Frenchman's patois. Never once did it follow the pattern tradition has ordained for the speech of the French Canadian. And now, as the fire mounted and the teakettle steamed, there rung through the woods the words of his favorite chanson:

> *"Please, Mister Conductaire, don' put me*
> *off de train;*
> *De bes' fren' I got in de worl', sir,*
> *she's waitin' fer me in pain.*

*She's not expected ter live, sir, an' she*
*may not live troo de day,*
*An' I wanna kiss Mother goodbye, sir,*
*afore God takes her away."*

This is the climax of a dolorous refrain. "A leetle boy with golden curls," it seems, had boarded the train for Bangor. Down the aisle comes "de gruff ol' conductaire," who rudely demands the fare. But "de leetle boy" has no money, and this is where we came in.

There is more. The hat is passed among the lumberjacks, the fare is paid, the "conductaire" wipes away the tear that has fallen from his eye onto his mustache, the train reaches Bangor, and the mission is accomplished.

His thin falsetto again took up the burden of the refrain as he tended the bacon that sputtered in the spider, boiled the tea, and warmed up the johnnycake in a baker that sat on four legs in front of his small fire.

This contrivance made of galvanized tin was open at one side for the insertion of a pan on narrow little ledge-like shelves. Then, when it is set with its open side facing the flames, its slanting top, vertical back, and sloping bottom combine to reflect and concentrate the heat on the pan. This handy device the Maine woodsman called his Yankee baker. Sometimes known as a reflector baker, it also serves as his dishpan.

My aching back and shoulder muscles had found contours of ease in the bed of dried balsam that marked the tent site of this old lunch ground. Overhead the limbs of a maple swayed back and forth in the steady breeze. As the branches weaved and parted, I glimpsed through half-closed eyes the bellying bottom of a passing cloud and a moment later a rift of blue sky. Where the sun hung, now past the meridian, there was the yellow of the low scud and, when for a moment the wind blew it clear, the leaves of the maple were spattered with sunlight. Then it was dun again, and the pattern that had passed in the sky was repeated.

In the parlance of the State of Maine, it was burning off.

Suddenly a dig in the ribs fetches me upright. I all but upset a tin plate filled with bacon, brown and dried to a crisp crust, and a large quarter of golden corncake. Beside me on the ground is a tin cup of black tea.

We eat. This is a solemn ceremony performed in silence, with precision and dispatch. I watch the rise and fall of a prominent Adam's apple as my companion gulps and then swallows large mouthfuls of tea. He is the first to finish and he announces the fact by tossing his cup and plate in a clatter on the stones of the fireplace and wiping his hands back and forth across his thighs.

In short order the lunch ground was cleaned up, the dishes were washed, and a hiss of hot steam rose billowing when the dish water was flung on the embers of the dying fire. We shoved off and the two canoes ran clear of Moose Island. The mist had burned off, the sun was shining, and the wind had dropped. Moosehead Lake lay ahead in a placid stretch of silver. With a good lunch within and fair weather without, we were off on the next leg of the journey.

"You see that leetle islan'?"

The Frenchman pointed with his paddle toward the south shore of Deer Island and I made out a small patch of green in a cove there.

"That's Whiskey Island. We make that feller and then we rest up good."

His arm rose and fell with unfailing regularity as he set a stiff pace. Soon the water became a little choppy, which was curious for so small a wind. On and on we went and suddenly once again we were in the midst of rolling seas. My paddle grew heavy and my arm stiff. I shifted sides and paddled harder. Deer Island was a long way off and it seemed to recede rather than come nearer. Would we never weather that next point and get again in the lee? The big twenty-footer ploughed steadily on ahead, and I struggled to keep up.

So it is in paddling Moosehead Lake. Your course is a series of short traverses from point to point, from island to island. As Thoreau had found it in 1857:

"A very little wind on these broad lakes raises a sea which will swamp a canoe. Looking off from a lee shore, the surface may appear to be very little agitated, almost smooth, or if you see a few white crests they appear nearly level with the rest of the lake; but when you get out so far, you may find quite a sea running . . ."

Whiskey Island played tricks with a tired eye. Time and again I figured it was merely a part of Deer Island. Slowly, oh how slowly, the trees on that shore became clear and grew clearer. Now the spray of the waves could be seen on the rocks.

"Hang to her, old boy!"

The Frenchman's voice came thin upwind.

Then Whiskey Island was achieved and we ran the canoes. into the cove in its lee. It is nothing but a rock or two supporting a sparse growth of bushes now tossed and beaten down by the wind that was piling the waves on its rocks. I ran the canoe alongside *White Water* and shared the dipper the little Frenchman always carried on his belt. The cool water of Moosehead Lake wet my parched throat. We clambered ashore and I lay down for a short and welcome rest.

From Whiskey Island to the thoroughfare between Deer and Sugar Island is a bare half mile. Through that thoroughfare, my companion informed me, we must go.

I groaned. The wind would be on the beam.

The moment the two canoes poked their noses past the end of Whiskey Island, they were hit broadside by the smoky sou'wester. This was the worst yet—with the wind howling on the right, the waves pounding the rocky shore a few feet away on the left, and a half mile of it to go. By dint of constant and herculean effort paddling on my knees, I kept the prow of the canoe quartered into the wind and slugged away at it. The crests of the waves slapped on the bow and successive showers of spray splashed on the tarpaulin covering my gear. With the wind on the quarter it was bad enough, but this attempt to buck it was really rugged.

Our progress, measured against the growth on the shore, was agonizingly slow. Halfway to the thoroughfare the shore began to bear away to the left. Once this was achieved, it was possible to swing the canoe and thus bring the awful wind on the quarter. Then the work eased.

Suddenly the trees lining the shore opened up. There was a clearing, and beyond it, scattered among the trees, stood the little cabins of a sporting camp. On the veranda of the main camp several people who were wandering about stopped and watched. We waved our paddles; they waved in return. Then, with the wind astern with the turning of the narrows, we passed swiftly along between the two islands, leaving the camp behind.

The Frenchman stood in the stern, surveying the low shore. He was looking for a campsite. As the shore keeps turning to the left, we were completely out of the wind, in the quiet water of a lee shore. Suddenly *White Water*'s prow turned and grated softly in the sand of a small beach.

There followed an hour's hard work, despite my aching muscles. First the two canoes were unloaded, turned bottom side up on the small beach, and secured by lines from their mid-thwarts. Next the gear and stores were lugged up over the bank, sites for the fireplace and the lean-to were chosen, the lean-to was quickly pitched—a joint task. Then I turned to breaking boughs of balsam for the beds, while the guide collected stones for the two sides of his fireplace, drove stakes for the uprights, tied on the crossbar, and began to cut wood for the fire.

After an hour of this there was a chance for a pause. I looked around. The lean-to gleamed white at the edge of a thicket of fir. There was a fire crackling in the fireplace at the foot of a tall birch. Beyond the line of the shore, the surface of Moosehead Lake stretched away in a silvered expanse.

A little later, supper beside the dying fire is a concentrated affair. Again we eat in a silence that is broken only by the *lap-lap* of the waves stirred by the wind. This silence is primary and it well befits those who live and toil in the out-of-doors. For at the end of a day a hot supper is a goal attained after much travail. Consumption and satisfaction are the ends sought, and toward them all energies are single-mindedly directed. The silence is both natural and traditional.

A tin cup of black coffee stands perched precariously on the log before the fire. Toes pointed awkwardly together form at the knees a kind of shelf. Here, wedged, is the tin plate from which there arise, to blend in an ineluctable mélange, the steaming odors from a slab of rich red ham, a generous pile of "potats smuggled in onion," and a quarter section of golden johnnycake.

The Frenchman is seated on the ground, his legs, as it were, akimbo. The coffee cup is in one hand. His jaws work rhythmically and swiftly. His eyes are vacant and they gaze off into space out over the lake. He is planning his approach to the blackened pan of johnnycake that lies half-depleted on the hearth. While with his left hand his cup travels to his lips, his right hand reaches around his back to withdraw his knife from his belt. Then with it he lifts and transfers to his plate the third quarter section of the golden cake. Now the cup is down and the cake replaces it. Then this alternation between coffee and cake continues until both are consumed.

Supper is over. Pipes appear. A tin of tobacco changes hands. A brand is withdrawn from the embers; two heads bend together for the lighting. Then blue clouds of smoke ascend.

This was a time for ease, for contemplation. The darkness of early dusk was upon us. Out on the lake, a lonely loon called and the call came echoing back from the ridges. In a cove hard by, there sounded the *yaaank* of a crane. There was a chill in the air, and the Frenchman boughed up the fire. Sparks ascended and shadows wavered against the trees.

The waning of the second afternoon of our windbound stay on Deer Island brought the promise of a spectacular sunset. The sinking sun was flecking the leaves with warm light and the shadows of the trees started slanting across the campground. First the wind slackened and then it died away altogether, and the surface of Moosehead Lake lay limpid.

The smoke from the dying fire presented a curious phenomenon. Rising slowly from the charred logs in the fireplace, it drifted slowly across the lunchground toward the bank. There, caught in a downdraft, it swept in a burst of speed down to the surface of the lake. On the water there was a perfect calm, yet the gray smoke was seen traveling swiftly out just above the surface as far as the eye could follow it.

The sun had reached the end of its trail across the sky and now above the western skyline it was seen, through the earth's atmosphere, as a ball of molten gold. In the north and east the distant shores of the lake were dark in contrast to the color and light in the west. Mt. Kineo loomed black and as its steep massif rose it became a deep purple that changed to gray, and then there was white as the path of a long tangent of cloud stretched to the zenith. To the right stood the Spencers, Big and Little, over in Spencer Bay, and beyond, still distinct in the distance, the wooded sides of Mt. Katahdin—more properly, in the ancient fashion, Ktaadn— and so it will appear in these pages.

The sun was now half-hidden by the skyline. Into the burnished half disc three spruce thrust their black tops, to be for this moment outlined against the gold. Above the horizon a cloud hung, and with the rays of the sinking sun striking it, it gleamed throughout as if from the heat of some vast inner forge.

The sun sank. The shores of Moosehead Lake were bands of deep green dotted with patches of black spruce. All around the skyline lay a rim of purple haze that in the west was tinged with warm colors. The afterglow now flooded the sky and in turn its reflected light bathed the water with rich shades of olive and yellow and gold.

Sky and lake were like opposed mirrors reflecting the light thrown aloft out of the west to the zenith and from there deflected so that the limpid water was like molten copper shot through with gold. In front of the camp swam the black form of a loon, its wings slashed with white, its neck arched forward in the familiar graceful curve. Suddenly the long mandibles gaped wide and the aching cry traveled across the water and through the woods to echo and re-echo from distant ridges and faraway wooded hills.

Slowly the afterglow faded. At length the long cloud in the west was a gray ash. Then against the darkening blue of the evening sky I saw hanging a crescent moon. Again the loon called—a long, low, mournful call, like the sob of some sorrowing soul.

This was the time for action. Hastily striking our camp and loading the two canoes, we made a dash for Hogback Island. This meant a swift paddle of two miles across the widest stretch of Moosehead Lake. In the cool calm between the dropping of the strong southwest wind that had been blowing steadily and had kept us windbound for two nights, and the rise of the evening breeze after dusk, the lake had the placidity of a millpond. With the light in the sky and in the water slowly dying, it was a memorable passage. By the time the bows of the canoes rasped into the sandy shore of the little island, the stars had come out to stud the darkening blue of the heavens.

Darkness descends rapidly in the woods, and once ashore we were forced to grope our way with the aid of the glinting of a lantern. Aside from the fact that it provides a haven from the winds that sweep Moosehead Lake, Hogback Island has little to recommend it. It is a narrow ridge of sand and gravel, sharp and steep, that gives support to a thick growth of scrub pine.

Whenever nowadays I think that I am having an uncomfortable night I think back to that night on Hogback Island, and directly I drift comfortably off to sleep. Even the Frenchman cursed it and he had never slept on anything other than the soft side of a hardwood plank. He had a rule for bedding down on the ground. He always picked a spot that sloped gently, the idea being that his head would then rest at a higher level than his feet—"so's when I wake up," he would always explain, "I won't have me guts in me t'roat."

On Hogback Island no such place was to be found. Dragging our tarpaulins and blankets, we scrambled up the side of the ridge, tearing a path through the thick growth until at length we reached the crest, only to discover that it shelved away on the other side at the same steep angle. Hogback Island is well named. We spent that night athwart that back and for me sleep never came.

But it did for the Frenchman. For a space the mound of blankets beside me emitted a series of grunts, groans, and sighs, and then for an equal time I watched the mound rising and falling, slowly and silently. After a bit there rose a muffled muttering. I listened carefully.

"Ever' day I be gittin' handier ter de grave."

A pause.

"Maybe dat other place be jes' as good as dis one."

Another pause.

"I tink as maybe dey have a canoe up dere already for Baptiste."

After breakfast the next morning there was time for a little ease. I sat in front of the dying fire with my butt up against a log and smoked my pipe while the Frenchman sat on the other end of the log with his legs spread wide before him and between them, with care and reverence, he washed up his little store of tin dishes. This period was often the occasion for small revelations.

"Eat yerself a belly-full an' wear out yer ol' clo'se. Tha's the bes' fun a man kin have in dis worl'."

This bit of backwoods epicureanism was punctuated by a kick that overturned the pail full of dirty dishwater between his legs into the dying fire. The charred embers emitted a furious hiss that blasted upward into the calm air, a billowing cloud of smoke and steam.

In short order we were clear of Hogback Island and on our way again. It soon breezed up and I could see the uneven lines of whitecaps between Sandbar Island and the weather shore. So, following the lee shore, we passed in back of Sandbar Island until we reached the point beyond which the Moose River comes pouring down out of the west into Moosehead Lake.

Here, at the narrowest width of the lake, we quartered our course and made a traverse to the weather shore. This brought the wind on our port quarter, and we literally sailed past Mt. Kineo, where the great big old-fashioned summer hotel nestled against the dark side of the mountain. Just to show what a hell of a feller he was, the Frenchman stood up in the stern to paddle, and all the boys and girls on the tennis court and out on the golf links and fooling around the floats gave him a big hand.

Past Mt. Kineo the shore soon turns sharply toward the eastward, and when we rounded this point we were again in the lee. From this point there stretched away before us in an unbroken expanse of water the upper arm of Moosehead Lake known as North Bay. At the head of this bay lay our destination—Northeast Carry.

The hour was still early. The wind, a fair one, was out of the southwest and thus we were able to hold it on the port quarter all the way and let the heaving waves roll under us. But there was plenty of hard work ahead. Keeping the easterly shore within easy reach, we made it from head-land to headland across Kineo Bay and then farther on, down across Duck Cove. Then we came to the hardest passage, a long stretch across open water directly toward Northeast Carry.

With the broad sweep of North Bay astern and getting wider with every moment of our passage, the waves began really rolling. They all crested into white caps and I could see the white foam running up their backs. Treacherous ugly waves they were; and if in a moment of panic I should swing the bow too far, they would greedily slap their tops over the gunwale. A few of these and I would commence to wallow and then . . . So, kneeling in the bottom of the canoe, I concentrated all my attention on keeping her quartered just right.

With the larger canoe the Frenchman swept on ahead. He got there first and I was glad to have his help when my little cockleshell of a canoe bounced in toward the rough pier at Northeast Carry.

At the head of Moosehead Lake there are two portages, Northeast and Northwest Carry. Long before the days of the white man, these and a hundred other carries scattered through the Maine woods had been swamped, and their paths were thereafter kept clear by the padding of countless moccasins. In this wise the several watersheds of the wilderness were linked by the Indian into a widespread inland waterway. These were the primitive paths used in the early sixteenth century by the Jesuits in carrying the true faith to the lodges of their aboriginal allies and later, throughout the long French and Indian Wars, for the fanatical forays against the heathens from Boston who were thrusting forward one of the nation's earliest frontiers. The men, women, and children taken as prisoners to Quebec came to know these portages well. So did Benedict Arnold and the small army he led in 1775 to the attack on Quebec.

Today these portages are reverting to the wilderness. The truck that lumbers lurching along the bulldozed road and the plane that hops from lake to lake are all too rapidly taking their place. Even in Thoreau's day, the seed of their disintegration had been planted. In 1857 he wrote:

"As we were returning over the *track* where I had passed but a few minutes before, we started a partridge with her young partly from beneath the *wooden rails*."

Even in those days there was a trellis on Northeast Carry. By my time the rails were iron and there was a handcar. We piled all our dunnage aboard and lashed the canoes on the cradles provided for them. Then came a curious experience.

With the Frenchman operating on one side and I on the other, we laboriously poled this contraption up to the low crest. Once over this height o' land, as it is always called in the Maine woods, we coasted lickety-larrup down the incline on the other side to the shore of the West Branch of the Penobscot. I shall never forget the wild exhilaration of that ride. For awhile I thought we were going, in the lumberman's phrase, "to sluice our team" by jumping the rails. But somehow or other, by dint of braking and snubbing, we brought her under control and to a safe stop.

And so ended our crossing of Moosehead Lake. The next day, as had Thoreau on the last two of his excursions in the Maine woods, we paddled down the West Branch toward Chesuncook—known always, in the vernacular, as Suncook Lake—whence, ascending Umbazookskus Stream we made the portage over Mud Pond Carry into Mud Pond and then entered Chamberlain Lake, a headwater of the watershed of the Allagash. In the next lake of the chain—Eagle—we left the trail of Thoreau, who in 1857 had made Pillsbury Island there "the limit of our excursion in this direction" and had then backtracked into Chamberlain and gone down the East Branch to Bangor. Instead, we continued on through Eagle, through Churchill, and down the foaming Allagash into the St. John River and so to Fort Kent—thus completing the famed river trip of the Allagash.

# On the West Branch and
# the St. John

IN MIDSUMMER the year before (1922), Baptiste Roncourt
and I had crossed Moosehead Lake on the little steamboat
that ran out of Greenville. This time, too, we followed in the

steps of Thoreau, who in September 1853 had traversed the Lake on the steamboat *Moosehead,* "a well-appointed little boat," on the first leg of his excursion "a-moose-hunting" on the West Branch. But in our case, since our river trip was to encompass the upper watershed of the St. John River from its source in St. John Pond, we made our portage across Northwest Carry and launched our canoes into that part of the West Branch known as Seboomook Deadwater. Thereupon, instead of descending, we went up the West Branch.

The West Branch of what? The West Branch of the Penobscot. In the parlance of the Maine woodsman, the last three words of that phrase are redundant. He knows and speaks only of the East Branch and the West Branch. In keeping with this terminology, as you ascend the West Branch from Northwest Carry to where it turns in a northerly direction, it becomes the North Branch, and then at its conjunction with the Middle Branch, or Dole Brook, where it again twists to the right, it is known as the Northeast Branch. At the head of the Northeast Branch, the Penobscot takes one of its several rises in Abacotnetic Bog. There we would find, debouching through the alders to the shore of a small brook, an obscure carry which would lead us stumbling under our loads over the height of land into St. John Pond. Then at its outlet we would course down Baker Stream into Baker Lake and thence on down the St. John River.

This, in the Frenchman's book, was "de longes' reever treep out o' de town o' Greenville."

On that July afternoon the reflected heat of a sultry sun shimmered above the glassy surface of Seboomook deadwater. The silence was deep, broken only by the rhythmical dip and drip of the paddles. As the two canoes slid smoothly forward, dragonflies, coupled in mid-air, flashed past in erratic spurts of flight, and in sudden fright an army of water crawlers scattered to the right and left of our course. The gaunt bare trunks of the dry-ki standing in the shallow water along the shores appeared through the shimmering heat waves in wavering distortions.

At the edge of this one-time forest a boom of long logs, linked together by chains, twisted and wound, making a faint line in the water across the open mouth of a pocket, or logan, as it is known to the woodsman. Then it encircled a jutting point. Here the vagary of the falling water had left one log levered on a stump with its butt end buried in the mud and the other pointing aimlessly at the sky. From it descended the rusty chain that bound it to the next up-lifted log of the boom.

Here swam a flock of teal. In complete unconcern, they paddled about in a turmoil of preening and feeding. Now and again and here and there a head ducked under. Often there was but half a duck, tail twitching as its bill probed in the mud after food. Then up it came with a backward flirt of its head and a precise folding of its wings. As we passed, the noise of the paddles sent them swimming off into the small cove in back of the boom.

Across the deadwater, standing on the boom were four white gulls. Completely motionless, they stood stolid and inert in the hot sun. Then one of them flapped away awkwardly. This disturbed the composure of its companions and there ensued a confusing clamor of harsh cries and clumsy bodies flapping underway.

As we passed, the turtles sleeping on the warmed logs of the boom came alive, scrambled slightly, and splashed overside, disappearing in the dark depths of the water.

In the topmost hamper of a tall dead tree, a scraggly mass of dried sticks told of the fish hawk, and then there he was, launched from the limb below the nest and borne away on great still wings. He scaled off away from us and then began to mount in circular soarings, higher and ever higher in the sky.

Thus did we disturb the denizens of Seboomook Deadwater.

The sultry air was dead. Not a ripple ruffled the flat surface of the deadwater. The two canoes skimmed steadily on, with the dry-ki passing by in slow progression on either hand, and all the while the denizens of the deadwater were departing in deep dives or in silent flight. Thus it was until the sun hung low, a fiery ball over the horizon. Then from afar over the silent forest there came faintly to ear the low muttering rumble of distant thunder.

The heavy haze dulled the glare of the falling sun and merged with the dark clouds looming in the northwest, whence came the low rumble as if someone were throwing down lumber in a distant loft. A thunderstorm was advancing down the Penobscot.

Soon on the far horizon the tops of the trees were seen tossing and weaving in the wind, and puffs of heat were felt across the deadwater. The two canoes paused while tarpaulins were spread over the stores, the gear, and the blankets. The squall came on apace, advancing down the valley ahead like a great gray wall extending up into the sky. Now and again, baleful glares and rapier-like strokes of lightning illuminated the approaching clouds. Then came the crack, the crash, and the rolling reverberation.

In the deadwater, what a few moments before had been intermittent puffs of heat had now become breezes that brought scattered drops of rain. Soon we heard the rain approaching through the woods—a low dull roar of downpouring. Then the wall of rain was in the deadwater ahead, advancing steadily. The wind blew in sharp and sudden gusts and we bent to our paddles as the advance wall of rain hit hard, churning the surface of the deadwater.

Now it was upon us—pouring, pelting, descending in sheets. It encircled us, reaching forward on either hand and obscuring the shores. Above the roar of wind and rain there was now and again the crash of falling dry-ki. A split-second flash of searing intensity coincided with an ear-splitting *cra-a-a-a-ck* and the envelopment of a tall birch in a sheet of flame. We were lost in the pall of driving rain. Even the Frenchman's canoe, but a few feet away, was all but obscured from my sight.

The thunder gust was traveling down the valley of the Penobscot with a terrible intensity. The height of it seemed interminable. But it was not. In fact, it had passed rather quickly. First the rain slackened slightly. Then the force of the gale abated sharply. The spume dropped back into the water, the shores became dimly visible. The roaring of wind and rain, the brilliant glare of the lightning, the crack and crash of thunder—all were now in back of us, accompanying the gust on its downstream course.

Ahead, in the upper valley, the top of the forest was now visible. Wraiths of white mist were rising in slender columns, haunting the wilderness as they drifted slowly, now obscuring, now disclosing the green of the trees. Soon the downpour was only a scattering of drops. Then it stopped altogether and in the sky there were rifts of blue through the gray.

The air was the air of a brave new world, cool and sharp, clear and fresh. The sultriness of the early afternoon was gone, swept away by the now retreating storm, and we paddled on toward the end of the deadwater with renewed vigor and heightened spirits.

At length the deadwater began to shoal. I saw, in time to avoid them, the brown domes of great boulders just below the surface. Pretty soon the current became visible, carrying leaves past the canoe. Suddenly we came to the foot of a rip.

In the book of a woodsman, no man can begin to call himself a canoeman unless he can manage his canoe in quick water with a pole—his "settin' pole," as he calls it—and here my first lesson was about to begin.

The Frenchman went ahead. First he laid his paddle on top of his load so that its handle was handy to his grasp. Then, seizing his pole, he rose to his feet in the stern of the canoe. With a quick snap of the wrist, he dropped the butt of his pole overside, hung his weight on it, and the bow of the canoe shot swiftly up the little rip. Then, just before it lost headway, he pulled the pole forward hand over hand, there was another snap of his wrist, another heave on the pole, and again the canoe shot forward, this time to clear the quick water and float on into the deadwater beyond. He went on in the same manner, in an endless iteration, overhauling the pole, dropping it, shoving, and surging ahead.

This looked easy. But it was not.

In the hands of a novice, a canoe pole is the most awkward of implements. I seized mine, dropped the steel pick— for river work a canoe pole is always shod with a pick—and shoved.

WHOOP! I almost lost my balance and the canoe swung all but broadside in the rip. So I let her drift back to try her again.

This time the first shove was fairly successful. The canoe shot ahead, straight up the rip. But I was so pleased with my progress that I paused to watch it. This was fatal. I failed to drop my pole into the bed of the stream before the canoe lost its headway. Result: again it swung broadside to the course of the rip, and this time fetched up on a submerged rock. I made frantic efforts to get it loose and succeeded only in wedging it all the more.

The ignominious end of all this futility was this. I clambered over the side into the water and, hanging to the gunwale, waded to the bow, lifted it, and let the rush of the water swing the canoe clear. Then I dragged it up that rip.

And it was several days before I ceased dragging the rips and went up one on the end of my pole.

Poling in the shallow deadwaters between the rips was good practice and good sport, though this too had its hazards. Here I learned to have a healthy respect for the way on of a well-laden canoe. Shortly after I had negotiated that first rip I saw, all but awash and dead ahead, the brown dome of a submerged rock. Reacting to well-remembered instructions, I attempted to "snub her." This involved throwing the pole forward to drop the pick near the bow and then holding the pole to stop her headway. But on this first attempt the end of the pole was just ahead of my solar plexus.

It knocked the wind out of me, and I went over the stern to take an unexpected bath. The canoe fetched up on the rock. But in time I learned, and this I can affirm—it is a fascinating skill, this poling a canoe.

The next day we ran into a northeast storm. Is there—can there be—a sound more soothing than the tattoo of rain on a shingle roof? That steadily pulsing reverberation forms the backdrop for a host of related sounds. There is the seething dripping from the eaves, the throaty gurgle in the downspout, the sharp swish of a sudden gust of wind through wet leaves, the faraway rumble of thunder. And always the sound of the rain on the roof, at first a patter, then rising with the intensity of the downpour to a reverberating roar, at length slackening, returning to a gentle patter, and finally ceasing altogether, to leave a silence pregnant with dreams of great deeds.

This always puts me in mind of the rain on the roof of the old cabin by the dam at Abacotnetic Bog. We had first paddled, then poled, and finally dragged our way upstream to where the West Branch of the Penobscot hooks around into the North Branch and then bends again into the Northeast Branch. The night before, in camp at the junction of the Northeast Branch, we had supped on a squaretail pulled from the rapids just above Green Mountain Pool. The water being too low for the loaded canoes in the Northeast Branch, we had a rendezvous there with two Frenchmen from over St. Zacherie way. They had a team of horses and would tote our gear up the bed of the stream. We were to drag the canoes.

That morning it began to rain. God, how it rained! When a northeaster shrouds the north of Maine, this is no ordinary rainstorm. It is a deluge—a storm of apocalyptic proportions. Through the driving, drenching rain, I floundered upstream, dragging a canoe that required dumping, it seemed to me, every hundred yards. We got separated, each of us ploughing on alone, and the team lurching upstream over the boulders far behind. On and on and on I stumbled over the rocks in the bed of that brook into the teeth of that rain, blinded by the water leaking through the brim of my hat and streaming down into my eyes, dripping wet, my belly growling with hunger, and utterly miserable.

Then at long last we came, one by one, to the dam at Abacotnetic Bog—and the old camp there. Soon the split birch and rock maple were blazing in the firebox and I could hear the hot cinders tinkle against the tin stove pipe as the roaring flame carried them aloft. Before that warming stove I stripped and rubbed myself dry with my bare hands. Then I stretched out on a blanket spread out double on a bunk of split spruce poles—one of the best of beds.

And then did that old roaring rain sound good pouring down and bouncing off the old cedar slabs right over my head! That was a day for sleeping.

The next morning an incredibly clear and beautiful day dawned on Abacotnetic Bog. In a broad expanse of placid blue, this one of the hundred and one sources of the Penobscot River lay stretched out before us. We were to cross it, find the inlet, an obscure brook at the head of an alder-lined deadwater, and where this came to fast land, commence our portage—three miles across the height of land into St. John Pond, the most remote headwater of the St. John River, down which we were destined to run.

While the bacon was sizzling, the coffee gurgling in the pot, the johnnycake turning to a golden brown, and the mingled odors, spiced with wood smoke, were whetting my appetite, I listened to the retelling of an oft-told tale of a game warden. This is a grim, sad tale. It seems that one day there trickled out, in the unaccountable way that word passes in the woods, a rumor that a French Canadian—a Frenchman, in northern Maine parlance—was poaching at Baker Lake. This is the next body of water in the St. John watershed downstream from St. John Pond. He had been shacked up in there all through the winter, stripping the streams of beaver. The warden went in after him, following the same route that we were to take.

He got him. Folks knew that because the search party from Seven Islands, down on the St. John, later found their tracks in the woods and their campsites. In the telling of the tale it is always explained that on the way out the Frenchman could sleep, but the warden, he had to stay awake—all the time. Well, this search party came to Abacotnetic Bog, close to forty miles through the woods from the Frenchman's shack at the foot of Baker Lake, and there at the end of the carry the two pair of snowshoe tracks led out onto the ice. They put their glasses on the trail. Out in the middle there was open water, and open water shows no tracks. It was easy to see what had happened. The warden was a tired man, and instead of going all the way around by the shore, he took a chance on the ice in Abacotnetic Bog. In the spring they found the two of them by the dam.

Candor compels me to add that the foregoing is a legend. It appears to be a compound of two different events, the winter drowning in Abacotnetic Bog of two game wardens, Dave Brown and Walden Johnston, and the arrest, as related, of a Frenchman in the Baker Lake area by yet another warden.

With the canoes tracing ever widening wakes across the placid expanse of the pond, a smooth and pleasing paddle soon brought us to the head of Abacotnetic Bog. Here we again met the team from St. Zacherie that was to help us across the carry. This was on the sixth of August.

Forty days later, mid-September would find us on another height of land in New Brunswick, between the watersheds of the Tobique and the Nepisiguit Rivers. Here we would have to bull the three-mile carry by ourselves. The account that follows is of that later portage. The night before we made it, we camped on the carry in the woods.

Dawn in the deep woods is somber. There is none of the glamour of breaking day. No sun is seen to rise. There is only darkness that wanes and shadows that merge indistinguishably with light. Slowly, the trunks of the trees and then their branches emerge and take on form against the distant darkness. The sky overhead lightens and a small wind starts soughing softly through the tops of the pines. Below, in the depths of the woods, all is silent. There is no beam of a warm sun to cheer the rising camper. Nor does the lull of rushing water in a nearby stream come to ear to soothe him. As the shadows lighten and the darkness slowly dissipates, silently and without display the wilderness assumes the garb of day.

Soon the campfire had warmed a black bucket of oatmeal, there was a golden gleam in the overhanging shadow of the Yankee baker, and the coffeepot was gurgling throatily. We fell to and ate silently, our thoughts on the long hard day's work ahead. As we ate, the tops of the trees began to be flecked with the warm light cast by the unseen sun. The rich yellow of the johnnycake disappeared as generous squares were knifed out, leaving the blackened surface of the pan littered with scattered crumbs. The oatmeal bucket was quickly emptied, leaving only shreds clinging to its sides. Soon there was nothing left but the coffee, and then the pot was drained. For a few moments the smoke from two pipes paralleled the column of gray ascending from the dying embers of the campfire.

The Frenchman rose, seized his axe, and started off into the woods. I remained, lolling for a short moment with my back up against a stump, feasting on the rest that anticipated the day's work. My companion returned. He had a pair of slender birch sprouts. He split them with the axe, cut them in two, and turned their edges with a knife. Then he was off again; this time he returned with four crotched sticks. He sharpened the ends.

Meanwhile I had not been idle. The breakfast gear had been washed and stowed, the grub had been packed, the beds rolled, and the lean-to struck. As the fire was quenched, a cloud of steam billowed up from the hot stones and embers. Now at last we approached the canoe. She was a White, a cedar canoe—twenty feet long and broad of beam. The split birch sprouts were lashed, flat side up, to the thwarts in the bow and stern, with the width of a man's shoulders between them. The sharpened stakes were thrust into the ground fore and aft. The canoe was lifted, overturned, and set down with her gunwales in the crotches of the stakes.

The two of us slipped underneath. There was a short moment while the birch sprouts were adjusted. Then at the word of the Frenchman in the stern we rose in unison with the canoe on our shoulders. Reaching down, each pulled the two stakes nearest him out of the ground and thrust them overhead on the thwarts. On the carry, when we wished to stop for a rest, we had only to reach up, retrieve the two stakes, hold them on the ground at a slight angle, lower the gunwales into the crotches, and then step out from underneath.

Then we walked away with her.

Like some great long flat-backed animal, the canoe moved slowly along the carry, weaving its way between the trees as the path twisted. Despite the fact that its feet were in step, it proceeded with a curiously uneven, veering, lurching motion. This was caused by the rough terrain. Strange inarticulate noises reverberated within the cedar sides as the bow man, whose head was hidden, passed some word to his companion, who was lugging astern—to watch out for that rock, or the rotting remains of an old stump, or a windfall they must straddle. Ours was no sociable converse. It was born of the necessities of the portage.

Lugging a canoe thus across a carry is rugged work. It calls for endurance that is the offspring of long experience and equanimity beyond the scope of ordinary men. For every time one of the men eases the load, say on that aching left shoulder, this correspondingly galls the right shoulder of his companion. And as they mount a rise, or one of them steps up on a windfall, the weight of the now ungainly craft shifts, and the other man takes the brunt of it with a grunt and a steadiness of composure bordering on the miraculous.

But there was a respite. The Frenchman had lugged this carry before and he knew where it was best to stop and rest—after mounting a steep hardwood ridge, or hard by a hidden spring. When this decision was made, the strange creature would come to a sudden stop and then shed its back. The crotched sticks were raised to its gunwales, the canoe was lowered slowly, and we would walk out from beneath her.

Nothing was said. We stood about, rotating our shoulders, stretching our arms, taking the kinks out, and rubbing our necks. By now the sun had risen high in the sky and was slanting down through the trees. Both of us were sweating. It was hot inside that canoe. Reaching down by the side of the carry, we snatched great swabs of sphagnum and wiped our dripping faces with the moist, cool green moss. Each of us has a long drink at the spring, and when we are through, the old handle-less china mug was replaced upturned on the rock above the spring, ready for the next "feller."

The rest was a short one. Frequent rests but short ones, that's the way to get across a carry handily. It breaks the monotony, keeps a man fresh, and takes away the feeling that he is a damned pack animal. But there is a pride that goes with bulling a carry. It is born of the knowledge that a man can walk away with his load and keep up with the best of them.

Soon we were off again, raising the canoe by the birch sprouts that pressed hard on our shoulders. A sojourner on this carrying place could have marked our passage well—by an old felt hat cast aside here, a shirt spread over a small balsam to dry, or the deep red of a sweat-stained bandana hanging on a bush. At long last we came to the familiar bottom land. This meant the lake was near. The pace increased. Then the canoe was laid, overturned, by the side of the carry at the edge of Nepisiguit Lake.

Now for the walk back and for another load to lug.

There's always an easy way to tote, and all the other ways are hard. This is an adage of the woodsman, a distillation of his experience. There is another maxim that is not so easily observed: never lug anything in your hands. Let them swing free. And still another: Let the pack ride high on your back so that you lean forward under it when you walk away with it. Then finally, the universal rule: Take it easy; slow and steady does it.

The gear that goes with this lugging is the pack strap and the pack basket. The former is an assemblage of straps, buckles, and a tumpline that fits a man and his carefully packed load like a harness. The tumpline is a broad band of leather that encircles the forehead, with lines leading back and supporting the pack on a man's back. The pack basket is an old

Indian device. The Penobscot Indians still make them. I
have watched them weaving white strips of ash into long
light rectangular baskets that taper toward the top. They fit
naturally to a man's back and are equipped with a harness of
webbing into which a man slips his arms as if he were don-
ning a coat.

But on every portage there are rebellious and recalcitrant containers and articles that demand special treatment.
As we strode into our deserted camp at the head of Caribou
Brook, the Frenchman made for the two wooden firkins that
stood underneath the rough board table by the campfire.
Joining their wooden withe handles with a strap of heavy
burlap, he shouldered the two of them, one on his chest, the
other on his back. Then he staggered off down the carry. I
followed, and I must have been a sight to see. Hanging from
me and sticking out in front and back were pots, pans, ket-
tles, spiders, axes, guns, fishing rods, and paddles.

The rays of the setting sun were slanting through the
trees when we arrived at the end of the carry with our last
load. Twenty-one miles we had made this day, twelve of
them loaded, and nine without a load on the three return
trips to our camp of the night before. Then did we rest? No
sir! There was work aplenty ahead, and each turned to his
appointed task—pitching the tent, cutting wood, breaking
boughs for the bed, unrolling the bedding, pitching the
lean-to, cooking the supper. It was late when we were
through, and the sun had long since crowned the crest of
Mt. Sagamok when we sat down to a hot supper.

Ours was the silence of weary men. We had packed upwards of five hundred pounds of dead weight across that
carry. The lugging was over and the satisfaction of accom-
plishment was ours. We turned in, leaving a small fire to
crackle in the silence of the night and cast its wavering light
up amid the trees. Then the pale light of the hunter's moon

rose, slanting shadows through the trees across the dying embers and over the silent tent on the shore of Nepisiguit Lake.

On that earlier August night, after bulling the three-mile carry from Abacotnetic Bog into St. John Pond all day long, we were dog-tired. Baptiste aimed to cook up a mess of beans, that certain restorative of consumed energy, but he could not find his frying pan. A clatter arose as he poked around in the gunnysack that held his cooking rigging. Then the woods rang with invective—purple adjectives, sharp explosive oaths, a veritable torrent of profanity mingled with fantastic imagery concerning the antecedents, procreation, and gestation of "dem two gesely Frenchmen" who had, he claimed, stolen his spider the day before on the Northeast Branch. All of a sudden he stopped short. There was a pause —and:

"By God, I reckon that's jest as it should be!"

This tight-lipped acceptance of things as they are is the bench mark of a Penobscot River man.

A bit later, the white sides of the lean-to glowed a faint pink and grotesque shadows were reflected as the guide peeled off his pants and crawled in under his woods' quilt. I kicked aside the half-consumed logs of the fire and joined him. Soon the lantern was doused and I was lying on my back between the blankets on a bed of fresh fir boughs. Now the only light came from the dying embers and on the wall of the tent flickering shadows were like great stretching fingers. A small breeze rustled the leaves in the trees and little waves lapped lazily on the rocky shore.

The fire snapped and a leaf rasped slowly down the slanting canvas. Then . . .

The gray light of pre-dawn was filtering through the damp canvas. Above my head, the slanting canvas wall was littered with fallen pine needles and hazelnut shells cast down by the squirrels. A flash across it, and the scratch of tiny feet told of the scurrying passage of a chipmunk. I threw aside my blankets and stepped outside.

The dew was thick on the low brush—the air cool and soft, and no breath of a breeze was stirring. A leaf fluttered down through the foliage of a maple. This being the only event, it was one of note. The eastern horizon was warm with the glow of pink. In the west were the shadows of disappearing night. Overhead, the stars were paling. Columns of mist rising slowly and silently from the surface of St. John Pond merged with the white pall that hung at the height of the trees. Suddenly the golden beams of the hidden sun touched the skyline of the spruces with fire. Tangent rays illumined the sky.

This is the moment of dawn. With the slow rise of the sun, the white mist above the pond is suffused with pink until it is consumed and disappears. The birds are alert. A phoebe calls. A partridge is clucking near the spring. Out in the middle of the pond a duck swims. Now he rises, his wings beating up behind him a series of bejeweled rings of water. Mounting, he wheels and, winging into the path of the sun, disappears in the intensity of the light, to reappear a black speck skimming near the horizon.

There is a stirring in the lean-to, and I turn. Framed by the flaps of the tent and beneath a crumpled black hat, a pair of dark eyes peer forth.

"Hey! Joe! How's de eyebrows dis mornin'?"

After the long portage from Abacotnetic Bog, this warm August day on the shore of St. John Pond was one of needful rest. I spent the morning puttering about. At the shore in front of the campground the triple trunk of an old cedar made a comfortable backrest. I boughed it up with balsam, and there I sat in the ease of inertia, sweeping the wooded shores of St. John Pond with my glass. The sun was hanging hours high in the western sky. It was a hot sun, but the gentle pulse and repulse of the cat's-paws rippling the surface of the pond kept the air soft and cool.

All around the circular wooded shore in the reedy places deer—bucks, does, and fawns—were feeding. About two hundred yards from camp, on the western shore, a spikehorn and a doe were slowly splashing their way in my direction, now poised before a green bank, now hidden behind over-hanging brush, again stopping to feed and pulling at the weeds that floated on the surface of the water. The spikehorn was nervous. Now and again he slid into the bushes on the bank, to reappear a few feet further on. The doe unconcern-edly ate her way forward. Together they circled a windfall that lay in the water within a stone's throw of where I was sitting.

In that instant a gust of wind dislodged a tin pail from the table and sent it clattering over the stones of the fireplace. In a flash of dun, the spikehorn disappeared in the brush, his tail flicking a parting white flash against the green.

The doe has turned toward the campground, her ears cocked forward, her luminous eyes staring, her stance a pic-ture of questioning alarm. Then a quick jump in a beautiful arc, and in another flash of dun and white she too disap-pears. There comes the noise of breaking brush and the sharp click of hooves on stones. Then silence.

I swept the shore with my glasses. The other deer were standing still. Inquiring heads were turned, black noses pointed, and long ears cocked in my direction. Then slowly, one by one, the heads lowered. The desultory motion com-menced again; the feeding was resumed; and now all was as it had been before.

Again circling the wooded shore in a long sweep with the glass, I made a count of the deer. On this long lazy summer afternoon, there were sixty-five of them feeding around the green shores of St. John Pond, and they were pleasant com-pany. Apt indeed is the Indian name for this wild, deer-haunted pond—"good hunting ground"—Watoolwangamook.

Cocked up in my comfortable fir-bough seat against the triple trunk of the old cedar, I spent the next hour alternately watching and snoozing. Shifting my seat, scratching my back against the rough trunk, and stretching out my legs, I could feel the kinks in my muscles give and unravel. It was good, this—ease for the body and balm for the soul—to lazy away a whole day watching.

By now the sun was slanting toward the wooded skyline and the cat's-paws that had been ruffling the water had given way to a perfect calm. High in the sky over the pond was a mere black speck against the blue. As it traveled slowly in a wide circle of flight, I put my glasses on it. Instantly I was in a world of pure blue framed by the field of my glass. In this upper other world a single great black-and-white bird was endlessly turning in an extending circle on a vast spread of set wings.

It was an osprey, anciently called an ossifrage and in ornithological nomenclature termed *Pandion haliaëtus,* but commonly known as the fish hawk. On and on he sailed on extended pinions, endlessly turning in his lonely empyrean world. Never once did the wings move. He appeared to be descending ever so slowly.

Then of a sudden all is different in this upper world. A wing tilts. The great bird falls. Down, down, down, straight down he plummets. On the limpid placid surface of St. John Pond there is a great splash, and in that same instant the hawk is rising, his powerful wings pumping him aloft. He flies above where I am sitting, and as he passes from sight beyond the edge of the forest I see a large trout that now swims through the air, hiding from my sight the talons that clutch through its back.

Somewhere in back of me, out of the forest plain the dead stub of an ancient white pine towered aloft. On it was a tangle of dead sticks, and toward this haven the hawk was now flying. Soon a young osprey would be supping off of fresh trout.

*Lil-lil-lil-lu-lu-loo-loo.*

It was the cry of a loon echoing in the aisles of the woods.

"De loon, he call—de wind, she change," murmured the Frenchman.

There were other days for remembrance on the waters of the upper St. John. Late one afternoon I was dropping downstream miles ahead of the guide. All about was the quiet of the deep woods. The tinkle and the gurgle of the stream, and an occasional rustle as a susurrus from downstream swept through the leaves of the birch, beech, and maple lining the banks, were the only sounds. These I punctuated with the uneven click of the iron pick of my canoe pole against the stones.

I came out into a small clearing where the stream took a sudden bend to my left, and there ahead on a small bluff stood an old weather-beaten log cabin. I decided to shack in for a bit and let the Frenchman catch up with me. So I shoved the canoe ashore, climbed the bank, and dropped down where I could sit propped against an old log. Then I saw them.

Directly across the stream they were, out on the point made by the bend in the stream. Here the timber had been cut, and there was a bit of clear space. First I noticed some sort of a commotion, and it took a moment or two to realize what it was. They looked for all the world like young puppies. But, no. I saw I was mistaken, for there by the playground, erect on its haunches, with a bushy red tail curled alongside, stood the upright body of a red fox. She was a vixen and she was on watch. In the dust, rolling, twisting, tumbling, wrestling, snarling, and fighting, were half a dozen red balls of fur, her cubs.

For a full hour I sat and I watched the fox cubs at their

play. Never for a moment did they stop. Now and again a set of sharp teeth bit home through the fur and a shrill yelp would arise in the still air.

Finally the *click click* of a canoe pole came to ear. In the mind's eye I could see the guide running downstream, picking his channel, snubbing the canoe with his long pole, letting her stern swing with the force of the water in the rip. Once, in white water, I put my camera to my shoulder in the bow and, without looking or aiming, snapped the shutter. The picture is startling. Tensed, knees bent, with that sixteen-foot steel-tipped pole poised athwart the canoe and a pair of coal-like black eyes peering from beneath the black brim of his felt hat, and in back the skyline of the spruces, the Frenchman was the epitome of poised concentration.

Now upstream I could see the top of the long pole as it swung with each set.

"Halloo!"

He had seen my canoe, and his voice rang out, breaking the stillness of the woods.

The vixen—*Vulpes fulva*—and her cubs disappeared with a flash into the brush.

That night I was awakened by a queer noise—a rustling on the ground by my head, just outside the tent. It was some sort of a small animal crawling about in the night. It would start, then stop, then start again, and the really curious thing about this small noise was that the rustling had a queer metallic sound. As I lay on my back listening to it, I could look out at the foot of the lean-to to where the light of a pale moon was tracing a silver path on the surface of Baker Lake and then slanting through the pines on the shore.

Then there bulked in the half light beside me the form of my companion. Throwing aside his heavy woods' quilt, he rose to his feet, grunting, and stepped outside the tent. I heard him at the back. There was a muttered curse or two and a thrashing of brush. Then he returned. Pulling the woods' quilt up over him, he made a laconic explanation: "Quill pig. You don't want that feller clamb over your face in de sleep."

The word porcupine derives from the Latin *porcus* for pig and *spina* for thorn, and thus the Frenchman's term for him —quill pig—was strictly in the classical tradition.

The next morning, as, coffee mugs in hand, we lazied over the end of breakfast through those moments of delicious ease that precede the striking of the tent, the packing of the outfit, and the loading of the canoe, I was regaled with tales of quill pigs and with an exposition of their place in the scheme of things in the backwoods.

The quill pig, it seems, is at once a bane and a boon to mankind. There was the risk I in my innocence had unwittingly run in the night, that Mr. Porcupine would "clamb" over my face while I slept and leave me with a beard of quills. In addition, they are great thieves, a nuisance around camp, and destroyers of timber. The phrase for this last has always stuck in my memory:

"Dey destroy all de timber absoluted."

On the other hand, the quill pig is good to eat and it is "de onliest animal that a man can kill wit a stick if he be los' out in de wood."

This antithesis is reflected in the public policy of the State of Maine.

"One year de big lumber people, dey holler de quill pig eat all de popple. So dey put de bounty on dem. De nex' year some feller make a speech 'bout de time he get los' in de woods an' de quill pig save his life. Den dey take her off."

Tossing the dregs of his coffee into the dying fire, he ended his discourse with a man's usual estimate of his fellow lawgivers—"de damn fools."

A few days later, on a warm August morning, we struck out along an old tote road on an expedition after wild raspberries, this being the height of that delectable season in the

Maine woods. When the rotting remains of an old log cabin came into view, we knew we would find them there. And sure enough, nurtured by mounds of ancient manure and mulched with sawdust, great rounding clumps of raspberry bushes sparkling with the red spots of the ripe fruit were growing against the side of the dovetailed logs. Here in jig time a man could fill his black felt hat to the brim with the gleaming red berries.

At the entrance my companion pointed and said:

"Look!"

The frame of the doorway, the poles supporting the bunks inside, the great round logs—everywhere I looked the wood was scarred by the marks of gnawing teeth. Then came the laconic explanation.

"Quill pig."

From inside the cabin came the familiar rustling sound with its metallic overtone. I received my instructions. I was to stand guard while my companion went for a club. I was to have a live demonstration of how a man lost in the woods averts starvation.

The club procured, we entered. The metallic scrambling started up again. My eyes, accustoming to the gloom of the cabin, picked him out in a far corner. His size was startling; nearly that of a small cub bear. The operation commenced. The club was poked under the quill pig's rear end. The tail twitched with a violent slat and when the stick was withdrawn it was studded with quills. The hedgehog scrambled up over the logs toward an upper corner. Then followed thrust and slat, thrust and slat. The end of the club soon resembled a studded shillelagh.

Suddenly losing hold, the hedgehog fell heavily. Instantly, the stick landed across its snout in a powerful blow. Rolling heavily, the quill pig turned over, and lay dead on the floor.

Then we went berrying and after we had filled our hats we set out for camp. The Frenchman walked on ahead. Slung in a gunnysack over one shoulder was the quill pig, and in his other hand he was carrying his black domed hat filled to the brim with red raspberries.

The following evening a gentle wind was blowing off Baker Lake from precisely the right quarter to guarantee that the smoke from the fire would blow in the cook's eyes. Choking and cursing, he was leaning over to give a flip to half a dozen slices of dark brown meat that lay sizzling and sputtering in the fat in a spider. The while I was regaled with the details of how best to prepare this delicacy of the wilderness.

Then came the feast. Little need be said. Socrates drank his hemlock. On this occasion I ate mine, and my advice to those who get lost in the woods is to eschew the hedgehog and tackle a hemlock log in the first place.

*Caaaaaw Caaaaaw!*
And then the answer:
*Caa—Caa—Caa—Caa!*
A shadow slid down the gray wall of the tent. They went at it again, and the air resounded with raucous cawings, now short and staccato, now long and drawn out. My companion twisted under his woods' quilt and cursed softly. Sleep was out of the question and, throwing aside the quilt, he stepped out into the gray air.

Instantly the congregation went into caucus. There was a regular cacophony of cawing, for this lunch ground was in the midst of their roost. Large black shadows slid across the aperture of the tent as, cawing madly, the crows took flight and disappeared into the fog. The cawing grew fainter: they were crossing the river in search of a distant Canadian cornfield.

The early morning air was chill; the fog had settled on the earth like a heavy blanket. The Frenchman was cursing the lack of dry wood.

"A hell of a lunch groun' this rig is. No fir bough, no dry wood, no spring water—nothin' for a man to make himself constable with."

His fire was making a smoking, sputtering attempt to get underway and he eyed it disconsolately. Then he disappeared into the woods in search of the woodsman's remedy for a wet morning—birchbark. Soon he returned, his arms full, and kneeling, tucked the curls of bark into the crevices and under the damp wood. Clouds of thick black smoke, with streaks of red flame through them, rose in billows, and soon the fire was burning merrily. This added a bit of cheer to this damp and foggy morning.

The crows were still about. One of them was swaying in ungainly balance on the top of a nearby spruce. It called and was answered from afar. Then, catching a glimpse of the Frenchman rising from the fire, it set up a succession of strident cawings.

*"Blaaa."*

The crow made an ineffectual attempt to leap and only succeeded in falling out of the spruce. In mid-air it recovered its balance and then it disappeared, flapping into the thick fog out over the river.

"Come on, old timer, and drink your coffee."

The scalding black coffee dissipated the fog that had encroached upon my very soul. The Frenchman's disposition was distinctly affected by the fog. He peered out toward the river and sighed. Squatting on the ground before the fire, with his old black hat pulled down over his tousled head, his clothing webbed with the mist and a drop of moisture pearled at the end of his nose, he was the human embodiment of the fog.

The sun was now shining in the sky above, and below, the fog was slowly dissipating. As they say, it was burning off. This gave an indistinct outline to the quaint town on the other side of the St. John. The red of the roofs was somber in the fog. Here and there the tops of the spruces and the twin spires of the church towered above the low and now thin fog into the sunlight, and the moisture that still clung to them glistened like quicksilver. The wisps and small clouds of fog that still hung about the town now concealed, now revealed, as they drifted—the shadowy outlines of the square frame houses giving to them an aspect of unreality.

That evening the Frenchman prepared for a trip into "de clear." Be it noted, in passing, that when he was not in the woods, he was "in de clear." In short, we were on our way to town.

Already he was divesting himself of his ancient khaki trousers, the legs of which he had cut off halfway between the knee and the cuff. In the vernacular, these are "stagged pants" and very handy in traveling the backwoods. Thereupon he donned a pair of black serge so large that they dragged at his heels. A pair of white sneakers replaced his moccasins. The antique black jersey that was more hole than jersey was next peeled off, and a brilliant crimson one pulled on and tugged down over his chest.

Now came the triumph of his adornment. Groping about up to his elbows in the depths of the gunnysack in which he carried his spare clothing, he dredged up a collar button. This was inserted in the shirt band and, after considerable effort that seemed to herald incipient strangulation, the neck band was fastened. He then grabbed and cocked on the crown of his head the high-domed black felt hat affected by all lumberjacks and river drivers even in the days of Thoreau. Thus accoutered, he strode from the tent, leading the way to the ferry.

The ferry was a unique craft, and its propulsion was peculiar. Between guyed uprights on either bank there stretched a cable. Running on this were two heavy blocks from which descended the towing gear attached fore and aft to the double-ended flat-bottomed scow. The ferryman was distinguishable by the galluses that outlined a gaudy red X on the back of his sweat-stained shirt, and by the long pole against which he leaned. He was testing the accuracy of his expectoration on passing chips. These he almost unerringly submerged with swift jets of tobacco juice.

The ferry this night lay with one end nosed into the soft sand of the State of Maine and the other extending into the murky darkness of the St. John River. We passengers sauntered slowly aboard. A team rumbled onto the rough planking, the hooves of the horses sounding a muffled tattoo. The ferryman leaned nonchalantly against the forward rail, chewing a straw with which he seemed to be charting the stars.

Suddenly he was in motion. With a quick snap of his wrist, he dropped his setting pole into the stream and, walking along the side, shoved the scow out into the stream. Now dropping the pole on deck, he went amidships and there hove on a sort of windlass. This was odd. The ferry was barely moving and, if anything, was drifting downstream. Then of a sudden the prow veered upstream, and gathering sluggish speed, she forged ahead.

There was a soft gurgle as the water swept around the stern. By the turning of that windlass, the ferryman had set a scoop underneath the scow so that when the current struck it, this gave it the necessary propulsion. This accounted for the mysterious startings, the silent crossings, and the easy landings.

The current "set" her across.

The passage to the Canadian shore was made silently. The black mass of the blockhouse, a disintegrating relic of the Aroostook War, merged with the darkness of the receding shore. There were scudding clouds in the sky and, as they passed before it, a full moon let down rifts of light. For those moments the white water of the rips shone against the black water, and the trees on the shore ahead began to loom out of the darkness. The silence was punctuated by small sounds—the sudden stomp of a horse's hoof, the gurgle and drain of the current under the stern, and now and again an ominous rasp as the blocks scraped on a rusted portion of the cable.

The ferryboat slowed down. Now she was out of the current in the deadwater near the shore. The ferryman stood by to collect his fares—*dix sous*—and here, let it be known, is one place where a man is worth less than a sow, for whose squealing passage *cinquante sous* are demanded. The team started jerkily and rumbled off the ferry to clatter away over the stones into the darkness.

We brought up the rear. "Say, old-timer, can you tell us where a man can get a drink o' beer."

The ferryman shifted his quid, that speech might be possible, and extended a long arm.

*"La première maison à gauche."*

We climbed the bank and soon came upon a ramshackle frame house. The blinds were drawn and through the cracks slabs of yellow lamplight descended to the ground. We mounted the steps, entered, and as the rough door slammed shut, an attached bell jangled harshly. The interior was bare. On one wall was a large poster of Sir Wilfrid Laurier, whose silk hat, curling white mustache, and black topcoat were quaintly inept in this backwoods bar. The room was empty, and as the sharp sound of the bell died away, it was succeeded by a deep silence.

Then there was a step on the stairs, a pause, another step. There was no call. The slow steps continued. From somewhere above someone was descending. A pair of cowhide shoes were visible first; then, topping them, a pair of blue denim pants. The feet moved in halting fashion, and as the step down to another level was made, the right foot dragged after the left. A small rasp rose as the fingers of the right hand slipped over the rough plaster. The hand slid into view and, missing its hold on the wall, dropped inert at the man's side. The other sleeve was empty. Then he stood in full view, facing us, his eyes staring from beneath the down-drawn brim of an old felt hat. They were vacant eyes and they looked out past us. Finally he stumbled down off the staircase and, reaching the floor, stood swaying back and forth ever so slightly, with his eyes staring ahead and the empty sleeve swinging with his swaying.

The Frenchman addressed him: *"Bon jour, bon homme!"*

There was a moment of deep silence. Then, without moving and without fixing his gaze, he responded in the high falsetto of a very aged man: *"Je ne suis pas bon homme, parce qu'un bon homme est ce qu'on met dans les champs pour faire peur les corneilles."*

He paused and stood there, swaying. Then: *"Je suis— TOUT un homme."*

Setting himself in motion, he stumbled toward a doorway and disappeared.

And so it went, as we drifted down the waters of the St. John—the Wallastook—the stream where, in old-time Indian parlance, you get smooth boughs.

# Men of the Maine Woods

"AND STANDING FAIRE alongst by the shore, about twelve of the clocke of the same day, we came to an anker, where six Indians in a Baske-shallop with mast and saile, an iron grapple, and a kettle of copper, came boldly aboard us, one of them apparalled with a waist-coat and breaches of blacke serdge, made after our sea-fashion, hose and shoes on his feet; all the rest (saving one that had a pair of breeches of blue cloth) were all naked.

"These people are of tall stature, broad and grim visage, of a black swart complexion, their eie-browes painted white; their weapons bows and arrows; it seemed by some words and signs they made, that some Baskes or [men] of St. John de Luz, have fished or traded in this place, being in the latitude of 43 degrees."

So reads in part the record of Bartholomew Gosnold's voyage along the western coast of Maine as he trended southward in the little bark *Concord* in the spring of 1602. The significance of this account, one of the earliest about the Maine Indian, lies in the wealth of the detail that suggests earlier contacts between the white man and the Indian. The source of these is lost in the mists of the past.

In two years' time the Indians on the shores of the Penobscot, and a year later those on the Kennebec, would be greeting the great French explorer, Samuel de Champlain, and the stage would be set for the struggle between the French and the English for the North American continent. It was a long struggle, punctuated by bursts of savage and bloody warfare in which the religious passions of Puritan and Catholic had full play, and it came to an end a century and a half later, in 1759, with the fall of Quebec. In this tumultuous contest, when the uncertain bounds between the partisans traced now along the course of the Kennebec and again along the Penobscot River, the Indian, though for the larger part the ally of the French, was actually in the middle.

Soon the black robe of the Jesuit priest would be seen on the waterways of the Maine woods and his powerful presence would be adumbrated by the great wooden crosses erected in prominent places in the wilderness. "As soon as the warmth of the Spring began to thaw the snow," so runs

one of the famed *Jesuit Relations*, "they [the Indians] returned to the banks of the great river where they had left
their canoes and shallops. The first thing that they did, on
issuing from the forest, was to frame a great Cross . . ."

The first white man known to have crossed the height of
land from the watershed of the St. Lawrence to that of the
Kennebec was Father Gabriel Druilletes. "The Abnaquiois
having come to ask for a Father of our Society, to take him
into their country, and to learn from him the way to
Heaven." The several references to Father Druilletes's jour-
neys indicate that he was accompanied by parties of Indians
with seven or eight canoes and that the journey from Quebec
to the Abenaki village on the Kennebec took from two to
three weeks. He is believed to have followed the route of
the Indians that in later times would become a familiar one
—from the St. Lawrence up the Chaudière to Lake Megantic
and thence over the height of land into the watershed of the
Dead River and by successive portages between the lakes,
ponds, and thoroughfares of that stream into the Kennebec.
A century and a quarter later, Benedict Arnold would follow
this route in reverse in his march to Quebec.

The mobility of the Indian in his birchbark canoe is further illustrated in the other journeyings of Father Druilletes,
"down the whole length of the stream Kinibeki, conducted
by a Savage who was acquainted with the places where his
fellow-countrymen lived." At this point a claim should be
staked for this anonymous Indian as the first in a long and
honorable line of Maine guides. But the *Relation* continues:

"The Savage who conducted him, taking him another time
to that English settlement named Kinibeki [at the site of
modern Augusta] had him go down as far as the sea of
Acadia; where, on its coasts, he visits seven or eight English
settlements, at all of which he was received with a cordiality
all the more extraordinary since it was little expected. The
Savage, his guide, seeing himself on the shores of the sea of

Acadia in his little bark canoe, conducted the Father even to Pentagouet, where he found a little home of Capuchin Fathers . . ."

Down the Kennebec and up the Penobscot! What a canoe trip!

Early in 1647 the priest accompanied the Abenakis on "their great hunt . . . they ascend eight or ten days' journey along the river Kinibeki. They enter a great lake, where they appoint their rendezvous after the hunt. Having separated into several bands, they declared war on the Deer, the Elks, the Beavers, and other wild beasts. . . .

"Their hunt finished, they all met on the shores of that great lake."

Assuredly, this "great lake" cannot have been other than Moosehead Lake, in which the waters of the Kennebec take their rise.

The Indian of the Maine woods was a nomad. He was also a river man. He had his villages along the banks of the Saco, the Androscoggin, the Kennebec, the Penobscot, and a host of lesser streams. In the fall of the year and in winter he went upstream to hunt; in the spring of the year and in summer he paddled downstream to the coast to camp amid the wealth of shellfish and seafood with which the coast of Maine abounds. His birchbark canoe was his conveyance and the waterways of the country of the Maine were his highways.

"Picture to yourself a tall strong man, agile, of a swarthy complexion, without beard, with black hair and teeth whiter than ivory"—so writes Sebastian Rale, the Jesuit priest who met his death in the raid on Norridgewock in 1724. This was in that segment of the intermittent French and Indian Wars known to the New England of that day as Lovewell's War.

Long after the *Bostonais*, as the French were wont to call the English, had thrust forward along the coast and up the rivers into the forests of Maine—our forgotten eastern frontier—the Indian continued to live along the streams and to pursue the ancient ways of his ancient race. In several entries in his *Journal*, Thoreau recounts having seen and visited encampments of the Penobscots on the banks of the Charles, the Concord, and the Merrimack Rivers. In my own time I have seen and visited similar camps in the woods of Pine Point handy to the sweet grass that is found in abundance on the Scarborough marshes.

I have always thought that of all Thoreau's sympathetic relations of his contacts with the Indian the most poignant is that recorded in his Journal on the tenth of May 1838.

"I had much conversation with an old Indian at the latter place [Oldtown] who sat dreaming upon a scow at the waterside and striking his deerskin moccasins against the planks, while his arms hung listlessly by his side. He was the most communicative man I had met. Talked of hunting and fishing, old times and new times. Pointing up the Penobscot, he observed:

" 'Two or three mile up the river, one beautiful country.' "

Today, by ancient treaty, legislation, and custom, the Indian lives on what little is left of the hunting grounds of his ancestors. He is to be found in Maine on the Indian Islands in the Penobscot River and at Peter Dana's Point at Princeton and Pleasant Point at Eastport in Maine's easternmost Washington County. There is a similar reservation at Tobique Point in New Brunswick and there are Indians scattered here and there in the eastern provinces of Lower Canada.

It was once my privilege in the early fall of 1922 to visit the Indian village at Tobique Point.

"Can't you smell Skidjim?"

This inquiry came from the stern of the canoe as we ran swiftly through the turbulent waters churned up by the confluence of the St. John and the Aroostook Rivers. We were about three miles above Tobique Point, where the stream of that name comes in from the other side. Here was the Indian reservation. My pointing out the distance and the fact that the wind was from astern only produced the rejoinder that with a fair wind my companion could "smell Skidjim twenty miles away."

We were gliding through a canoeman's paradise. The St. John was wide and deep and swift. The fair wind fairly drove the canoe through the rips, where the surging waves lapped hungrily at her gunwales. The chill of early dawn had been dispelled by the warmth of the sun, now high in the sky, and the white water that was breaking and rushing upstream with the cresting of the waves in the rips was sending forth flashes of reflected sunlight. September was in the woods and the sparkle of early fall in the clear air. Here and there, amid the deep green of the hillsides that shouldered against the sky, there gleamed the blood red of a maple sprout and the glowing yellow of a poplar. This was but the prophecy of splendors to come. Now and again, overhanging the stream from the high bank and gleaming in red and orange clusters, were the ripened berries of the mountain ash. The sight of these provoked my companion into comment.

"De hash tree is jes' de ting for de Skidjim. See de canoe over dere?"

He pointed to a ramshackle canoe overturned on the bank.

"De Skidjim, dey up on de hill, cuttin' hash. Dey make basket out of that."

He was not to be diverted from his subject, and a dissertation followed on his life "wid de Skidjim down Pedennis Point."

"They's de best people in de worl' if a feller know how to treat dem. A Skidjim, if he like you, he give you half what he got. Sure, I trop one whole winter wid Noel Bear down

Pokamoonshine Lake. We had a carker trop line runnin' troo Shin Pond an' over Modagamon. I was only de white feller dey let stay wid de Skidjim overnight. All de res' dey has to pull dere freight away from de point at half past seven. But Baptiste, he know de way back. An' Noel an' me had plenty huckabee to keep company wid us dat winter."

*Huckabee*, he explained, was "Skidjim for booze. Sure dey talk dere Skidjim language, dese Skidjim. You know what *hadok* mean—well, that's a deer. An' *hodoksamo*—that's a moose. An' dey call a dog *holamos*. No, I can't tell you how to talk it. Only, when Baptiste git wid dem fellers, dey onerstan' him, an' he onerstan' dem. Down Old Town dey talk de Penobscot, an' de Passamaquoddy dey talk same as dey do down Pedennis Point. De fellers we comin' to, dey talk de Menasee."

He pointed to a slender column of smoke rising from the trees on the hills back from the bank where the overturned canoe was.

"Dey makin' *scut* for dere lunch groun'. *Scut*? That's Skidjim for fire."

Ahead, on the left bank, a canoe manned by two men was putting out into the stream. This generated curiosity astern, and I felt the canoe leap forward. The craft making obliquely across the river was a waterlogged affair, its back broken in the middle. As it passed into the rush of a rip, the force of the water bent in its side, but the two men paddled steadily on, unconcerned. Then, as they crossed our bow, my companion rested on his paddle and called out. The Indians turned, grinning, their white teeth agleam against their dark faces. The two canoes drifted rapidly apart and in an incredibly short time the Indians made the shore, overturned their canoe on the bank, and disappeared into the woods.

By now we were nearing Tobique Point, a low, level bank of sand on the east shore of the St. John that ran down into the mouth of the Tobique. Outlined against the sky stood the quaint frame houses of the Indian settlement—low, rambling squat buildings with bizarre façades and luridly painted blinds. The picayune tower of the little church rose with an air of proprietorship, and the houses around it rambled away toward the outskirts of the settlement. As our canoe grated on the sand, two little round copper-colored faces peering down from the top of the bank were surreptitiously withdrawn.

The shelving shore was lined with overturned canoes. An Indian was bending over one of them and now he rose and turned. He was a physical tribute to the lost power of his race. He stood a full six feet, straight as an ash. A gray flannel shirt open at the neck gave hint of the massive strength of his broad chest. Gazing quizzically at us, he shoved a ragged Panama hat askew on his bronzed forehead, the while scratching his graying hair. The strands of gray among the black hair, in contrast to the copper color of his skin, gave a sheen of silver to his head. Now he was standing in the water by the bow of our canoe, his waders covering his corduroy trousers. He gave laconic response to my companion's queries.

"Allo dere, old timer."

This form of salutation is traditional in the backwoods.

"How do."

"How many Skidjim you got up dere?"

"Bout tree hunder'."

"What you doin' to your canoe—puttin' de pitch to her?"

"Yes."

There came a pause, so I spoke up. "Seen any moose around here this year?"

The Indian stared. Then he shook his head slowly from side to side, as if pondering the question with great care. He replaced the Panama and turned his attention to my companion, who promptly shot another question into the air.

"You know a Skidjim by de name of Noel Bear?"

"Yes."

There was another pause. Then at long last came the Indian's first question.

"You know Noel?"

"Sure, I trop wid heem one winter down Pedennis Point."

The Indian now gazed at him solemnly for another long period of silence. Then: "Noel, he my brodder-in-law."

He turned to me. "You like to come ashore?"

Before I could respond, the invitation had been accepted by the Frenchman. Thrusting his paddle in the sand, he vaulted ashore. I stepped out of the bow, the canoe was beached, and the three of us slowly mounted the bank. A soft sound of thudding feet arose as the curious scuttled for their houses, where there would appear momentarily here and there, between the shade and the frame of a window, the slice of a face.

Everyone had disappeared save an aged squaw who was packing a bulky bundle of firewood high on her back. She gazed at us with frank curiosity. Then, without bending under her heavy load, she walked along the path ahead of us, her two plaits of silver hair dangling down over her hips, until turning she disappeared around the corner of a woodshed.

The Indian led the way to a neat little frame house near the brow of the bank. Without a word, he entered through the kitchen door. We followed.

The Indian pulled up a couple of chairs for us and then seated himself on the edge of the woodbox. His squaw, a thickset, square, heavy-jowled woman with straight black hair that was plaited and fell to her knees, eyed the visitors casually. A round-faced urchin clung to her knees, making exaggerated efforts to hide his copper-colored face in her skirt. But curiosity won out, and from time to time a dark eye peeped out. A lean and scrawny hound crawled out from beneath the stove, sniffing suspiciously.

Our host reached to a shelf for his tobacco tin, filled his pipe, and then passed the can to his two guests. In silence pipes were filled and lighted. The squaw reached for the tin, filled a blackened corncob, and lit it with a live brand that she withdrew from the stove. The blue smoke ascending from four pipes now filled the small kitchen.

As the squaw moved about, she stumbled over the little boy. Leaning over without a word, she seized him by the scruff of the neck, and lifting him, deposited him outside the back door. In a moment's time, I saw him manhandling a bucksaw bigger than he was. Its momentum pulled him forward across the log on the saw-buck and then he jerked it back, struggling manfully and engrossed in his task.

My companion now made inquiries about his friend Noel Bear.

"Noel, he up to Old Town now. Get marry next month."

Mutual acquaintances at Pedennis Point and Old Town were canvassed and discussed. The squaw listened gravely, her face passive and expressionless. Now and again, as a familiar name was mentioned, the deep dark eyes would gleam and then die away to their natural somnolence.

I took a look around. We were occupying the only chairs. Opposite where we sat, a doorway opened into the only other room in the house. Here stood a gaudy brass bed and beside it a trundle bed. Outlined by a flaming red quilt lay a baby with a little rotund belly. The walls were covered with cheap colored prints depicting scenes in the life of Christ. Above the head of the bed hung a wooden crucifix, and behind it a dried palm leaf. In the kitchen the pumpkin-pine floor had been scrubbed until it shone, and the shelves and closets were neatly arranged with the necessities of their existence. The stove stood supported on four bricks, caving in precariously in the middle, and a rickety funnel, ingeniously suspended by haywire, stretched its rusted length upwards to disappear in a disjointed angle through the roof.

The conversation at last turned from personalities to hunting, and the Indian announced that they had had good luck on the Point last winter. They had moose meat until the middle of April. Every fall a party goes up the Tobique after the winter's supply of red meat, and what is brought back is shared equitably among the inhabitants of Tobique Point. They returned last fall with five bulls—this is in comparison with the expeditions of their forefathers in the old days, when, it is related, 140 carcasses and 3,000 moose hides were brought down the Tobique every fall at the behest of their French conquerors.

Now that hunting had become the topic of conversation, the Indian did the talking.

"Callin' 'll be all right pretty soon now. After a couple of cold nights. Then they'll start to rut. The Tobique is good moose country. Plenty o' logans. Its dry now and you may see one in the stream or even along the tote road on the way up. You say you ain't got no horn?"

At this the squaw rose and padded softly into the bedroom. In a moment she reappeared with a straight and slightly tapering horn about eighteen inches in length. It was made of birchbark, deftly rolled and skillfully stitched, with the deep brown of the inner side of the bark outside. It was greatly admired.

"Say, ol' timer," said my companion, turning the horn slowly in his hands, "that's jes' a carker moose horn. Winter bark, too. You fellers know jes' where to get that. An' sewed up with raspberry root. I tell you it takes a Skidjim to make a good moose horn."

The Indian smiled.

"You take that one. I can get plenty."

At this juncture I was the recipient of a swift sidewise glance from my companion, and thereupon I delved deep into a pocket. Dredging up a tin of my cherished and fast-disappearing tobacco, I silently handed it to the squaw. Her

dark eyes glowed as she handled the tin. Then she murmured: *"Merci, m'sieu."*

The Indian nodded at me gravely over his pipe.

I still have that moose horn; it is the memento of that
occasion.

A silence ensued while the squaw knocked the still-smok-
ing coals out of her corncob into her left palm, half filled
the bowl with fresh tobacco with her right hand, and tamped
it down with the warm coals. Then she thrust a splinter of
birch into the embers in the stove, withdrew it flaming, and
sucked the small flame down into the bowl of her pipe. Her
head was nodding and she spoke softly.

*"Bon tabac."*

Her husband reached for the tin and the operation was
repeated.

A social equilibrium had been reached. I asked the squaw
if she was a full blood.

"No, my modder, she French. De ol' man"—here she nodded admiringly at her husband—"he full blood. Dey not
many left. De most of de people round here is half blood.
My husban', he de p'liceman on de Point."

Then, noticing my camera, she asked: "You want picture
of squaw. I go get pretty one."

With that, she padded across the kitchen, disappeared,
and returned a moment later.

"My niece, she ask you wait. She get her Skidjim dress on."

The talk turned again to Old Town.

"They treat our people well there. Plenty work. No tax.
They can't get *huckabee* [liquor]. That raise hell round
here."

The soft padding of moccasined feet sounded outside,
then a single gentle knock. Rising from the edge of the woodbox, the Indian opened the door. He announced simply: "My
niece, she ready."

The Skidjim dress she had been at pains to put on turned

out to be a cheap and faded khaki dress with a tangle of fringes at the waist, at the ends of the sleeves, and at the hem. A headband and a single feather rising from a shock of unruly black hair completed her costume for her role as a Menasee maiden. I have her snapshot still.

Then commenced a tour of Tobique Point—past the curious little wooden church that somehow reminded me of a toy, along the footpath between the meager frame houses, into the store, a darkening hole that was the abode of an old squaw with a virulent tongue. She was like a noisesome animal in a cave. In the yard of one of the houses we came upon two men seated on a low veranda. One of them was working swiftly with a crooked knife, pulling off long strips of white ash, and the other was weaving them into the frame of a basket, holding it the while within the spread of his knees. To one side of them lay a tumbled mass of freshly made white baskets. This was the industry of Tobique Point.

As we approached each house, our coming was watched by dark eyes that peered out at the edge of the drawn shades. Then, as we passed, the open doorway would fill with dark figures. And finally they joined the gathering crowd that trailed us at a respectable distance, until at last we came to the edge of the bank, where our canoe was drawn up.

The Indian shook my hand in grave silence. Then he assured my companion that his messages to his friend Noel Bear would be delivered upon the latter's return to Tobique Point after acquiring a wife in Old Town. We stepped into the canoe and shoved out into the stream.

"So long, Skidjim."

My companion was waving his long paddle in the air, and from the shore there came a low murmur of many voices.

"*Bonne chance. Au revoir.*"

I turned in the bow for a parting look. Our host stood erect, his powerful frame outlined against the sky. Beside him was his squaw, the smoke from her corncob pipe escaping back of her in short puffs. The urchin clung to her skirts and the hound was turning in and out among their legs. Back of them was gathered the crowd of the curious.

As *White Water* was borne downstream by the swift running current of the St. John, and the forests on the hills began to fill in the background and the forms of the settlement to lose their outline, they still stood there watching our departure—silent watchers, as must their ancestors have stood when first they were visited by white men.

Our debt to the Indian is very great. There is much in our culture that has an aboriginal origin. What we know of the wildness and wilderness of America the Indian knew long before us. The whole craft of the woodsman—that complex of primitive skills and practical know-how coupled with a slant of mind in which there is a blending of close observation, stoical patience, and a complete acceptance of the hazards of the environment—all this derives in the first instance from the aborigine. The Indian was America's first woodsman and our forefathers learned their woodcraft from him.

One thinks first of the canoe. Without doubt it is the Indian's outstanding contribution to modern America. His birch is a thing of the past, and its construction is all but a lost art. But its lines, thwarts, gunwales, ribs, and planking are all to be seen in the canoe of today. And here and there still, in the backwoods, you come up with a man who, choosing his cedar, maple, and ash in the woods near at hand, fashions one with hand tools, just as the Indians did.

Within a few years I came upon such a canoe set up on a pair of wooden horses in a back yard in Jackman. An eighteen-footer it was, a cedar canoe covered with fiber glass instead of the traditional canvas. I was invited to slide in under the middle thwart and walk away with her. What was extraordinary was that its weight was on the underside of sixty pounds.

The building of a birchbark canoe was a considerable undertaking. In Thoreau's time the Penobscots were adept at the art. At Old Town in 1853 he watched old John Pennyweight at work on one that was nearly completed, and four years later, up on the West Branch near Northeast Carry, he came upon one in an earlier stage of construction. His account of the process in his *Journal* accords with the findings of later researches, the most notable of which is Fanny Hardy Eckstorm's detailed description. Her knowledge of the handicrafts of the Indians of Maine is unsurpassed, and to this source must go anyone who would have an authoritative account of this example of aboriginal woodcraft.

Winter bark was the first requisite; that is, bark that was taken from a canoe birch before the sap began to run. Old John Pennyweight went fifty miles upriver to the head of Passadumkeag, and there, says Thoreau, it took him "two days to find one tree that was suitable," that is, free of knots, burls, and blemishes for at least twenty feet. The birch was felled on to a cradle for the butt as well as the top. The trunk was then girdled at each end of the bark to be taken and a gash scored lengthwise along the trunk. Next came the careful peeling with wooden wedges, a process that was aided by the heat of a slow fire.

Mrs. Eckstorm paints an interesting picture of how the Indians got the bark out of the woods. The single sheet was turned over and rolled from the butt, with the inner side of the bark outside. This roll was lashed with cedar bark and lifted on a man's shoulders crosswise, with the ends sticking out on each side. Then with a tumpline that encircled the roll and came forward around his forehead, and another around his chest, the Indian would walk away with the heavy load.

The next step in the process was out in the woods, to hew in the rough the white cedar that would be needed for the gunwales, the ribs, and the lining or planking. Thereafter these, and the thwarts, for which rock maple was sought, would all be fashioned with the axe and crooked knife, and the ribs would be steamed and bent to their proper shape by the eye.

With all these materials and a good supply of spruce roots —preferably white—all was ready for the construction. A spot was chosen in the shade of a tree, on hard and perfectly level ground near a stream, where the roll of bark would be soaked out. Thoreau watched a St. Francis Indian so engaged up on the West Branch, and his description of this stage of the work has the interest of a first-hand account.

"As near as I could *see,* and *understand* him and Polis they first laid the bark flat on the ground, outside up, and two of the top rails, the inside and thickest ones, already connected with cross-bars, upon it, in order to get the form; and, with logs and rocks to keep the bark in place, they bend up the birch, cutting down slits in the edges from within three feet of the ends and perpendicularly on all sides about the rails, making a square corner at the ground; and a row of stakes three feet high is then driven into the ground all around, to hold the bark up in its place. They next lift the frame, i.e. two rails connected by cross-bars, to the proper height, and sew the bark strongly to the rails with spruce roots every six inches, the thread passing around the rail and also *through* the ends of the cross-bars, and sew on strips of bark to protect the sides in the middle. The canoe is as yet carried out square down at the ends, and is perfectly flat on the bottom. (This canoe had advanced thus far.)"

Next would come the lining and the fitting of the ribs, and then the ends would be finished, a task that called for great skill and care. In the extensive sewing, an awl made of bone or the tail of a horseshoe crab was used to puncture the birchbark for the entry of the spruce root. The sewing of the seams presented a crisscross pattern.

The last phase was pitching to make the canoe watertight. Before the combined use of grease and pitch was learned from the white man, spruce gum was used, the squaws doing the chewing. Pitching a canoe was an art in itself. The craft lay bottom up on a pair of horses. The pitch was heated in a pitch kettle and was applied to the seams with a flat stick and then worked in and shaped with the hands after they had been dipped in cold water. And so it was with the constant repairs necessary to keep this tender craft watertight.

The only decoration was a pair of eyes, a circle, or a star on each side at one end. This at once made that end of the double-ended craft the bow, and, says Mrs. Eckstorm, "enabled the canoe to see the dangers and rocks ahead."

Such in rough outline was the aboriginal construction of a birchbark canoe, and the interested reader is referred to Mrs. Eckstorm's account in *The Handicrafts of the Modern Indians of Maine* for a most precise and meticulous description of the process.

A canoe is the proper craft for the man who hankers after an interlude on the waterways of the wilderness. The canoeman's point of view is in absolute contrast to what may be termed the bird's-eye view, that of the man who reaches for a telephone and makes a reservation on an airline.

The bird man gets there quickly. The very next day he is dropped down into his favorite lake. There he will spend a couple of days at what he deems to be the contemplative

man's recreation, plug fishing over a deep hole. No luck at-
tending, he calls away his airplane in order to try his luck
on the other side of the state. He returns at night with a
string of chub, "smelling of strong drink, and the truth is not
in him."

Now, to the canoeman all this is anathema. Think what
the fellow has missed—all the successive gradations that
held the interest of the canoeman in his slower passage from
the city, through suburbia, into open country, then along
shore, perchance to spend a night by the side of some curving crescent of sand, and finally to arrive at that fascinating
frontier where a man can step from his back yard into the
deep woods.

Then there is the canoeman's gear; his own axe, for example, the talisman of the woodsman; and a pack basket,
woven long ago by some nameless Penobscot, well worn and
neatly packed with long-used gear. All this has been tested
in the acid of experience and found not to be wanting.

And there is his companion, one of the vanishing race of
guides, a man now verging on years but with a sharp eye,
a keen ear, and the alert step of the woodsman. He can take
off from the shore of lake, pond, stream, or brook, cruise the
woods for hours on end, and return, after dark if need be, to
the precise point where he went in—and this without the
aid of a compass. This man knows every rip and pool where
*Salvelinus fontinalis* is lurking, awaiting the lure of the enticing fly, and there with infinite patience he will hold the
canoe steady while the canoeman casts.

With the dawn the canoeman rises, refreshed by solid
sleep on that most fragrant of pallets, a fir-bough bed. He
takes a plunge in the cool pool above the rips, and by then
the aroma of boiling coffee and frying bacon is mingling with
air that Henry Thoreau once described as having the quality
of a diet drink. A leisurely breakfast follows, and then the

breaking of camp, with each man intent upon appointed tasks. In short order, the canoe is loaded and the day's run begins.

This is it! Ensconced in the comfortable butt-fitting bow seat—laced after the fashion of a snowshoe and hence, too, an heirloom of the Indian—the canoeman now feasts his eyes on vistas of woodland beauty changing on either hand in a slow kaleidoscope of ever varying, ever alluring contour. It is still as only the deep woods are still. Little rhythms of noise soothe the passage—the click of the pole up some swift-flowing rip, the dip and drip of the paddle in the ensuing deadwater, the soft susurrus of wind through the leaves, the sweet song of a hidden whitethroat deep in a distant thicket.

At noontime he eats a lunch that will be long remembered—hot tea, dry bacon, cold johnnycake—accompanied by unfettered conversation. And if that afternoon a passage is to be clawed from headland to headland against a head wind, there will be that staple of the woodsman's diet—baked yellow-eye beans. At length, when the trees on the shore begin to cast long shadows out over the water, a comfortable camp will be made. That night he will sleep, dreamless and content, on a fir-bough bed.

Are you of the favored company who have made and slept on a fir-bough bed? It is a slice of life that is a fit experience for the gods.

Like all facets of the woodsman's lore, the proper building of a fir-bough bed is a piece of magic. It has its special techniques. There is the choice of the site—on slightly sloping ground, the head being higher than the foot. One must know how to break the boughs—not down toward the ground, as you would suppose, but up and in toward the trunk of the tree; they break easily then, with a sharp snap. Great armfuls are needed, and after three or four trips you kneel to the task. Lay the butt ends at the head, and as you work toward the feet, thrust the butts of the branches in through the fir toward the ground. Thus you build, layer upon layer, until your bed becomes a mound. Then you cut logs and stake them at the head, foot, and sides, and continue stuffing in fir boughs until the surface is even all over.

In the end you have a bed as sweet as the smell of fresh balsam can make it, and resilient with the secret spring of the life in the fresh branches. That night you will sleep the unbroken sleep of the gods, and the next night too, for each day a fresh layer of fir boughs makes you a new bed.

"We camped"—says Henry Thoreau in the late summer of 1857—"about two miles below Nicketow, on the south side of the West Branch, covering with fresh twigs the withered bed of a former traveler . . . Wherever you land along the frequented part of the river, you have not far to go to find those sites of temporary inns, the withered beds of flattened twigs, the charred sticks, and perhaps tentpoles. And not long since, similar beds were spread along the Connecticut, the Hudson and the Delaware."

Who will say that the Indian was not the inventor of the fir-bough bed?

I have often wondered if the camp fireplace cannot also be traced to an aboriginal source. There is archaeological evidence that the Indian was wont to camp over and over on the same site—a spot of high land, well drained, with a spring hard by, and handy to a plentiful supply of dry wood. The fireplace you find today on any long-used campground along a State of Maine waterway has a functional simplicity—two low piles of flat stones set apart at a convenient distance of from four to six feet. Out of each a forked stick rises, and in the forks rests the crossbar.

Writing in 1883, Lucius Lee Hubbard, the once celebrated cartographer of the Maine woods, whose "MAP OF NORTHERN MAINE, specially adapted to the use of LUMBERMEN and SPORTSMEN" is today a much prized rarity, said that his two Indian guides, when constructing the "frame of two upright crotched poles, one on each side of the fireplace with a horizontal pole laid over them," called it a *kitchiplakwagen.*

From the crossbar two or three forked sticks of variant lengths are suspended. The stone piles support a back log and a fore log, usually of green wood, with a space between. These are handy for the cook's spider. Beneath and up through and around them burns the fire. And when a bed of glowing coals results, the Maine woodsman uses a word that is doubtless of French-Canadian ancestry. "Set the coffeepot in there handy to the *braise,*" he will say.

Here, too, facing the flames, he will have his broiler propped up by a stick, its black grids bulging with the pink flesh of the squaretail trout you have caught. And on the other side of the fireplace, also fronting the *braise,* his Yankee baker squats, shedding its reflected heat on the golden surface of a baking johnnycake.

It is well, when the cook is busy about his cooking, to give him and his fire a wide berth. When suddenly disturbed or distracted, camp cooks are prone to bite, as is proved by the experience of a nameless lady from Boston. This story is a classic of the Maine woods. The protagonists are a French-Canadian cook by the name of Jo Leisure and a lady from Boston.

I tell the tale as it was told to me by a man who was one of the guides.

"We was guiding a large party of sports, men and women, down the Allagash. One of them women was always looking for information. Every time we made camp she'd go after the guides. She wanted to know how the tent was pitched, and how the beds was made, or how long the blankets was aired, and how the dishes got washed. Then she'd tell 'em how t'was done in Boston.

"And in particular she was always after Jo Leisure to tell

her all about his cooking. Every meal she was round his fire watching and asking questions. How long did he bake his gingerbread and his johnnycake? How did he do this and how did he do that? Well Joe, he always told her, patient-like and respectful. And every time he give her an answer, she'd always turn round on him and tell him how she done it in Boston.

"You could see by the signs that the Frenchman was getting ornery. Well, anyway, we come to the last lunch ground just before we was to come out into the clear at Fort Kent. It was the end of the run and everybody had got his wages. Joe, he was busy cooking up the last lunch, and pretty soon he grabs his iron spider and starts beating on it with a big spoon, telling 'em to come and get it. There warn't no table set up like they usually was, and this here lady from Boston, she come up to him arunning.

" 'Oh Mr. Leisure,' she says, 'where am I to sit?'

"And then Joe, he let her have it.

" 'You can set on yer arse, ma'am,' he says, 'the same as they do in Boston.' "

. . . . .

I asked: "What did you do, Allie?"

"Me, I goddamn near fell out of my canoe."

"Sure, but what did they do?"

"Well, her husband, he come up looking like a thunder gust, but he couldn't stand the gaff. I could see he was half grinning and pretty soon he starts in laughing. And then, by God, that lady from Boston, she was a real sport. When she seen her husband laughing, why, she started laughing too."

In the summer of 1857, on Thoreau's last excursion in the Maine woods, he was crossing the head of Chesuncook Lake headed for the Umbazookskus River—"meadow place" —en route to the Allagash waters. Joe Polis, his Penobscot guide, suggested that there was a good camping place a short distance up the Caucomgomoc River, which came in on their left. And there they went.

Upon going ashore, Thoreau noticed a fir tree that had been blazed by an axe. Here in charcoal was a crude drawing of a bear paddling a canoe, followed by a legend in the Indian language. Joe Polis explained. The bear was the emblem of his family, and the inscriptions recorded his use of the campground in 1853 and 1855. He then added still another inscription.

The episode is very human. The desire to leave a record of one's tracks is perennial. Before me as I write is an old yellow sign of the Maine Forestry Service. This battered bit of tin was once nailed to a pine standing on the old Donnelly campground on the shore of Chamberlain Lake. Faint and crudely penciled letterings tell of the use of this campground by four different men. One of them—Allie Ayer—it tells, first came to Chamberlain Lake in 1888. There are also anonymous recordings in the form of five bullet holes.

One of these records gives me a feeling of kinship with Joe Polis and Thoreau. For on the first day of October 1940 I had camped there with Allie Ayer.

The next day we paddled across the lake to explore the old Chamberlain Farm. This was a relic of the days of long logs, when it had been a considerable operation, the main depot for all the lumbering in the area. Now it was completely deserted, its buildings rotting and falling down, and the open fields fast turning into sprout land. The Maine woods were taking over again.

A deserted ruin that is not overrun with sightseers has about it an aura of romantic melancholy. It is as if the people who had lived there had suddenly vanished. I could see that the evidences of its former activity lying about were sparking the recollection of my companion. In his younger days he had worked in the woods in many a lumber camp and for years had been on the East and the West Branch drives.

In the blacksmith shop we came upon a complicated contraption of windlasses and great leather belts, and I was invited to guess what this was. I went wide of the mark, and was then regaled with a vivid description of how a frightened and bellowing ox could thereby be hoisted into the air in order that it might be shod.

The great barn, vast and cavernous, was still standing, and my attention was drawn to the strap hinges extending across the width of each door. Hand-wrought they were, as indeed, according to my informant, was all the iron used in the woods by the blacksmith from whose cold forge we had just emerged.

In the barn my own recollection was sparked. I had been there before, in the summer of 1923, and had then made note of a legend scrawled on a beam: "June 5, 1901—Saw a Cariboux on Smith Brook."

The legend was still there. In the fall of that year, Allie told me, he had seen a caribou above the timberline on Ktaadn. This was about the time they left the Maine woods forever and moved over to the caribou barrens in New Brunswick. In January 1964, an interesting wildlife experiment was attempted. Twenty-four caribou, six bulls, and eighteen pregnant cows were transported from Newfoundland by air and turned loose on Mt. Ktaadn. We shall see what we shall see.

On the way back, hard by the shore, supported on wooden skids, and almost hidden by the bushes that had grown up around her, we passed an old steamboat, dried out and bleaching. Her days of towing rafts of logs on Chamberlain were now long past.

As I stepped into the canoe and was making my way to the bow seat, Allie made a find. His sharp eyes had glimpsed on the bottom, half buried in the sand, a bit of rusted iron.

He dredged it up with the canoe pole. It turned out to be a curving piece of iron with what had once been a sharp point at the bulging end of the curve and an eye at the other. His reaction was explosive as the hook was lifted into the canoe.

I listened. Here was a real relic. It was a hook for a swing dog, the tool that antedated the modern cant dog way back before the Civil War. A great heavy long-handled tool, the swing dog had had this old rusted hook, or dog, secured by an eyebolt that ran through the butt of the handle. The trouble was that whenever a man swung it around a log he had to reach down and fit the dog into the log before he could heave with the handle.

Then one day, so the story goes, a young fellow by the name of Joe Peavey was watching a bunch of river drivers using these cumbersome tools on a jam. He had an idea. Like all good ideas, it was simple. Instead of the eyebolt through the handle, he saw in his mind's eye a fixed collar with lips and the lips with holes for a bolt on which the hook, or dog, would swing up and down, but not sideways like the swing dog.

This worked like a charm. A man could swing and heave all in one motion The name, Peavey, attached to the new tool and has stuck to it ever since. A peavey and a cant dog are one and the same.

Allie Ayer had a true craftsman's respect for the tools he used. More than that, for him they were endowed with living qualities. I will not forget that night back in camp when, after using his axe to split some wood for the fire, I swung it high over my head and sunk it half-blade deep into a log. He gave me a kind of a look. Then he walked over, loosened his axe, and laid it blade down flat.

"You don't never want to leave your axe like that. All the strength'll dreen right out of it. It wants to rest over the night."

There was another tool that always accompanied him into the woods, his crooked knife. This again is an inheritance from the Indian. A crooked knife has a single fixed blade. Its cutting edge, facing the user, is sometimes straight and sometimes curves upward at the end of the blade. The name, a crooked knife, derives from the handle, which extends up and out at an angle. In it a groove is carved into which a man's thumb fits neatly and comfortably. Thus, when the hand, palm up, grasps the handle, the thumb extends up the crooked handle. Then, as he holds the axe handle he is making in his other hand and draws the blade of the knife toward himself, a little sliver of wood curls up ahead of it. The tool is actually a one-handled drawshave with far greater flexibility in its use than a drawshave.

With these two tools—his axe and his crooked knife—Allie Ayer in his lifetime fashioned many a paddle, pole, oar, axe handle, and handles for all the other tools of the woodsman, the lumberman, and the river driver. Many of these are still cherished in the Penobscot country, and I say cherished advisedly, for this is a craft that is passing.

The next day, under his skilled direction I made use of these two tools of the woodsman's trade. First I picked up on the shore of Chamberlain a well-seasoned cedar log. I split it, quartered a half, and kept on splitting down until I had a stick of a fit size for working up with the crooked knife. Then, seated on a box by the small fire, I worked it up, shaving the stick toward me, with the long slivers curling away from the wood, until at length I had fashioned a rod with which to clean my gun. I have this rod still. Its use by others is forbidden. If ever it is to be broken, I am going to be the one to commit the sacrilege.

Booms, cribs, sluices, dams, tramways, yards, tote roads —all these and many another are reminders of the men who once worked in these woods. Today many of these evidences of their assaults on the forests are rotting into oblivion. The forest is taking over again. Indeed, over the long haul man's traces have ever been in a state of flux. Where, for example, in all the forests of New England is there today a towering white pine or mighty oak marked with the Broad Arrow? Time was when the Crown's prerogative was the law in these backwoods and trees so blazed were the property of the Crown. These forests furnished the masts and spars for the ships that Nelson led to victory at Trafalgar, and the original sticks for the *Constitution* were cut and hauled out of the woods near the town of Windsor in Kennebec County.

"Ride into a swamp to see a mast drawn of about twenty-six inches or twenty-eight; about two and thirty oxen before, and about four yoke by the side of mast between the fore and hinder wheels. 'Twas a notable sight."

Thus the redoubtable diarist, Samuel Sewall, describes what in his day was called *baulking* a mast. For generations, *masting* was the cream of the calling of the lumberer. The great sticks, measuring three feet through at the butt and upwards of a hundred in length, would be felled, when the snow was deep, upon a bed of smaller trees and branches that had already been felled transversely. Then, after the butt end had been skidded onto a heavy sled and secured by chains, it was *baulked—twitched,* in Penobscot parlance—out of the woods by great teams of oxen on a road that had been *swamped*—that is, cleared and leveled by the swampers—to a stream where it could be rolled in and floated down to the *masting* port.

Not a shred of this once widespread activity remains. And today we are approaching the end of another great evolution in lumbering, the replacement of water by gasoline. The bulldozer has made possible the gravel road; the truck and the tractor driver have replaced the river driver; the power saw is supplanting the logger's axe. Thus it is that what the canoeman of today sees of lumbering on his river trips are—pulp drives aside—the relics of an earlier stage.

The first of the contrivances that were destined to drive the axe and the horse, not out of, but deeper into the woods, was the log hauler. I once saw one at a deserted depot camp on the St. John River. A great, wood-burning locomotive-like contraption operating on treads and runners it was, and in the deep woods in winter it must have been an awesome sight, snorting and chugging its smoking way along a frozen tote road with a slew of towering log-loaded sleds in tow. And there she stood, set up on skids, in rusting disuse. The log hauler is said to have been the forerunner of the tractor.

From the earliest days of lumbering, the rivers and lakes of Maine have furnished a natural means of transporting the logs to the mills. This was particularly true in the earlier day of the long log, and it is still true in these days of short logs, for a large amount of pulp still comes downriver. But there is a considerable difference. The short logs come, as it were, of their own accord. No roaring river drivers, no Bangor Tigers are now needed to pick the jams and keep the drive on the move. The picturesque river drive is all but a thing of the past. Save for the spring drive down east on the Machias River, it exists today only as a gleam in the eye of some old-timer when the East or the West Branch drive is mentioned, and he will thereupon, with a contemptuous spurt of tobacco juice, dismiss "them goddamn short logs" as kindling wood.

The propulsive force for this means of transport was what the woodsman calls a good head of water, and a good driving pitch. Hence the ancient dams that the canoeman encounters on his river trips. The disintegrating sluices and the still functioning cribs and booms that stud and sometimes impede his progress were the means by which the torrents of logs were kept under a semblance of control, driven downstream, and finally stored in booms, pending their ascent of the inclined plane leading toward the whirling, screeching circular saw.

A graphic demonstration of what all this involved was given me a few days later at the head of Telos Lake. One must have in mind the lay of the land; it is important. We had come through Chamberlain Lake, passing on our left the deep pocket Allie referred to as the "arm of Chamberlain," on into the thoroughfare and then across Telos. And here we were standing on the shore at the very end of that lake. Here there was a dam, and thereby hangs the tale.

What we stood on was the height of land that once divided the watersheds of the Allagash and the Penobscot. Allie traced it out on the ground with a stick. Chamberlain, whence we had come, he explained, was the first of a chain of three large lakes connected by thoroughfares— Chamberlain, Eagle, and Churchill—and only then at the foot of Churchill does the main body of the Allagash start. All these lakes, he said, were fed by numerous other lakes, ponds, and streams. Then, on the other side of the height of land less than a mile away, down that ravine there, you come to the head of Webster Lake, and this is one of the headwaters of the East Branch of the Penobscot.

Now what they did, Allie Ayer was explaining, was to cut through this canal you see here right in front of you, into the ravine, and build two dams, one here and the other at the foot of Chamberlain. This gave them a good head of water here, ready to flow down into the Penobscot whenever they raised the gate. Later on, there were two more dams built, Chase Dam at the foot of Churchill and one in the thoroughfare from Eagle into Churchill. This last dam, Churchill being the lowest lake, acted as the lower gate of a lock.

By these means, which were completed in the 1840's, all the timber on the vast upper watershed of the Allagash could be cut and then driven, floated, and rafted into Telos, whence it would be sluiced through this canal down into the East Branch of the Penobscot. An estimated 286 square miles had been added to the watershed of the Penobscot. A contemporary account, John S. Springer's *Forest Life and Forest Trees,* published in 1851, has it that the motivation for the enterprise was the levying by New Brunswick of a tax on all timber driven down the St. John, in contravention, so it was claimed, of the recent Webster-Ashburton Treaty. This had put to rest the bloodless uproar over the nation's northeastern boundary that is known in the State of Maine as the Aroostook War.

At this point, this historical account was interrupted. My companion invited me to visit his home downriver at Passadumkeag, where he would allow me to handle the flintlock his father had carried when he marched up the Military Road to Houlton to fight "them goddamn Blue Nosers."

But to Allie Ayer it seemed equally likely that behind the enterprise was the natural desire of the lumberman of that day "to get his logs downriver to his Bangor mill." Control of the Canal had been acquired by one Rufus Dwinell, and he announced that there would now be a slight charge for sluicing logs through it. Directly a competitor, David Pingree, met this with an ultimatum. His men, by God, would sluice his logs through there, by God, by force. Whereupon Dwinell, joining issue, moved in and lined the canal with his own private army of loggers. Everybody was full of rum, brimstone, and fight, and the Telos War was on. It, too, turned out to be a bloodless affray, for it was soon transferred to the purlieus of Augusta, where it was settled by the Maine legislature.

Then another bunkhouse tale came out of Allie Ayer. This time it was his own story. Way back in 1905 he was on the East Branch drive right here at the Telos Dam. Out there— he swept his arm toward the lake—"there was logs for as far as a man could see, six million feet of lumber held there back of a boom. That night there come a terrible rain and early in the morning the dam here went out. When she *cra-a-a-cked*, everybody come running down to the shore. There was one of them terrible deep bows there, below where the dam had been, like there always is when a big head o' water breaks loose.

"The walking boss come up to me and he says: 'Allie, do you think you can run her?' They never ordered a man into his bateau. They always asked you, did you think you could get through? I was a young feller then, ready for anything. I takes a look at that deep bow and I knowed that if I made that without the water swamped us, we'd make the rest of it. I figured it was worth the chance. They had to get word down to the dam keeper at Webster to raise the gate afore that head o' water built up and took it out too, and then we'd lose the whole damn drive. It would take too long to send a man down there by the tote road and through the woods. Webster Dam would go long before he got there.

"Well, I hollered for my crew—two oars and a bow man I could trust, and one of the cookees come along, setting on the lazy seat in front of me. Every man jack in the camp was out there along the bank to see me drown my crew, but I give her a powerful shove right in the bottom of that deep hollow and we never wet a hair. But by the time we made Webster we was half full of water.

"We come through like a streak of greased lightning. The cookee kept time with a stopwatch from the time we was in the stream until we made the fairway into Webster. That's three quarters of a mile, and we made it in a minute and a half. Then we made it down to Webster Dam in good time."

Others were not so fortunate. There was Joe Aitteon, a noted river driver in his day. He had been Thoreau's guide when he went "a-moose-hunting" on the West Branch in

1853. The tales of his death at Grand Falls on the West Branch are legendary in the Penobscot country. According to one version, they were in trouble from the start. As they shoved out into the stream the water caught the bateau under her side and shot her straight across the channel. There, before they could get her straightened out with the current, she smashed against a rock and began to fill. John Ross, the walking boss, was closest to them and he sent another boat after them. He saw Joe climb up on the gunwales and start paddling like hell. Then he said, "I knew they were going to have a hard time—so I turned and looked the other way."

Few men in such circumstances ever have the decency and the guts to do just that.

Days later, they found Joe Aitteon's body. It was in Shad Pond below the falls. So they took his calked boots and hung them in a tall pine on the shore where they found him, and then they cut a great cross on the tree. This was traditional. There are other such humble memorials on the wild streams of the Maine woods. Up on Nesowadnehunk—"the stream among the mountains"—if you know where to look, you can find scored on the face of rocks the names of men drowned on the drive.

The next day we paddled back over the long length of Chamberlain and, making the portage over the dam, ran through the thoroughfare into Eagle Lake, the Pongokwahemook of the Indian. Twenty years had passed since I had been in Eagle on my way down the Allagash. At that time the "belt of dead trees" which Thoreau in his day had deplored as creating a "ragged and unsightly condition" on the shores of both Chamberlain and Eagle had long since rotted away, and the wooded shores of Pongokwahemook had enshrined it in my memory as the wildest and most beautiful of lakes.

A shocking sight now met my eyes. On either hand there rose a tangled jungle of dead trees, upright, slanting, and prostrate, hiding from sight the shores of this lovely body of water. As far as the eye could see, the shore was inaccessible.

It should be borne in mind that raising the level of the water in these wild wooded lakes kills all the trees whose lower trunks and roots are thereby inundated. For the resulting desolate tangle of dead stubs the woodsman has a word: dry-ki. Eagle and Churchill, it appeared, had been raised from six to eight feet to facilitate the operation of some Frenchman from over the border in cutting pulp.

We paddled hurriedly on and soon reached the deadwater at the mouth of Smith Brook, which comes in from the east. Here the despoiled shores of Eagle Lake receded from sight as our course wound in tortuous curvings between shores of yellow sedge. Then the quick water commenced abruptly and we dragged the canoe, the ascent being sharp and the channel well defined. In a short time we came to the foot of the falls, where in a broken descent of about twenty-five feet were the rotting remains of an old sluice. Here we camped on the carry, using a campsite set deep amid the firs.

The next morning early, we lugged the canoe over the carry to come upon another deadwater lined with yellow sedge. This was a mysterious place alive with wild duck. They flew continuously, rising before our passage, flashing past the distant trees, and passing on downstream. Here, upon suddenly doubling a marshy point, I had the rarest of rare fortunes to make with a single shot a double in wood duck.

Again, as on the day before, the water suddenly shoaled; there was quick water ahead. It was warm, and stripping to a pair of sneakers, I led the canoe up the gravelly bed, midleg deep in the sparkling, rushing water. In pools formed by the bends of the stream, I came upon trout covering a spawning bed. At my approach, they sped away flashing, some upstream and some downstream. Then came a sharp turn, and there, stretching away before me, lay Haymock, glittering in the sunlight.

Haymock is a lake to dream about. On this early October afternoon, as our canoe slid slowly across its shining surface, we two were alone on Haymock Lake. Out in the middle, where one could look around the compass, I saw that the shores at first ascended gently and then sharply up the sides of the hardwood ridges that cupped the little lake. Ablaze with the flames of the autumnal foliage that flashed in the sunlight, they were spotted with the black of the pine and the spruce and the fir.

We made for the west shore. Here there was a lovely campground with a clear clean spring hard by. Allie showed me where a spotted trail ran up over the ridge and down into Stink Pond, a headwater of the East Branch. It was a rugged portage, he said.

All that long autumn afternoon of blue and gold we leisured and lazied on the shore and surface of Haymock Lake. It was an afternoon to mark a point in a man's span of life.

That night in camp, again on the carry, I took a look at my Hubbard Map and puzzled out the Indian names for Smith Brook and Haymock Lake. What jawbreakers they are. Haymock appears as Nahmajneskicongomoc and Smith Brook, which drains it, is Nahmajneskitegwek. Pronounce them if you can. Their meanings, I think, are interesting. The stream Nahmajneskitegwek means "the deadwater extends up into the high land," and the lake Nahmajneskicongomoc means "lake of the deadwater that extends up into the high land." The modern name Haymock is believed to have been taken from the last two syllables—*hemook*—of the Indians' name for Eagle Lake, Pongokwahemook, which means "place of the woodpecker."

A day later we were back down in Eagle in camp on the eastern shore, where there was a bank high enough to be clear of the dry-ki. This was an old campsite known in the north woods as the Zeigler campground, the name being that of a party that used it for many years. The prospect from here was superb.

Across the lake a wooded knoll made the skyline. It was now a glory of blending color, an immense bouquet assembled and arranged by the practiced hand of Nature. And that evening a quartering moon shone its silver crescent in the dark sky just above the knoll.

Here I was regaled with the tale of how the Austrian "got bit by the wasps." Allie was on one side and I on the other of the little fire that flickered between us, lighting up the trees in back of the camp.

"Maybe you don't remember that German boat that put into Bar Harbor about the start of the last war with a load of gold?"

This was his opening gambit. I did remember. Her name was the *Kronprincessin Cecile,* and it had been in early August 1914.

"Well, there was a feller on her, an Austrian, and he didn't have no place to go, seeing as how he couldn't get back to his own country. Well, one day he fetched up at Kineo, where I was guiding that summer. People didn't like him none. He was always taking pictures and he couldn't speak much English. They all said he was a spy.

"He wanted terrible to take a river trip but there warn't nobody would guide him on account he was a spy. They come to me. I figured his money was as good as the next man's, and anyway there warn't much to spy on in the Maine woods. So we got our outfit and went on down the West Branch.

"He was a nice young feller. We couldn't talk much on account he couldn't speak much English. And he was all the time taking pictures. One thing was funny. He hated like the devil going out into the woods to relieve himself, and after a good while I made out he was asking me about backhouses. I told him there warn't none, only very seldom, in the Maine woods."

Pausing, he rose, stepped to the woodpile, picked out a stick of rock maple, and rested it on the fire. Then he gave it a shove with his foot. Sparks ascended and the flames grew. He resumed his seat on the log on the opposite side of the fire.

"Well, one day we come to Webster Dam and they had been fixing her up that summer. All of a sudden he lets out a yell, and I wonders what's chewing that foreigner now. Then I seen him. He was running toward an old backhouse that was set up on the dam. Couldn't wait to get inside her and he was hitching down his galluses as he run. He ducked inside and I didn't pay no particular attention.

"Then he let out one hell of a yell and I seen him bust out of that backhouse like he was shot out. I seen easy what had happened. That privy hadn't been used recent and the hornets had nested under the seat.

"When he set down, they come up.

" 'Hey!' I yells, 'don't hitch up your pants.'

"But he hauls 'em right up, paying me no heed on account he don't know the language, and he runs round like a wild man, yelling to raise the dead. Course he caught all them wasps up in his pants and they was stinging hell out of him.

"Well, I got to him, and got him into the thick bushes, and finally I got his pants down again and him to running through the brush. Took him nigh to half an hour to get clear of them hornets."

By this time the woods were ringing and I was rocking with laughter. It was incredible—the comical effect of his matter-of-fact, dead-pan recital.

THE WOODS AND THE SEA

"You kin laugh  but I ain't never seen a man suffer so. He couldn't set and he couldn't stand and he couldn't sleep for three nights. I poulticed his butt with wet mud and sody but it didn't help him much. Why, that first night you couldn't 'a got 'em"—here, in a classic gesture of simulation, he doubled up his fists—"into that two quart pail there."

The next morning Eagle Lake lay shrouded in a deep white mist. It burned away in spots and, drifting with the rising breeze, revealed patches of the shoreline and the trees with their autumn foliage agleam in the morning sunlight.

A few days later, we shook hands and parted, Allie Ayer and I, in the old railroad station in Bangor.

Somewhere in a packet of old letters I have a poignant lament by this old-time woodsman. Time was catching up on him, and his activities were limited. He did not like it, and he said so. Then:

"Well, I reckon I shouldn't complain none. I've cooked up a lot of hot suppers in my time."

And now he is long since gone.

# Small Point Beach

ALONGSIDE THE KENNEBEC, as you run down from the old shipbuilding town of Bath toward the sea, you follow a winding river road. It now traverses the side of a ridge, then descends into bottom land, to mount again in a long enticing curve toward a skyline of spruce. Next it crosses on a causeway a stretch of marsh. Much of the country through which it passes is wooded, and in its more remote stretches the moose still roam. Not so long since, I saw one—a young bull trotting along a dirt road, for all the world like an awkward horse on the loose—before it turned aside into the bushes to mount a ridge and disappear.

This river road should be traveled at a slow and contemplative pace, for then you can drink in with your eyes the vistas that stretch across the blue water. Now and again the Kennebec, trending toward the sea, curves into a cove to enclose a green island. Here a point makes out into the river and the sharp white spire of a country church stands up above the surrounding green.

Around and about are the clustered frame houses of a small community, and the elms that overshadow them are like great inverted bowls of green. On the left hand, perched in part over blue water, is a small, story and a half frame house. Beyond, on a small island a stone's throw from the shore, another white house, with green shutters, makes the skyline.

I pass on, and half a mile below, another vista opens up. This time it is of a fresh-water pond formed by the embankment of the river. This little body of water is rimmed with green, and the water is of a deep dark blue. Here water lilies grow in profusion. Great stretches of them cover the surface, and now and again, as I watch from the side of the road, the small breeze catches at the edge of one of the great flat leaves and lifts it aloft. A myriad white and gold blossoms are open full, and in startling contrast around the shores there rise the purple spikes of the long, green-leaved pickerelweed.

Later, in one of those ancient wide washbowls which are still to be found in old summer cottages, the purple of the pickerelweed and the white and gold of the water lilies make a spectacular show. When later one sniffs the lilies, the exotic odor they exude, he says, is as evocative as the smell of a ripe red Astrakhan apple.

High on a bluff, this old-fashioned, capacious summer cottage has a veranda extending around three sides. Two of the sides give on shady groves; the third faces the sea. Here the low railing of the veranda provides the lower frame and the edge of the roof the upper frame for a panorama of marsh and beach and sea stretching far to the eastward. Cocked up in one of those old, rush-bottomed chairs that lend themselves so naturally to a perch on their two hind legs, I can take in, with a sweep of my glass, all that the Maine coast has to offer.

The sea in a broad expanse to the taut line of the horizon; the white triangular sails of a sloop; surf trending shoreward in tiers of white foam; black reefs covered with brown seaweed down which the receding waves leave paths of running quicksilver; a low, rounding island topped at its peak by a round lighthouse. This is the light on the island of Seguin.

Then shoreward, three rugged outcroppings of granite, known as the Herons. Next, curving in a long crescent toward the dunes, the flat beach, its broad, brown sweep broken by the black bones of a long since foundered schooner. Then up ashore, the dunes forming the outermost bound of a salt marsh covered with salt hay, its subtly blended hues of green and brown traversed by the winding blue path of the rising tide now flowing up a little creek.

At the inner edge of this marsh, with my glasses, now at the end of their broad sweep, I survey a pine-clad mountain, its granite top in bald contour; and on either side the jagged skyline that long ago gave to the coast of Maine its name as the country of the pointed firs.

Now coming into view at the edge of the overhanging roof, a gull scales, silent on set wings, sweeping for its own purpose this scene of marsh and rocks and beach and sea.

This is at noon, when all is in fine clear line.

At sundown too this prospect has a compulsive appeal. With the slanting rays of the setting sun reaching across this segment of the sphere, the foreground lies in shadow while the distance is still agleam with sunlight.

On the marsh it is already twilight. The shafts of the sun reach across and above it, to touch with light the crests of the firs and the tops of the dunes. Then beyond, on the brown beach with the sloping of the dunes, here too is the shadow of twilight. But out across the sea, which lies calm and stilled for these moments of sunfall, the granite ledges are still flecked with sunlight that glows in contrast to the mounting shadow. For a few moments only is it thus—one half of this foreshore scene in daylight, the other half in dusk.

Against this immense backdrop there are birds in silent motion. Off the mouth of the Morse River I see on the surface of the still-sunlit sea a strange long dark shadow. I put my glasses on it. It turns out to be a great congregation of coots that have rafted there. As they swim, they form and reform their battalions. Seaward of this there rises out of the sea a large ledge. Above the tide line, its gray granite is dotted with the black forms of cormorants—shags, in alongshore parlance.

Now, swinging out from the mouth of the Morse River, three large birds proceed in a triangle of flight—necks outstretched in a down and up curve, long legs trailing astern, and heavy wings pumping. They fly like crafts of the air, and I watch these great blues in their long westerly course swinging past the island of Seguin, their triangle of flight continuously changing, yet always in a three-pointed form, until they pass from sight, barred by the corner of the cottage. Swallows dip toward the sand and mount again. Now and again a gull scales into sight past the edge of the roof, on and on and on, to pass far out over the sea with never a change of pinion. A lone black duck etches a swift path west-ward.

With the descent of the hidden sun, the line of light rises above the marsh, the beach, and the sea, and the well of shadow deepens. Albeit this is a slow process and hardly dis-cernible, its termination is sudden and dramatic. The reful-gent light on the bare granite sides of the Three Herons goes out. Then the rock is like a consumed ash. The side of Seguin is now dark and its white light, yellowed by the haze, replaces the sun. Around the horizon other lights come on—Ram Island, the Cuckolds, and, some say, Monhegan. And a host of lesser lights wink on and off. And on again.

The cup of companionship passes. There is small con-versation, desultory, easy, companionable. So it is on this cool August evening as daylight fails and darkness falls on Small Point Beach.

After dark I seek again the solitary solace of the de-serted veranda. From behind me, in back of closed windows, the chatter of conversation and the clatter of china tell of after-dinner coffee. The yellow light streaming through the windows lights the tops of three balsams rising above the level of the high veranda, in contrast with the deep dark-ness beyond.

Gradually my eyes grow used to the darkness. Overhead, stars glint, cold points of light in the blackness. The light on Seguin is a small yellow ovate, and in the wash of the fore-shore I see its image palely reflected. The tide is making, and I watch the surf come gleaming ashore in tiers of pale white, the crests of the oncoming waves. The beach is in darker contour, the dunes are vague shapes, and the wind-ing path of the rising river is dimly visible out there in the marsh. The distant lights are winking. Up the beach on the far side of the river a red flaring tells of a bonfire.

For a long time I sit thus on the high veranda, looking eastward over the beach and out to sea.

. . .

This coast, its islands, and its waters are all storied. The tales antedate the written record. No man can now tell when the fishermen of Devon and Brittany and the Basques of the coasts of France and Spain first dropped their lines in these waters. But the earliest of the relations of the voyages of exploration contain references to the presence of shallops and gear of European origin. This confirms the view of eminent historical authority that if there were records extant the fisheries in these waters could be traced back two or three centuries before 1600.

In 1607 the *Relation of a Voyage to Sagadahoc* recounts that on just such a mid-August night as this the ship *Mary and John* was beating her way westward broad off this beach with the shore under her lee:

". . . and about mydnight thear arosse a great storme and tempest uppon us the w$^{ch}$ putt us in great daunger and hassard of castinge awaye of our ship and our Lyves by reason we wear so near the shore, the wynd blew very hard at South right in uppon the shore so that by no means we could nott gett of. hear we sought by all means and did what possybell was to be don for that our Lyves depended on ytt. hear we plyed ytt w$^{th}$ our ship of and on all the nyght often times espyeinge many soonken rocks and breatches hard by us enforsynge us to put our ship about and stand from them bearinge saill when yett was mor fytter to have taken ytt in but that ytt stood uppon our Lyves to do ytt and our bott Sonk att our stern yet woold we nott cut her from us in hope of the appearinge of the daye. thus we Contynued untill the daye cam. then we perseaved our Selves to be hard abord the Lee shore and no waye to escape ytt but by Seekinge the Shore. then we espyed 2 Lyttell Illands Lyeinge under our lee. So we bore up the healme and steered in our shipe in betwyxt them whear the Lord be praised for ytt we found good and sauffe ankhoringe and thear anckored the storme still contynuinge untill the next day followynge."

Here they repaired their boat and went ashore, where they encountered "4 salvages and an old woman." The next day, the storm abating, "the wind Cam faier for us to go for Sagadehock." This was the Indians' name for the mouth of the Kennebec. Two days previously they had sailed westward past the mouth of that river and the island of Seguin, being uncertain of their identity. Now they stood away to the eastward and dropped anchor in the lee of the island of "Sutquin," or Seguin—which is said, appropriately, to be the Abenaki word for the phrase "it vomits." Other authority gives the meaning more prosaically as "hump."

Then, when the sea was calm, their companion ship, the *Gift of God,* sent out her boat and they were towed into the mouth of the Sagadahoc. And so the ill-fated colony of Popham was established. In little more than a year's time it would be abandoned, largely for want of leadership and a lack of resolution among the rank and file.

To the eastward, when in the wake of a cold northwest wind the light on distant Monhegan gleams at night for its appointed round, it reminds me of Captain John Smith and his celebrated espousal of Monhegan and her fisheries in 1614.

"I was contented, having taken by hookes and lines with fifteene or eighteene men at most, more than 60,000 Cod in lesse than a moneth: whilst my selfe with eight others of them might best be spared, by an houre glasse of three moneths, ranging the coast in a small boat, got for trifles eleven hundred Bever skins besides Otters and Martins; all amounting to the value of fifteen hundred pound, and arrived in *England* with all my men in health in six or seven moneths."

In the same quarter, a point or so to the north, hard by another winking light lies Damariscove, the site of yet another famous fishing station that in the winter of 1622 was the source of food for the hungry Pilgrims at Plymouth.

In days that were then to come, these waters would be the scene of other events of note, as, for example, when in September of that famous year 1775 a fleet of eleven sail would sweep past this beach in a day's passage from New-buryport to the mouth of the Kennebeck, bearing on board the little army of Benedict Arnold on the first leg of its long march to Quebec. Here, too, on an early September after-noon in 1812, the *Enterprise* and the *Boxer* would sail on parallel courses on the starboard tack, and there would blaze and roar the broadsides that in a quarter hour's time would leave each youthful captain on his own quarterdeck —one dead and the other dying.

The next morning I am awakened by a wild noise. It is more than a noise. It is a medley of noises, a cacophony to which new voices are continuously being added, while others cease for a time, only to commence again. I know well what this is. It is the gulls, and they are in caucus.

I swing around in bed, propping a pillow at its foot, that I may look out of the window and down onto the beach. There they are, a myriad of them, their black forms barely dis-tinguishable in the darkness, lining and waddling along the banks, and swimming on the surface of the little salt river as it courses seaward over the broad beach at low tide. They are feasting on the sand eels that abound in the swiftly ebbing creek.

Gradually my ear distinguishes two kinds of voices in the medley. There are the broken, haunting calls of the great ponderous herring gulls, strident, hoarse, screeching. Then in the background there is the softer mewing of the terns. It is ceaseless, this raucous chorus, and it never varies for a moment in pitch or tone or volume. The impact of its mo-notony is tremendous.

Along the eastern horizon the sky is black, and this darkness extends upward to a considerable height. Here it gives upon bands of pink that are dark and light. Running horizontally across the sky, they proclaim the coming rise of the sun in back of the long fog bank furled along the horizon. Thus, the growth of the daylight is very gradual. The shades of reflected light tinting the beach and the rocks and the sea in pastel shades are so faint, and they change so slowly, that I hardly notice the change. The light on Seguin is either out or blotted from sight by the heavy haze.

There is no indication of the moment of sunrise. But I am instantly aware when it occurs. Of a sudden there is silence, a deep silence: the gulls have ceased their outcries. They leave their caucus and are now winging in scattered flight in over the marsh, up and down the beach, and out over the sea. By this I know that the sun has arisen and daylight is at hand.

I turn over, and in the silence that is caressed by the wash of little waves, I drop almost instantly into a deep sleep. When I awake again, the room is flooded with sunlight, the clear light of a brilliant morning.

A day alongshore always begins with the night before. This is when, after dark, you step outside to see how things stand for the next day. This night the moon is blurred and it shines dully through the overcast. A stranger has asked for fog; never had seen any. So a wet finger is stuck up into the clear air to see from what quarter the wind, which is to say the weather, is making. Southerly—a light southerly wind—and the prediction is: "Sister, you're going to get your fog."

The next morning the fog comes blowing in through the screen and across my bed in fitful puffs. I like fog; it tends to sharpen a man's senses. When within its compelling shroud, the eye is keener, the ear more carefully cocked, and I sniff the salt air with a greater zest. There is a remoteness about it, a pleasurable loneliness. In a fog a man is utterly on his own.

When the tide is at its ebb, the wide level space of sand known as the foreshore lies uncovered. This flat expanse is for those who like to walk alone. With the receding of each tide, a virgin world is laid bare for you, and as you traverse it, you know that your tracks are the only ones that spot a trail on its hard surface—until, perchance, your path crosses the tracks of some other solitary sojourner.

This day the light air is a bit south of east, coming gently from the direction of the distant never-never land that is always referred to with a knowing look and a jerk of the thumb as "down east." As I walk along the foreshore in the fog, the world is foreshortened and brought within the focus of the immediate. To my right, in the southern quarter, the extent of my vision is the cresting of the small waves. Beyond them, grayness obscures all. From out there in the depths of the fog there comes across the water, in a tone muted by the fog, the hoarse and haunting booming of the foghorn on Seguin. I like this somber, yet friendly note of warning. It gives me a feeling of kinship with the mariner at sea for whose guidance in intermittent periods it pours forth across the water.

In the other three quarters—east, north, and west—wet brown sand merges in a few feet with the gray fog. That is all. In this small gray-brown world the air is cool and moist and fresh and I walk with a growing sense of elation and expectancy.

All along the foreshore the little shorebirds are in abundance—peep, ringnecks, and ruddy turnstones, the latter adding a checkered pattern of color to the dun shades of the fog, the sea, and the sand. Enhanced are their slender orange legs and the harlequin aspect of their russet and black and white markings. As I walk, I put them up. They peel off the wet sand and swing out around me over the waves, uttering plaintive *peeps,* and then disappear in the thick fog.

Then there sweeps into sight in silence and close rank a flight of beetlehead plover—a living constellation that emerges from the fog and is then swallowed by the fog.

At length, there looms up a high ledge covered with dripping brown rockweed and spotted white by squatting gulls. Silently they mount and disappear.

Now and again a single gull appears overhead. It is an apparition, a bird of omen, as it emerges out of the fog, is seen for a moment, and then merges again with the grayness.

I hear the screaming of gulls and the mewing of terns. Now they come into sight—a great concourse of them in caucus on a bar. I walk on and come very close before, screaming, they get up. In the air there is a great confusion of flapping wings and heavy bodies, and the bar is littered with their feathers and droppings. I hear them squalling, in flight, hidden in the fog out over the water. I walk on, and turning around, I see them scaling back in, to alight again on the bar from which I had disturbed them.

I watch one. His beak plunges into the sand in front of him. Then it is jerked up and I glimpse a wriggling flash as the gull gulps down a small sand eel. This bar deserves a name and so, for this short space between the tides, I call it Sand Eel Bar.

Hours after I started, I return, and the single light that shines through the fog as I approach the cliff is like a baleful eye.

Always akin to fog is haze. In late August, when the upland swelters and people in the cities suffer from excessive humidity, along Small Point Beach a spell of hazy and foggy weather produces singular effects of color and perspective.

Each morning the ebbing tide uncovers the great broad beach. Walking beside the wash of the small waves, I see wisps of fog rising from the surface of the sea. Inshore, they likewise rise from the damp sand and drift toward the dunes. Overhead, the air is thick. The sun is hidden. As I walk, the light of the invisible sun, filtering through the thick haze and this low fog, produces delicate pastel hues.

Toward the indistinct dunes, the atmosphere has a pale violet cast. The colors of the different strata of sand are enhanced; they range from a dark brown that verges on black close at hand, to a delicate fawn color in toward the dunes. Beyond the dunes and across the marsh which they hide, the dark black of the pines on the mountain is all but obscured. Once, when the sun burns through an open patch in the haze, the crests of the waves give off a pale green light. Away up the beach, a boy and a girl walking hand in hand are seen as disembodied souls, for below their knees they are invisible.

Along the edge of the tide the shorebirds are thickly clustered. For a distance of a hundred yards up the beach they stretch six and eight birds deep. I start a count at a point where they crowd the head of a cove. When I reach fifty they start peeling off, and now they are hurrying out over the wash. Suddenly the flight splits and the air between is emptied. One flock goes east, the other west along the shore, and seen against the haze, they are swiftly passing flutters of white specks.

I walk on, putting them up in successive arcs of flight winging out over the tide.

The foreshore is flecked with mounds of foam. These come and go at my feet in the expiring wash of each small wave. I bend over one, and a myriad iridescent hues flash forth. Here, in this microcosm of foam, are caught and reflected all the pale colors of this haze-filtered light. It is a rare and remarkable phenomenon, and I savor it for a space.

## Small Point Beach

A large gull, at first seen dimly, emerges out of the haze. I put the glass on it. In perfect balance, with wings spread wide in cambered curves, it passes over my head, seeming to float without effort through the air. Now, sinking lower, it settles toward the sand. The wings tilt and the feet come down. There is the landing. Then with slow precision it folds its great wings over and down on its rump.

The gull stands alone, facing the sea.

These days of haze are days of vistas and of cameos. I take a stand somewhat at a distance from where the small waves of the ebb tide are gently lapping. In between lies the hard tan sand of the foreshore, flat and bare and damp. Next there is the surf, scarcely more than a series of recurrent ripples. Beyond, stretching out into the distance, is the flat floor of a calm sea. Then, breaking the horizon, there is the curving contour of the rockbound island, and at its low crest, a cluster of frame houses topped by the lighthouse on Seguin. This is the vista.

Now I raise my glasses and focus both lenses on the foreshore. Within the small circle of the glass, at the edge of a crescent of the tide is a shorebird. He stands perfectly still, facing the wash of the waves. I observe the slender little yellow legs, the snow-white belly, the dark brown back, and the encircling choker of black: it is a ringneck or semipalmated plover. This is the cameo.

He is off, his legs atwinkle. Now he is airborne and swinging out over the tide. He sweeps in toward the strand, comes to a fluttering landing, and busies himself, first chasing the retreating wash, then in turn retreating himself before the incoming wash, all the while feeding on the run.

On another such day—a day of heavy haze overhead and wisps of fog rising from the surface of the sea and from the flat wet sand—I particularly noticed an apparent increase in the size of the Herons. Never had I seen the bare sides of these three granite ledges loom so large.

It was the time of the full moon and of spring tides, and hence a larger than usual expanse of their foundations was laid bare. But this was only a partial explanation, I am now sure. For the next morning early, the conditions were the same—ebb tide, haze overhead, and fog arising from the sand and the sea. In a casual sweep of the beach my eye was suddenly caught by a bird, a large bird, that appeared on the horizon of the sand. It was enormous. Could it be an eagle? I put my glasses on it. It was a black-backed gull. And then I saw others farther along the beach—and all of them appeared oversized.

Only then did I realize the cause of the phenomenon. It was the fog and the haze. Seen against the gray background, the three Herons and the black-backed gull had assumed truly Gargantuan proportions.

At ebb tide the little salt river that drains the marsh courses seaward with a rush. It sweeps over the sand with such speed that waves mount and crest upstream. Lining its banks of sand are a myriad gulls. Now and again a single gull settles in the fast-flowing rip and suffers itself to be borne, like a chip tossing on its course, downriver to the sea. Apparently the gull enjoys the ride. It is spun by the force of the water, now facing upstream, now headed toward the sea. A great bird running the rapids, as it were.

Upstream, in back of the dunes, the marsh extends in a flat expanse of tawny salt hay fenced at its farther bound by dark, timbered ridges and the steep slope of Morse Mountain. This early in the season, a flight of nine black duck is swinging out over the sea, angling toward the marsh. Like the leaves of a single swamp maple at its head, they betoken an early fall. Now they circle up over the marsh, dropping. Now they are lost to sight against the black background of the firs on the far ridge. I do not see them pitch. A few moments later, in that quarter I see another large flight milling and mounting, and then disappearing beyond the ridge to settle into another marsh drained by another little salt creek.

The duck entice me, and I walk alongside the winding stream up into the marsh. On its flowed-out flats I notice the holes of the clams. The soft sand is spotted with them, and as I walk, they spurt. I recall with a grimace the so-called clam chowder I had for lunch up-country the other day—made, I will take an oath, from the rubber boots some old clam digger once used on these flats.

Emerging above the last tide line is a set of small tracks. What are they? Small, round, very close together, with separate claw marks finely cut in the leading edges. This was no dog or cat. A coon perhaps, more probably a skunk. And so I pass on.

From over the dunes comes the rote of the sea. The tide is making. I have often noticed that the muted roaring of the waves is always more distinct in back of the dunes. Is it that you cannot see the waves? Or is it the current of air that carries this timeless message of the sea in over the beach, up over the dunes, and down again into the quiet marsh?

The coarse marsh grass tickles the soles of my bare feet. I look down and I see on every hand thick clumps of sea lavender now at the height of its purple blooming. Like heather it is, and often mistaken for it. At the edge of the marsh the beach peas grow in profusion, and despite the fact that the green pods are well formed, I spot here and there a blossom, a late message from early summer. Swinging around, I see beyond the low marsh grass the yellow dunes that hide the sea save where the little salt river runs.

In back of the distant dunes that front the beach and sea, and out of my sight, beyond the grass-topped dunes that range in toward the marsh, there is a small cranberry patch.

This secret spot is known to only a favored few. The tale is told of one who, on his hands and knees, was picking the little red berries there when he sensed a presence in back of him. Turning suddenly, he looked up into the staring eyes of a cow moose.

The tide is now making, flooding the flats with blue water. The fish are schooling, and the terns are in flight.

From the veranda, to which I have returned after my walk on the marsh, I look out over the foreshore with my field glasses on a level fifty-odd feet above the beach. In the round field I catch and follow a tern as it wings past in urgent flight. The black-capped head scans the surface, now left, now right. The sharp red bill extends perpendicularly down, and the mantle between the swiftly beating wings is gray, and then there is the sharply forked tail. Thus seen from above, this flying tern makes me feel as if I myself were in flight. Now he stops short and, wings set, dives straight down, toward the water. I follow with the glass.

In the trough between two waves I see a splash of white, and then there is no bird. A second later the water breaks. The tern is in flight again, and from either side of his red mandibles there gleams in the sunlight the silver sides of a sand eel.

There is a sudden flitter of the wings as he shakes the salt water from his body and wings. His head jerks up, then down. The eel is being lined up to be swallowed, and then it is gone. The tern sweeps on set wings in a grand scaling, downwind. Then turning, he courses upwind again, fishing. These terns always fish upwind. Then they turn, scale away downwind, turn, and beat their way back again.

Later I watch their flight from the beach. Over my head, their red feet are neatly outlined against their soft white bellies. Some have black tips at the end of their red bills. These are the common tern, *Sterna hirundo hirundo;* those of the pure red bill are the Arctic tern, *Sterna paradisaea.*

## Small Point Beach

In the little salt river that flows across the beach, the sand eels are schooling. I level the glasses and count five terns, facing upwind and hovering. One dives. I follow him down, watch the splash. Then comes splash after splash after splash, as terns rain down out of the sky, break out of the water, and mount again, always with the luckless sand eel. The smart terns fly off to feed, and I see why. Two terns apparently collide in flight, but the one that flew in from aloft tears the fish from the beak of the other and makes off with it.

The flight of the terns goes on endlessly. Out over the sea, toward the island of Seguin, I watch a multitude of terns and gulls in ceaseless flight, winging on this course and that, bent on urgent, unknown errands. Now and then, through the wheeling, shifting, and flashing white bodies, a black shag flies steadily, in a flight as straight and even as that of an arrow. And all the while there comes to ear their screaming outcries.

At the tail end of the summer, coots are plentiful off Small Point Beach. At low tide, on the calm sea that goes with dog-day weather, they are to be seen scattered in great rafts, so thickly clustered as to give the impression they are the tops of ledges laid bare by the low tide. There is something compelling about a raft of coot. It is out there to be watched.

I stand at the water's edge and they swim unconcerned not a hundred yards out. On the gentle curvings of the incoming waves they are seen as rolling undulations of birds. Now and again, from the midst of the mass there is a flash of white as a single bird rises from a swimming position, to beat its wings. Within the raft, individual birds are swimming in either direction, yet the mass always trends in a single direction.

As I watch, they move west. Then a few in the van, perhaps fifteen, turn and swim east. In a matter of seconds, by some subtlety of communication, the entire raft starts moving east. After a bit, its direction is again reversed. The raft moves as a unit, the impulses of its action a mystery.

I make a rough count. The raft is ten to a dozen birds wide, swimming almost wing to wing, and it is easily a hundred yards long. Thus I calculate that there must be at least two thousand birds in the slowly moving raft.

At my feet, the finite edges of the small waves come bearing floating feathers, light and downy, the evidence of preening. Then, when I look up from an inspection of this, the raft has split in two.

Perhaps the explanation of this is the sudden appearance of a seal. His bald concave head has risen above the surface between myself and the raft. It is dripping and from it two round eyes gaze steadily at me. Then, his curiosity satisfied, the head slowly submerges, withdrawn into the sea, leaving an emptiness of water.

Beyond the raft of coot, other rafts lie scattered here and there on the surface between the beach and Seguin. A lobsterman's boat with a swordfishing pulpit on its bow is poking around, following the smooth slicks in the hope of sighting a triangular black fin. Later, someone who had been aboard her reported that out there the eider ducks were as thickly rafted as the coots on this hazy lazy August morning.

Also far out is a lone loon, distinguishable by the long bill and the gracefully curving neck.

A dog, a waddling basset hound, comes down to the edge of the water. He barks at the sea, and his long, weeping ears shake gently. Three youths in truncated shorts pass in the rear on the run.

Alarmed, the raft moves offshore. I continue my walk along the beach.

The early morning of the next day betrays its character by

its muted, yellow light. By breakfast time, although the sun has risen above the fog bank that lines the horizon to the eastward, its beams are still filtering through a heavy haze. Now I know that the trip up-country which lies before me will be a blistering one. For no heat is more intolerable than that encountered on a dog day in one of the valleys of the rivers that drain the State of Maine.

Later, before I leave, I sit again for a moment leaning back in the rush-bottomed chair on the veranda for a long last look out over the sea. The tips of the three balsams that project their green branches above the line of the railing give contrast to this memorable scene. A song sparrow sings as if to burst its small self, and a yellowleg comes winging in across the beach from over the sea, whistling as it flies. Suddenly it is eclipsed by the line of the roof. Then I leave, content with what I have seen and heard.

A long day's journey followed. The scorching heat was compensated somewhat by the sight of the goldenrod, now at the height of its blooming. It stretched on either hand in yellow paths, each golden sheaf forming a delicate arch in its bending toward the sun.

# The Moose River Country

ON OUR JOURNEY up-country from the mouth of the Kennebec and along its winding reaches, for a large measure of the way we are in sight of the blue of the river. Here Benedict Arnold led his army on its march to Quebec in the fall of

1775. Sometime in the afternoon, as we follow the course of an ancient trail once known as the Canada Road, we pass the Great Carrying Place where Arnold and his men left the Kennebec to make their arduous portage over to the upper waters of the Dead River.

Arnold's black treason at West Point has tended to erase the fame of this earlier exploit. For his leadership of this remarkable expedition through the Maine woods to Quebec was outstanding. The man had a genius for leadership. What was lacking was judgment. To his contemporaries his course must have seemed like that of a meteor flashing in brilliance across a star-studded sky to plunge at the end into darkness and oblivion.

Today you can go from Boston to Quebec, following Arnold's route, in a good day's driving. Even in the middle of winter in 1845, Dependence Forbush was able to drive over the Canada Road in an open sleigh from Portland to Montreal, a distance of 275 miles, in thirty-two hours. But, seventy years before, in the fall of 1775, it was quite a different thing. Arnold's army totaled almost exactly 1,050 men. The bulk of them left Cambridge on Wednesday, September 13, and marched to Newburyport. Here eleven schooners and sloops had been assembled, and here they stayed, windbound, until the following Tuesday. On that day the fleet headed down east with a fair wind, making an excellent passage and heaving to off the mouth of the Kennebec late that night. Then they beat their way up the river and reached Fort Western, on the east bank opposite the Augusta of today, on the twenty-fourth.

Here they acquired a fleet of bateaux, 220 of these having been deemed adequate for the transport of the army and its supplies on the waterways of the wilderness to Quebec. They gave trouble from the start. Hastily put together with green pine, they were heavy and they leaked. Moreover, the handling of a bateau in quick water is a skill achieved only by long and arduous experience, and few, if any, of Arnold's men had ever seen one. In consequence, when they could have poled upstream, they clambered overside and dragged instead. This, coupled with leakage and the shipping of water, would cause them to lose much of their stores.

The arduous struggle up the swift-flowing Kennebec commenced with a portage of half a mile around the rapids and falls above Fort Western. This was the first carry. There would be four more on the Kennebec around Ticonic, Skowhegan, Norridgewock, and Carritunk Falls. What this meant in arduous labor may be imagined from a conservative estimate of the weight of the bateaux, the stores, and the equipment at a hundred tons. For a time they had the aid of oxen and sledges but later, on the Dead River, these would be lacking.

By the eleventh of October, the last of the expedition left the Kennebec at the place long known as the Great Carrying Place. You can spot it today if you are any good at figuring the lay of the land. It is some two miles south of the village of Caratunk. Across the Kennebec, the swift course of which on your left has been flowed out by the Wyman Dam downstream, a long stretch of quite high land runs north, parallel to the river. At this particular point, there is a big notch in this plateau that makes out due west from the Kennebec.

Here the trail took off toward the west through this notch, to follow a series of four portages and three ponds called the Carry Ponds. The aim was to reach and then ascend the waters of the Dead River, itself a branch of the Kennebec. On this leg of the journey the going would get really rough.

They were now beyond the limits of any settlement. Almost a month had elapsed since they had left Cambridge, the fall of the year was closing in, the fall rains were due, and it was cold, at times bitter cold.

Arnold's men were not swamping an altogether trackless trail through the wilderness. They were following a path that had been used by the Indians from time immemorial in their passing between the watersheds of the St. Lawrence and the Kennebec. The first white men to use it had been the black-robed Jesuits, who, guided by the Indians, had come in the middle of the seventeenth century to save the souls of the savages on the banks of the Kennebec. This route had been considered as an approach to Quebec in the last struggle between the French and the English, which culminated, with the deaths of Wolfe and Montcalm on the Plains of Abraham, in the fall of Quebec in 1759.

The last carry on the Great Carrying Place was a nightmare. It terminated in a cedar swamp. There, staggering ahead and sinking, with each step forward, half-leg deep into the moss, mud, and mire, a double file of six men would move slowly, their bruised and aching shoulders supporting the hard gunwales of an overturned bateau. They had come two miles on this fourth and last, and worst, portage on the Great Carrying Place. And there was almost a mile of it to go.

In the later days of lumbering and river driving in the Maine woods, this operation would come to be known as "lugging boat." On Arnold's march to Quebec, his Journal records thirty-two portages.

At length, the weary men would set down their bateau in a small stream, appropriately known as Bog Brook, and this, in a short mile, would bring them into the Dead River. Here the going would be better—for a while.

Then the fall rains began in earnest—on Thursday, the nineteenth, in the words of Arnold's Journal—"small rains the whole of this day." In the night this turned into a three-day southwester with a "Prodigious fall of rain." And since this part of the Dead River was the watershed of a number of bogs, ponds, and streams, early Sundy morning came the run-off. The freshet, says Arnold, "came running on us like a torrent, having rose 8 feet perpendicular in 9 hours." The expedition was at the edge of disaster, as may be seen from his entry that day:

"This morning presented us a very disagreeable prospect, the Country round entirely overflowed, so that the course of the river being crooked, could not be discovered, which with the rapidity of the current renders it almost impossible for the Battoes to ascend the River or the men to find their way by land or pass the small brooks, arms of the river, & — Add to this our Provisions almost exhausted, & the incessant rains for three days has prevented our gaining anything considerable, so that we have but a melancholy prospect before us."

Then, in characteristic vein, the ebullient colonel concluded: "but in general in high spirits."

The shortage of provisions was particularly serious. Improvidence in their rationing, and the hazards of this primitive mode of transport, had brought the expedition to this pass. The next day, as they approached their seventh portage in the ascent of the Dead River, "we had the misfortune of oversetting seven Battoes & losing all the Provisions." This led to the holding of a "counsell of warr," and Arnold decided to press on ahead of his men in an attempt to reach the French settlements on the Chaudière and send back supplies.

That afternoon it started raining again and "continued raining & snowing all night." The next day Arnold and his small party wove their way along the thoroughfares connecting, and through the several ponds in the upper watershed of the Dead River which are today known as the Chain of Ponds. Meanwhile, unbeknown to him, his fourth and last division in the line of march, under the command of a Colonel Enos, gave up the struggle and turned back toward the Kennebec.

The last link in the Chain of Ponds was Moosehorn, now

known as Arnold Pond. From its shore there rises the height of land—in the vernacular of the woodsman, a height o' land and sometimes a horse back—that separates the valleys of the St. Lawrence and the Kennebec. Eight years later, at the conclusion of the Revolution, this height of land would appear in the Treaty of Paris as the "Highlands" along which the international boundary between Canada and the District of Maine was to run.

Arnold reached this shore in the late afternoon and impetuously forged on ahead, making three miles on this carry, and not making camp until "near midnight." The three remaining divisions came on. This was the last long portage —upwards of four miles—over which these weary and half-starved men would have to bull their bateaux and supplies. By the late afternoon of Saturday, the twenty-eighth of October, they were all on the far side of the height of land. With the leader in the van, the march continued. On down Arnold Stream they went, into and across Lake Megantic, where the Chaudière takes its rise, and then down its wild course.

Just before it enters Lake Megantic, Arnold Stream divides deceptively in the midst of a treacherous waterlogged terrain of bog and swamp, into three outlets. It was a trap. The men, attempting to follow the shore of the stream, became almost hopelessly entangled. Once again, disaster threatened the expedition, and they extricated themselves only after the greatest difficulties. Then, after the passage of Lake Megantic, there came the Chaudière.

The word *chaudière* means cauldron, and it is the source of the New Englander's *chowder*. The Chaudière is a wild stream, turbulent, of swift-flowing and churning white water, studded with dangerous rapids. Here Arnold "had the misfortune to overset & stave three boats," and later in the same rapids Captain Morgan lost seven bateaux. Here, too, Captains Goodrich and Ward and Lieutenant McClellan suffered similar losses. What the loss of provisions entailed is only too clearly indicated by contemporary references to the consumption of dog meat.

In the van, Colonel Arnold reached "the first house" on October 30. Three days later, the first of the men in the long straggling column that had marched, many of them barefoot, sixty miles from Lake Megantic, met the cattle being driven upstream by a relief party laden with all the abundance of the rich French-Canadian countryside. The worst was over. The number of casualties is unknown, but the next year a number of skeletons were found on the banks of the Chaudière.

In three days' time an orderly advance had been established and the little army, marching by road this time, completed on November 8 a three-day march to Point Levi on the St. Lawrence, opposite Quebec. A number of boats and canoes had been gathered along the Chaudière, but for three nights the men lay in camp, windbound. Then, in the dark of night on the thirteenth of November, silently, and skillfully eluding the patrol boats of the British frigate *Lizard* and the sloop-of-war *Hunter*, Benedict Arnold put ashore at Wolfe's Cove, in the shadow of Quebec, his band of between five hundred and six hundred men.

And so ended Arnold's march to Quebec. It was two months to a day since the departure from Cambridge of the main body of 1,050 men with whom he had started the preceding September.

Soon after leaving the Great Carrying Place, where Arnold had left the Kennebec to carry over into the Dead River, we arrived at the Forks. This is a crotch of the stream where the Dead River joins the Kennebec. Here we commenced to climb. Here the air became noticeably cooler. Then, at the crest of the height of land separating the watershed of the Kennebec from that of the Moose River, a memorable vista stretched away before us to the next height of land, beyond which was the Province of Quebec. We gazed at mountains and ridges, and the hills that bulk before them, all timbered and in the late afternoon all of a clear dark purple of variant shades. Cupped within these somber slopes are the lakes, the ponds, and the streams of the Moose River country. Here lay Attean Lake, our destination, where, on Birch Island, a hot supper was awaiting us.

## ATTEAN LAKE

The next morning, as I walked down to the float, a soft breeze rustled the leaves of the poplars in front of the cabin, and in the early morning sunlight they danced as only the leaves of a poplar can dance, flashing their silver-gray undersides. The dark surface of Attean Lake stretches forth to meet at the far shore a green that rises sharp to a high ridge. There, in rugged outline against the sky, is the granite contour of the horizon. Passing clouds were flecking this green mountainside with scattered patches of shadow, and close to the ridge a faint mist hung lightly over the tops of the trees.

I took a quick plunge into the cool water of the sun-drenched lake. This was the matins of the day. Then I climbed the hill and dressed for breakfast.

When cruising the woods of the Moose River country it is important to have in mind the lay of the land. The key is the course of the Moose River. Its source is a complex of ponds and brooks, about ten of them, that lie and rise just under the Canadian border. Like the fingers of two outstretched hands, they run down, carrying considerable water, to form the main river, which flows on across Maine, trending in a general easterly direction. From the north it receives the waters of Holeb Lake. Then winding a tortuous path around bogs and logans and between ridges and mountains, it forms a great oxbow around the timbered terrain that lies to the south of Attean Lake. Finally, after coursing down over Attean Rips, it enters that lake.

Thence its waters flow northerly, leaving Attean Lake by the thoroughfare that leads into Big Wood Pond. At the northeast end of Big Wood, the Moose River resumes its leisurely, winding, alder-lined course, turning again to the eastward and passing first through Long Pond and then through Brassua Lake, until at length it courses into and loses its identity in the broad waters of Moosehead Lake.

The two aboriginal names of the Moose River reveal very clearly the dominant characteristic of an Indian place name. In the great majority of instances it would describe the place, or some aspect of it, or its resemblance to something, or, not so frequently, some event associated with the place. Thus, the lower reaches of the Moose River received the name Sahkhabehaluck. This meant that more water flowed from it than from any other stream emptying into Moosehead Lake. But in its upper reaches, where its predominant characteristic is its winding curvings, it was known as the Kweueuktonoonkhegan, or "snowshoe river" —invoking its resemblance to the curved frame of a snowshoe, just as we might have called it the Oxbow River. To give a lake a name such as Attean, which is the name of an Indian family, was rare.

The evening before, after driving up the valley of the Kennebec by way of the old Canada Road that runs through the village of Jackman, I had arrived at a landing on the shore of the thoroughfare leading from Attean Lake into Big Wood Pond. Here my companion and I left our car. A boat was waiting for us. In short order, our gear was loaded aboard and we went purring up the thoroughfare and across the tossing waters of Attean Lake to our destination— Birch Island.

Birch Island is appropriately named. As we weathered the rocky point off its northerly shore, a small cove opened up before us; the shores of its embracing curve were covered with stands of silver-leaved poplar and the slender trunks of white birch. In the cove there was a landing, and among the birches were log cabins, half hidden by the fluttering foliage. These were the Attean Lake Camps.

In the days that lay ahead we would leave Birch Island in the morning after breakfast with a box lunch and foul-weather gear in a pack basket. In the late afternoon, and just in time for supper, we would return. In between there would be a memorable excursion. From this hub on Birch Island, there are infinite possibilities for excursions: cruisings through the woods and streams, the lakes and mountains of this Moose River country. You can stay on Birch Island for a month at a time and never take the same excursion twice. The names come swiftly, tumbling through my mind like chips in a rip—Holeb Lake, Number Five Mountain, Long Pond, the Mud Pond, Clearwater, Benjamin and Horseshoe, Sally Mountain, Number Five Bog, Bitter Brook, and a host of others.

Late in that first afternoon I sat out on the veranda of our cabin. I was facing the western quarter, where the lake stretches away in a broad expanse before entering a long narrow pocket. To the right, the timbered slope of Sally Mountain descends in a long decline to the shore. To the left, across the pocket, the green slope rises again, this time to the top of Attean Mountain. All this is about two miles distant. Then, beyond this western skyline, there lie hidden in the depths of the forest the twisting curves of the Moose River.

Against the background of mountain and forest, the light green of the hardwood growth spotted by the black of spruce and pine, I watch the approach of a thunderstorm. It comes on toward me across the overcast sky in an easterly direction to encompass the lake before passing on down the watershed of the Kennebec.

At the start, out over the low height of land at the head of the pocket, the sky is darkening to a flat black gray. Rolling across the sky, hurrying in advance of the storm, are deep convoluted billows of gray cloud forming and re-forming as they pass. The trending clouds trail their skirts over the tops of the mountains and, in a few moments' time, the distant peak of Number Five Mountain, which rises beyond the Moose River, and then, nearer at hand, Attean Mountain, are eclipsed. The shores of the pocket fade slowly and then suddenly they are obscured.

The wind is rising, and it continues to rise. Scattered drops dimple the water, patter on the leaves, and spot the veranda. What a few moments before was a moderate chop now lengthens out. White caps gleam, and there are considerable troughs from the crests of wave to wave.

The shower is advancing. It is a dark wall of rain, and I hear its distant roaring. The tapping on the roof increases to a tattoo. Soon it rises to a roar. Gusts of wind drive mist from the falling drops, and in the shelter of the veranda roof I feel them against my face. In the middle distance between Birch Island and the pocket, a small boat comes swiftly on before the wind, with a swelling wave in hot pursuit. In it two figures crouch, huddled inside their ponchos.

A single clap of thunder cracks like a bullwhip, and then comes a long reverberating roar and rumble that departs echoing and re-echoing. The falling rain flattens the seas. For a few moments, amid the crashing and tumbling of thunder, with the watery scene illumined by baleful flashes, there is a steady downpour and the eaves and leaves are running with rivulets of rain.

Imperceptibly the downpour slackens. The shower is

passing on its course. The clouds lighten, and the obscured far shore of the lake comes into dim view. Then the slope of Attean Mountain becomes visible. On its side, white mists rise that now obscure and now, shifting, disclose the dark trees. They rise. A cloud forms, ascends, and disappears. The dark wall of rain retreats southward. There remains a gentle shower. In the distance, over Number Five Bog a great covering of white mist hovers.

Afterward, when the clouds in the western sky part to let through the light from the fallen sun, an afterglow is reflected on the surface of Attean Lake. Then for a few short moments the water is a sheen of burnished copper.

## THE MOOSE RIVER

A strong southwest wind is adding its force to the outboard that is driving us across Attean Lake ahead of rolling seas. In the bow of the canoe I am snug and warm in a new rubber poncho, and I watch the scud racing eastward in competition with us. At the skyline the clouds meet the mountains and ridges and drape them with great skirts. All is gray and the surface of the lake is dotted with small dark islands crowned with the black plumes of tall pines standing in sepulchral contrast to the gray light and sky.

The motor purrs a low monotony. There are those who decry the use of an outboard in these outermost reaches. I am not one of them. If you do not kick against the pricks of "progress," you become accustomed to them; to me, this low monotonous purring is part of the wilderness today. Whenever it ceases, I enjoy the contrast of the silence and the soft slap of the little waves overside.

The alder-lined shore soon looms ahead, and as the mouth of the Moose River opens up, the sun burns through and lights up the smooth dark path of the river between the overhanging alders. In an opening, a low tangle of alder and poplar branches is visible for the moment of our passing. This is the mark of a beaver dam. Here there is a splatter of wings, a high, piping, whistling note, and the swift sight of a duck in flight above the alders. By the whistle I know that we have startled a wood duck.

The tops of the alders lining the banks still toss, agitated by the strong southwest wind. The welcoming kingfisher awaits, and as we arrive at the successive turnings of this winding deadwater, he ushers us on our way in long arcs of flight, warning by his repeated rattles the denizens of the river of our alien approach.

At length, in the pool below Attean Rips, the motor ceases. A silent fisherman greets us with a wave of his free hand, the other being concerned with his casting, to which he immediately returns his attention. We take the canoe up over the rips.

Attean Rips descend sharply in two pitches with a dead-water between. On the east bank a well-worn path mounts in a slow decline the ledge that forms the second pitch. The grass is thick and lush and wet with dew, and our task is easy. We lug the outboard motor and all removable gear— pole, oars, oil can, and the like—to the edge of the dead-water above the falls, and then return and haul the canoe up over the grass. I once heard a Frenchman say that he could take his canoe anywhere on a heavy dew.

We are soon launched and sputtering along through the deadwater while I stand in the bow with the pole to fend us off any submerged rocks. A hawk makes a scaling flight across the deadwater. In a short space we reach the foot of the first pitch.

Here the water is high and strong. Dragging upstream is a new experience for my companion, so I lead the way, letting the canoe float out on the end of its line into the quick water at the foot of the rip.

Then we ease out into the white water. It is all but waist

deep. The current is rugged, the footing deceptive, and the rocky bottom slippery. By setting the pole and hanging to it we manage to achieve firm stances. Then we haul the canoe up the middle of the rip until we can reach out and grab the bow. From then on it is easier. We hang to the gunwale as we feel for our footing; one man on each side of the bow. This supplies us with a balance, and the canoe heaves ahead as we walk.

Now, with the motor purring softly, we are winding along and around the long bends of the Moose River. Beyond the still alder-lined banks there rise outlined, now against a gray sky, and then, as we round the next bend, against the wooded side of a distant ridge, the silent sentinels of this river: spruce that taper to a tip, hackmatack with wide-spreading branches shredded with gray moss, balsam, the spectral white of a canoe birch, and occasionally in a wild meadow back of the alders, incongruously yet naturally, a wineglass elm. This Moose River has an awe, a mystery about it.

As we proceed slowly on our winding course, there is in the background an ever-shifting backdrop of timbered ridges and dark mountains. The trees extend in reflection deep down into the water, and below their pointed tops, a mountainside shimmers.

A single white pine towers tall and stately, waving its black plumes far above the level of the surrounding forest. It is far ahead, beyond the end of a long reach, and we are in sight of it for a considerable time. Nearer at hand, it begins to dwarf. Then suddenly I look again for its familiar shape and it is gone, hidden by the thick growth of alder that overhangs the bank.

I see afloat a single red leaf of a maple sapling. Its edges are curled slightly and the inside of the leaf is dry. This red spot on the dark water is a reminder that autumn is fast approaching.

Just before we reach the mouth of Bitter Brook, with the wind dead ahead, there is an opening in the alders. It is the entrance to a marshy, bog-like pocket at the side of the stream.

"LOOK!"

Knee-high in the deep grass, watching us unconcerned, is a large animal, tawny, black-brown, with great long ears and a broad snout from the sides of which a mouthful of grasses is dripping. The animal turns slowly and starts off, ambling into the alders and out of sight. It is a cow moose, and thus does the Moose River live up to its name.

The sight of this cow moose in that logan, her high-shouldered bulk outlined against the alders, instantly put me in mind of calling moose on the Nepisiguit River in New Brunswick nearly four decades before.

It was later in the season—this was early August—in late September, when the hardwood ridges along the Nepisiguit were ablaze with the fiery hues of autumn. All day long the sun had been traversing a mottled sky. For a bit it would be warm and the sunlight would glance off the white water in the rips as the canoe went shooting through them. Then, with a veering of the wind, the sky would fill over with scudding clouds, and there would come into the air a chill, the chill of early fall. A weather breeder, that is what that day was.

We made camp in the late afternoon in a curving bight of the stream. Directly supper was over, and before the quick dusk came on, the wind having dropped, the Frenchman decided to try his luck at calling a moose. Dipping to his elbows into the burlap bag he called his "pooch," he pulled out a birchbark moose horn, the one the Skidjims had given him at Tobique Point. Thereupon I was witness to a curious bit of woodcraft.

First he disappeared into the woods, returning a moment

later with a large glob of wet moss. This he dropped at the edge of the stream. For a moment he stood there, outlined against the fading light, his conical black hat pushed askew on his crown, his galluses forming an X across his back, his legs widespread and extending out of the ends of his stagged pants. Then, bending over until the open end of the birch-bark horn was just above the moss, he commenced his call.

The call of a cow moose begins on a high, wild, nasal note. Then, as the caller rises, swinging the mouth of the horn upwards in a long slow arc, the pitch of the call drops, and it grows slowly to a full-throated, resonant roar that increases in intensity until the caller has described a full circle and the mouth of the horn is again over the moss. Then, as this hungry, yearning moan starts echoing and re-echoing out over the ridges and in the aisles of the woods, there pours forth liquidly from the horn the hoarse grunt ending in a whisper that simulates the final blown-out breath of the cow moose.

*E-e-e-e-a-a-a-a-r-r-r-o-o-o-n-n-n-n-g-g-h-h*

There was a pause. Then again this aching, haunting wail came from the horn, to travel in reverberating echoes out over the hills. The short twilight was soon over, and at the end of his last call, the Frenchman added a small embellishment. He filled the long horn with water. Then at shoulder height he poured it slowly, splashing the water into the stream,.

"There, that ought ter fetch heem."

Casting the moose horn aside, he turned to bough up the fire, and for a bit we sat, enjoying the warmth of the blaze and the relaxation of a quiet smoke while night filled the aisles of the woods with darkness. For a small circle around us the ruddy glow of the fire held the night at bay. Overhead the open sky above the Nepisiguit was barely visible since the overcast there was a shade lighter than the blackness beneath the overhanging trees.

Picking up the moose horn, I plucked from its mouth a slender aspen leaf.

"That leaf, she make de call sound wheezy in de distance. Me grandfadder, he tell me all 'bout how ter call de moose. You see de moss dat I trow in de mud. Well, de bull, he tink de cow, she come back to feed, after she geeve him de call. De moss, she geeve de reel moose sound."

When we turned in, the wind was rising. You could hear the trees thrashing and now and then, out of the darkness, came the creaking squeal of two interlaced limbs. It was as if the forest were in agony. Then the rain came, a scattering of drops at first, which soon developed into a steady pelting downpour. You could feel the fine spray on your face as the drops struck the canvas above it, to run down and off the selvage and form little pools that had an unpleasant way of spreading and creeping inside the tent. We were in for a rough night in that lean-to.

I don't know when it happened, for I had dozed off. My first sensation was a tugging at my blankets and a whisper: "Did you hear that?"

I sat up. The fire was out, and I could not see my companion. I reached out my hand. He too was sitting up.

"Ssh, listen!"

Then, through the rattle of the rain, the soughing of the wind, and the thrashing of the branches, I heard it—a deep, solid, heavy grunt.

*Unngh*

Then again: *Unngh*

At regularly spaced intervals it came. It sounded like the even strokes of a man chopping steadily but slowly through a big hardwood log. It was a bull moose answering the Frenchman's call.

But it was so dark we never saw him. Instead we heard him—for hours it seemed—grunting and stomping around somewhere in the darkness. The next morning we found he had been just across the stream. The soft shore there was littered with his spoor and his droppings. We figured the bull moose had put in as bad a night as we had.

Now, as we glide on up the slow-moving waters of the Moose River, a low line of dark water opens up beneath the alders. This is visible only to the practiced eye, and looking closely, I see that it cuts through the high bank that is hidden by the alders. This is the mouth of Bitter Brook. Here we go ashore.

First we pull the light aluminum canoe up on the bank and load in the gear—fish rods, paddles, lunchboxes, and a small knapsack. Then we start dragging her through the grass along a well-swamped trail that leads to an ancient beaver dam, so old that it has long since become a part of the topography. Here we launch the canoe and begin to fight our way through the protruding alders. Gradually, this body of backed-up water—a beaver flowage, in the local vernacular—widens. The alders soon disappear from the banks and we can see out over an expanse of tall waving grass, quite a distance in the clear, to where the fast land begins and the timber rises.

Hark! The tinkling of trickling water. A brook coming in? But no. When the canoe rounds the next blind turn, there is another beaver dam, stretching from sedge to sedge. There is nothing antique about this one. There are leaves on the topmost alder sticks and their butts are white. This is a clear "beaver sign." We clamber out on the dam, haul the canoe over, and launch it again into a level of water eighteen inches above what it was below.

The course of this flowage twists and turns. We round a point marked by a great round boulder. This, according to our mentor that morning, "we could not possibly miss." But we do miss the next landmark—an old birch stump marking the start of a spotted trail. Probably rotted away. But no matter. We are for exploring the whole of this flowage, and on we go, paddling slowly.

Just above the next beaver dam, we pass close to a miniature island covered with tall grass and a multitude of little blue flowers. Like miniature snapdragons they are, and later I learn that they are the mad-dog skullcap—*Scutellaria lateriflora*. Our discovery of Skullcap Island is the event of this upward passage.

We soon reach the head of navigation. The dry bed of a brook lies ahead, and we put ashore for a short reconnaissance. At a little distance, on the height of land, the trees part and again we look on a body of water, a logan between two ridges.

A *logan*—there is a word that goes back to the Indians. Algonquin in origin, it is a shortened version of the word *poke-logan*. This, it was explained to Thoreau in the 1840's, is "an inlet that leads nowhere. If you get in, you have to get out again the same way." These logans—low marshy places, pockets off the course of a stream, spots where marsh and grass and ooze all come together—are the places to see and hunt game. It was in a logan that we had seen the cow moose.

In short order, we are afloat again on the dark water of the logan. Directly we start paddling, four black ducklings scutter over the surface ahead, up into the tall grass, and are lost to sight. We paddle on. A short half mile brings us again to the head of navigation. Here is another bed of rocks in a dried-up stream. Once again we make a portage, toting the canoe awkwardly over the boulders. Then, slightly above, there is still another logan; from its shore a ledge rises. This is a good place for nooning and soon, comfortably seated on the soft moss, we are dividing the slices of cold mutton, devouring the corncakes, and washing them down with great swallows of hot tea. Then we watch a shower come down over the forest out of the west, engulf us, pattern the water with a myriad drops, and disappear down the logans and through the beaver flowage whence we had come.

After lunch we continue our exploration. Another paddle brings us to the head of the logan, where there is a small mountain of a beaver house. We proceed up the supposed inlet, paddling through the thick ooze, only to find that it is a dead end and disappears obscurely in the grass. At the left, the skyline dips. That must be it, and it is. Up we go—again over the dry bed of a brook, steep and filled with large moss-grown boulders. At the top there is another beaver dam, a large one that has backed up still another flowage. We stand on the edge and watch. A startled duck takes flight. In back there arises a plunging, floundering sound. We turn and see the graceful red body of a large doe rising in magnificent curving bounds out of the bog, her white flag flashing.

This is the peak of our excursion. We turn to backtrack, and traverse the two logans and the beaver flowage, making three portages before we reach the Moose River again.

By now the sky is overcast and louring; soon there is a fine light drizzle-drozzle of falling mist. The wind, which for some time has been hanging in the south and east, has brought this drisk up-country from off the Gulf of Maine. As we pass on down the Moose River, our wooded world is constantly shaping and reshaping as the louring overcast rises and falls and the drisk now obscures and now clears before the ridges. I take note of a lovely grove of birch dripping silently.

On our way downstream we encounter shower after shower. First, scattering drops dapple the surface, then the clouds drop down until they envelop the tops of the ridges, and the rain comes pelting down. At length the downfall tapers off, the scud lifts again, and the sky lightens. Then the sequence is repeated.

With the winding of the stream, my sensation is often that we are standing still while before us a scene shifter is at work. The backdrop is in a constant flux, now with the wooded ridges clear, the next moment with the skirt of a cloud trailing silently over them. The tall, sentinel-like spruces along the banks seem actually to be in motion. Slowly, as we pass, spruce replaces spruce, balsam succeeds balsam, to be succeeded by stands of dripping hackmatack and canoe birches, ghostly white on this wet gray day and some of them large enough to warrant their name.

In the shank of the afternoon we fish the head of Attean Rips from the shore, casting upstream and allowing the fly to drift downstream in the white water of the rip. I see several small birds fly out from the alders over the falls, snap up an insect, and return. One perches athwart my fly rod, which leans against an alder while I am tying on a new fly, and I note the little yellow band on the tail, the red spot on the wing, the crest, and the black bib surmounting the buff-colored breast. Cedar waxwings, that is what they are.

Then comes the carry. We lug in silence, with heavy steps and at a slow pace. Then home to Birch Island and to the hot supper that awaits us there.

## HOLEB LAKE

Dawn next day ushered in a day fit to make the reputation of any climate. It was one of those rare clear days when all horizons are fine-drawn lines. A little breeze stirred the surface of Attean Lake with fillets of the deepest blue as our canoe sped steadily onward. Overhead, clouds were traveling from horizon to horizon like great white argosies afloat on the ocean of the air, and their dark shadows likewise traveled over the green bottom of the aerial sea. They were racing up there in the sky with spinnakers set and billowing balloon jibs on a course from west to east. I felt the chill of autumn when one of them blanketed the warmth of the sun's rays.

And high on a far hillside was autumn's heraldic emblem—
the red limb of a maple.

Our destination was Holeb Lake, and I glimpsed high up
against the forested slope of Attean Mountain a sliver that
seemingly floated in the air. I put my glasses on it and made
it out to be a fish hawk in a long, curving, scaling flight
against the tops of the trees that mount in tiers on the side
of the mountain. The sharply-angled wings flapped once,
twice, three times, almost languidly. Its course changed.
Then the osprey was winging in a widening arc high and far
out over the surface of the lake.

Its *phee phee phee* came down faintly to ear. I followed
him in the field of the glass. At full circle he was back, traveling in a steady slow gliding against the trees. From my vantage below, in the bow of the canoe, I could see, against the
green of the forest, the bands on the underside of the tail
and the mottled marking of the wings. His slow flight was
carrying him toward the treetops. A tall birch stub stood
dead and white amid the green. Here he alighted and then
folded his wings, to sit motionless as if mounted.

We traveled on, the birch and the osprey slipping steadily
away in back of us. Then once again I heard the wild *phee
phee phee* and I knew that he was in flight. In the field of
the glass I watched as he encompassed the curve of the
shoulder of Attean Mountain and was lost to sight.

A few moments later, the rasp of the bow in the wet sand
announced the end of this leg of our voyage.

In jig time we were on the carry leading to Holeb Lake.

"Will you, for God's sake, look at that!"

This came from my companion, who was toting the outboard motor just ahead of me. He had stopped in his tracks
and was pointing down with his free hand. Almost underfoot
was a little animal, unconcernedly enjoying a hearty breakfast in a thick clump of red bunchberries. Its small oval-

shaped back was laterally streaked with black and white; this was the familiar denizen of the woods, a young hedgehog.

Immediately there was a considerable to-do. Down came the motor, and the motion-picture camera was pulled out of the bottom of a knapsack. The light meter was consulted. By this time the porcupine was lumbering off into the woods. I pursued him, heading off his flight. His black and white quills flared in defense, but with the aid of a stick I needled him back onto the carry. He liked the stick; it must have been a piece of hemlock, for he grasped in his little paws the end that was thrust toward him and started gnawing. He squealed, a small, baby-like noise. The while, the camera was clicking. Then we watched him lumbering off through the woods, over the leaves and rocks. As he heaved himself clumsily over the rough terrain, he had a pristine, almost an antediluvian aspect.

And so we passed on. We sniffed the fragrance of the wild roses and listened to the distant reedy piping of the white-throat, who again and again responded to my whistling call.

At the end of the carry there was time out to watch a hawk sitting silently on a dead birch stub. Startled, it winged out over the lake, flying with short quick beats not unlike those of a pigeon. This fellow, the size of a crow and endowed with a long sharp tail, was identified by common accord as a duck hawk, more properly called a peregrine falcon and scientifically dubbed *Falco peregrinus anatum*.

Soon the canoe—an eighteen-foot aluminum one—was located. "You can't possibly miss it," had been the parting injunction of the proprietor of the camp, and we didn't. Then soon we were purring across Holeb Lake. As the shores receded, there came into view, scattered here and there on the top of the forest and outlined against the sky, the towering tops of the great white pines that once in lofty isolation spread their great plumes to the winds above the surrounding forest all over New England. Here and there in the

State of Maine a cluster of this virgin timber still stands, zealously guarded by its owners. But it is my notion that around the shores of Holeb Lake these great giants are again reaching toward the sky—fit eyries for the osprey and the eagle.

In a little curving cove of white sand we took our nooning. Here too we saw a sight of the wilderness. At one arm of the small cove a bold shoulder of granite rises, and at the top of this bluff stands one of the towering white pines. It is a lonely outpost. The other trees—spruce, balsam, and cedar— stand back to give it space and air.

In and out of its spreading branches a number of birds were flitting. As in dipping flight they passed back and forth from the tops of the other trees into the top hamper of the great pine, I put the glasses on them. They were flashes of color in the air, some of a roseate hue, with barred wings. Their call was a small triple whistle, not unlike that of the yellowleg, but less shrill and more reed-like. They were pine grosbeaks, *Pinicola enucleator leucura.* Here in the mountains of northern Maine is the southern limit of their range.

I went closer to investigate, and the birds scattered, flying out over the lake, uttering their shrill triple whistles. On the crest of the knoll, I decided to walk through the woods.

The growth was of spruce, cedar, and white pine. As I descended the far side of the knoll, for a few moments I could see the blue of the lake glinting through the woods and hear the rasp of its lapping waves. But this was quickly lost as I penetrated farther.

The woods were damp. They were thick and dark and cool. The whole forest floor was covered with deep green moss, and time after time I plunged into the soft sphagnum halfway to my knees. Even the thick outcroppings of granite wore an outer garment of moss. Ancient windfalls lay prostrate, enshrouded and embalmed in the thick moss. They reposed in the confused pattern of their accidental falling.

It must have been a generation and more since the lumberers were in this spot. The rotted remains of an occasional large stump told of a once great white pine towering aloft to wave its green plumes in the open air beneath the blue sky. Often, another tree had taken root and was climbing aloft out of the ancient stump.

In this darkened glade the smaller trees had no chance of survival. Balsam grew to a handful of feet and then died for want of light and air. There were mute evidences of lonely disaster, as when I came upon the dying tops of four trees that stood close together, their still-yellow butts twenty to thirty feet high. A violent twister, no doubt. And once the white scar of a lightning-struck pine gave off a spectral gleam in the shade ahead.

The farther I went, the darker the woods become. Pools of dark water appeared amid the moss. There was no underbrush, only the tapering trunks of trees with snagged branches that stuck out like spikes.

In this dark, dank, silent forest, there was no life—only evidences of life. In my noiseless passage through the thick moss, I came upon a clustering of the husks of a pine cone atop a rotting stump—the litter of a red squirrel's meal. Again, beside a limpid pool there were the brown round droppings of a deer—some quite fresh, attested by the presence of sluggish flies. In the stump of a dead cedar that hung at a tangent, supported by its living companions, I counted, to the height of twenty feet, thirty-two holes. I measured the depth of one with my pencil—three and a half inches. This was the work of woodpeckers.

Keeping it in mind to bear slowly to the left as I made a slow passage through this mossy glade, I came out at length on the shore of a swamp. From there it was a long and difficult walk around the shore through the thick underbrush back to the lunch ground. I found my companion on the prowl, hallooing and hollering for me in the belief that I was lost.

Then we loaded the canoe and put out onto Holeb Lake toward the carry.

In the late afternoon, as we were coming off the carry, Attean Lake was pure blue, slightly rippled, with the green slopes of the ridges trending northward on each hand, leading the eye to Birch Island and then beyond, to the timbered slopes of the distant shore, which were dappled by the shadows of the clouds. Overhead, the sky was freighted with argosies of fleecy cumulus.

This was a fleeting scene, for the clouds were drifting slowly and ther earthbound shadows were rising toward the skyline. In the foreground close at hand, the white breasts of three loons glared in the sunlight. I put my hands to my mouth and gave the familiar call. The middle one rose in the water and beat its wings.

## THE MAGICAL NUMBER FIVE

That night it came on to blow a gale of wind, and at sunup a dry northeaster was in full blast, tumbling the clouds across the sky like furies. This was a steady, hard wind, and I knew it would drive the heavy, louring clouds beyond the horizon. Accordingly, we took off for Number Five Mountain.

This curious place name derives from the following circumstance. In the Maine woods, the wilderness was long ago divided into square blocks in parallel ranges running east and west. Many of these unorganized townships in the wilderness, like this one, bear no name and have no inhabitants. The one where this mountain rises to the greatest height in Maine west of Ktaadn is known as Township Number Five in Range Number Seven. Hence the name—Number Five Mountain.

To get there, we went first by canoe across Attean Lake, back to the landing on the thoroughfare. Thence we drove south, up through the wooded hills by way of the old Canada Road, past Parlin Pond. Then, turning right and following a lumberers' road that ran in to the westward below the course of the Moose River, we came at length to the foot of Number Five Mountain. Straightway we commenced our ascent.

Halfway up we came out into a clearing. Here there was a camp, that of the fire warden whom we would later find on watch on the top of the mountain, and we took our ease for a bit. The sun was out, and looking back out over the vista formed by the little clearing, I watched the clouds casting slowly drifting shadows on the wooded slopes of the ridges and in the valley beyond.

The fire warden was a perfectionist. He had dammed up a brook, giving himself a trout pond; he had a bird feeder, wood under cover, grass cropped close, the brush cleared, a fresh coat of paint on his cabin, his wash flapping on the line, a small vegetable garden, a cold cellar built into the side of the mountain, and a vast American flag floating lazily over it all. This last, I suppose, was to show that he was in residence.

With a mile and a half to go to the top, it was time to get on. Up we went, traveling easily on the fire warden's well-swamped trail. We soon experienced the event of our ascent. I was in the van and, having surmounted a ridge, was about to descend the hollow. Of a sudden, like a bullet in flight, a small bird flashed out of the trail into the brush. Then another and another. Then two together. Altogether I counted seven. Grouse—pa'tridge, as they are called in these parts. I could see the little hen stalking in outraged dignity in the thick growth of balsam and fir where the side of the mountain ascended sharply.

Here was a chance for some fine pictures, and in we went, struggling through the dense growth. Operating separately, we prevented her from leading us away. Now and again a young one flashed out of a balsam. There was a dispute as to whether she was a birch or a spruce partridge, until in the right light the telltale patch of scarlet gleaming above her eye proclaimed her to be a spruce—*Canachites canadensis*.

At last we cornered her between us, and then she turned on us. Wings spread and beak agape, again and again she leaped up at us. A fascinating show this, and of course by now her brood was safely hidden in the cover.

Finally we took our leave of the spunky little critter and went on. Soon afterwards the tops of the trees began to flatten. We were reaching the timberline.

An ascent above the timberline is an exhilarating experience. First the trees begin to look stunted, and they are gnarled. The branches of an occasional spruce that stands exposed atop a ridge extend out on the lee side only and give to it a weird lopsided aspect. As you plod on upward, the stunted trees are only shoulder-high and then only waist-high.

In this wet season the tops of all the conifers were burgeoning thickly with great clusters of cones, ranging from a fresh green to a dark brown, to blue, to purple and almost black. Now the trees could no longer be called trees. Like juniper growing on a granite ledge by the side of the sea, they were small, crawling plants, ankle-deep. Then there was no vegetation at all, and we trod upon bare rock. We were above the timberline.

The wind was by now assaulting us in full force, and it was cold. It had been a wise decision to lug that extra shirt or windbreaker. At the highest point of this rounding, rock-strewn dome, a trellised tower rises aloft. We climbed up with some trepidation as it shook in the wind, and we got a royal welcome from the fire warden. No wonder; we were his only visitors of the season.

Here is a vast and open panorama of wilderness. For miles after miles upon all sides there stretches away the great green silent forest. The eye follows its descent over the shoulders of the mountain into the valleys beyond, then it ascends the ridges and the hills in the middle distance until at length I gaze at the mountains that rim this world of forest and form its rugged skyline.

In the south there stretches the watershed of the Dead River. Over that rugged terrain, through those woods and swamps and across those ridges, in the freezing weather of the fall of 1775, the rugged men of the little Continental Army led by Benedict Arnold had marched, hauling and heaving their bateaux and stores over the height of land into the Chaudière and on to the historic assault on Quebec.

To the westward, I looked across the ridge that by the Treaty of Paris of 1783 marks the international boundary, and gazed upon the distant watershed of the St. Lawrence. To the eastward, my eye was arrested by the bulking massif of Ktaadn, rising beyond the blue expanse of Moosehead Lake. And beyond Ktaadn, in the far distance is the valley of the East Branch of the Penobscot. In living outline, the contour of the north of Maine—the Maine woods of Henry David Thoreau—lay spread in a familiar pattern before my eyes.

Hardly a habitation was in sight—a cluster of white that bespoke a French-Canadian village in the Province of Quebec, or the distant houses of Jackman Village, that is all. Only the forest, across which great patches of shadow thrown down by the passing clouds were in silent motion. And scattered amid the green of the forest were the patches of heavenly blue that are the lakes, the ponds, and the streams of northern Maine.

With care, I examine through the glasses the detail of the Moose River country. The course of that stream wanders in a complex of evolutions, linking the blue expanses of Holeb and Attean Lakes and enfolding within its broad general curve—which is called the Oxbow—the peak of Attean Mountain and a vast yellow-brown bog surrounding the blue of the pond at its center. I had been into Number Five Bog the summer before and have written about this excursion:

"A wild, a desolate, lonely place, where the scattered hackmatack struggles to the height of a man and dies. A place of pitcher plants—they are in bloom—and rare flowers and deep moss that later will be a glory of color. The abode of the black duck, the moose, the deer, and in years past, of the caribou. In this great saucer of sedge, cupped between wooded ridges and lofty hillsides, for the space that we are here we are unspeakably remote in a vast silence.

"Stretching endlessly, the wet sphagnum lies in every direction. Here and there it is peopled by the stunted trunks of dead and dried hackmatacks and by the sparsely needled branches of those that still struggle to survive. At the far distant edges of this wide-open space in the midst of the Maine woods it is rimmed by a line of dark spruce. Then, at an even greater distance, there slowly rise the hardwood ridges, then the hills, and finally the timbered mountains that cup this scene of desolate beauty. In the southwest the wooded escarpment and the bare bald top of Number Five Mountain tower aloft, and there the fire warden's lookout rises like a thin clean needle in the clear air."

Now the fire warden was speaking: "You see that next peak? I seen a big bear clambering over it the other day. And the moose, they come out in that pond most every night."

The pond toward which he had pointed was intriguing. It had no name; it is on no map. Now, would not that be a fit spot for an exploratory excursion, come another year?

## MUD POND

This day was clear, the sky blue, and after traversing Attean Lake and passing through the thoroughfare, we were running swiftly over the placid surface of Big Wood Pond. Great rounding masses of white cumulus were drifting across the sky, casting dark shadows on the bordering forest. Our destination was Mud Pond, which lies beyond the northerly escarpment of Sally Mountain.

As we approached the start of the carry, I watched through the glasses two black specks that I had seen with the naked eye circling in the blue, high above the lake. Fish hawks they were, tracing out on poised wings two great coinciding circles. In their circling soaring, they are the skaters of the sky.

Soon we were on the carry, taking turns under the canoe, which weaved a steady pace through the trees. In short order, we were afloat again in the deadwater of Mud Pond Stream. Then the shores began to widen to encircle the Mud Pond with green reeds. We were alone. First we explored the pond, paddling against the small head wind that had sprung up, and tracing around stretches of white lily pads and yellow spatterdock until we came to the mouth of a small stream. Into this we poked the nose of the canoe. We scared up a blue heron, who ascended on pumping wings, dodging through the spruces. In a few short turns we reached the head of navigation and then turned about.

On the pond we had passed a point with low land in back of it. Here, beneath a clump of cedars, were space and shade—the requisites of a proper lunch ground. So we backtracked and were fortunate in so doing, for it was a botanist's paradise.

This wet cold summer in the Maine woods had produced a most remarkable profusion of wild flowers. No sooner had we stepped ashore than we spotted, rising on the rocky shore, the delicate spike of the smaller purple-fringed orchis, *Habenaria psycodes*. This is one of the glories of the wilderness. Hard by was a single specimen of another marsh orchid, the cream-white *Spiranthes cernua*, which has a curiously twisted spiral spike. These are lady's-tresses, and this one gave off a delicate, haunting odor.

Lunch was forgotten. The flower book was brought out of a knapsack, and seated on the shore, one of my companions identified the specimens we were bringing to her from every direction: mad-dog skullcap, *Scutellaria lateriflora;* yellow loosestrife, *Lysimachia quadrifolia;* wild mint, *Mentha arvensis;* a member of the St.-John's-wort family, *Hypericaceae,* that bears both a small yellow flower and a round red seed-pod. And there was many another that was taken back to camp to be pored over by the light of the kerosene lamp in the evenings.

Beyond a low marsh in back of the point there was a line of alders along a stream, and when our nooning was over I poled the canoe up in there. Mud Pond Brook was a wild stream, and it was quite a task to pole the canoe against the strong current. Here too there was a garden of wild flowers, and I shall not soon forget the green island in the middle of the stream, with the purple-fringed orchis all around and the strong scent of wild mint rising as I stood casting my fly in the rips that flowed in swift descent on either side.

Later, when we were about to go on the carry that runs by the side of Mud Pond Stream down to Big Wood Pond, the thought of again toting the canoe suddenly appalled me. Why not take her down the stream? The water was high. I had a pole. Good! The rest of the party went ashore, and I watched them disappear through the trees, laden with knapsacks, cameras, fishing rods, and the rest of the gear. Then I shoved out into the deadwater, which soon came to an end at the edge of the first pitch.

Here a roughly square jumble of great rotting timbers was

all that remained of a former logging operation—a sluice. In the faraway days of long logs, the timber that had been cut during the winter along the course of Mud Pond Brook, where I had been fly-fishing, and had been "twitched" out of the woods to its shores would in the spring of the year be rolled into the stream and come coursing down its turbulent waters into Mud Pond. This was the "brook drive." Then the logs would be "rafted"—that is, floated in a raft—across the pond to the deadwater. Here there was a boom, a dam, and a sluice. Tended through a "sorting gap," these logs would then be "sluiced" into the outlet and there driven again on down into Big Wood Pond. This was the essence of a river drive, now a thing of the past, though there is still a spring drive of long logs each year down east on the Machias. Elsewhere, aside from pulp, tractors and trucks have supplanted the river drives.

The dark water coiled over and gurgled through the rotting remains of the sluice as I let the canoe down gently, standing precariously perched on a slippery piling. Then I stepped into the canoe just aft of the mid-thwart, and stood, feet spread in a sturdy stance. With the pole poised, I was ready to snub her, to let her stern swing with the stream, and to guide her bow, as borne on the rushing water I picked my way through the rocks downstream. At the start there was a moment of awkwardness. The canoe swung broadside to the stream and it took a deal of heaving to push her stern back against the force of the water that was wedging her against a rock. It was a good quarter of a century since I had come downstream on a pole.

But soon I sensed again the delicate balance, the close concentration, the thrill of shooting through the V of a rip, and all the exhilaration that makes the handling of a canoe in white water so delicious an experience. There was no noise save the rush of the stream and the click of the pick on the stones. The stream wound into a wide curve. There was a quick judgment as to where the channel ran, and down we went—I and my canoe.

Time was, and it was not so long ago, when pole and paddle alone carried a man in his canoe wherever he wanted to go in the Maine woods.

At length the last pitch was run, the shores began to level out, and the surface of the stream ahead no longer had the aspect of an inclined plane. Suddenly a low bar divided the waters, and on it something moved. It was a large bird—a gull. Was it wounded? No. Its wings arched. It rose to its feet. But it did not fly. Rather, it flapped awkwardly into the water, to float on downstream. In pursuit, I soon came alongside, and as the wings arched again, I caught one and lifted the bird into the canoe.

When I emerged from the deadwater into Big Wood Pond, I exhibited my trophy to my companions, and all the way back to camp the gull sat quietly crouched in the bottom of the towed canoe. After supper, from the small fry around the camp to whom I had given it, there came a report. Alas, the bird, a young herring gull, had just died.

## THE HERMIT'S ISLAND

From Attean Rips to the mouth of the Moose River, the right hand bank is the shore of a large island. You never would know it was an island unless someone told you. It is one because of what is unceremoniously known as the "back passage." This leaves the Moose River above the rips, and when the water is low in summer it is the merest trickle, sometimes disappearing underground to find its way around the boulders and over the ledges marking the edge of the ridge that forms the rips. Then after a short bit there is a deadwater, with its dark depths reflecting the hemlocks leading out from the banks. This is a beaver flowage; next you come to the dam.

I came upon all this one summer day from the other direction, when, through its outlet into Attean Lake, I went up this back passage—a long curving watery avenue lined by alders leaning out horizontally over the placid surface. It was a dead stream, where things floated as if in suspension. Here I found a curiously minute water lily—the flower with the odor of nymphs—*Nymphaea odorata*. These specimens, some of them hardly an inch and a half in diameter, were about a quarter the size of the usual water lily, and I never have found them mentioned in the books.

Now and again, as the canoe drifted, the alders parted to give a glimpse of the sky, a plain of waving meadow grass, and in isolation, the beauty of a wine-cup elm. Once as I passed a game trail, a brown doe and her delicately speckled fawn eyed my passage curiously until my scent drove them in bounds up over the bank. Flashes of white from under their lifting tails marked their passage through the thick grass and out of sight.

There is a tale that goes with this island and this back passage. When this north country was young, so the old-timers will tell you, there was a young fellow up across the border in Quebec who was about to get married. On his wedding day, when he went to the home of his intended bride to take her to the parish church, he found that that very day she had gone off with another man.

So he took a vow, this young man—to go into the woods and never again speak to a woman. It was the dead of winter. With snowshoes, an axe, his gun, the clothes he had on, and a knapsack of grub, he set off.

He came to this island, and here he stayed. He cleared it; built a log cabin and lived out his days there, making a meager living as a trapper. Never would he go to town. The lumberers brought him his supplies, and if there was a woman with them when they came to his camp, he would light out into the woods. In the vernacular of the Maine woods, he was "woods-queer." He died there one day when he was an old, old man—froze to death—alone.

## CLEARWATER, BENJAMIN, AND HORSESHOE

Here is the terrain for a superb excursion. Clearwater, Benjamin, and Horseshoe are three ponds that face the sky in the forest valley hidden by the shoulder of Sally Mountain to the westward of Attean Lake. A height of land separates each from the other, and at the head of the west pocket of Attean alongside the carry over to Holeb Lake, there is a long portage going into Clearwater. This portage is a clear trail that soon comes out on the tracks of the Canadian Pacific skirting the west shore of the lake.

When on the warm July morning of my first exploration of this chain of ponds we reached this point, I listened to the oft-told tale of my companion, who, as a boy back in 1910, had watched the east side of Sally Mountain all ablaze in the darkness of the night. There are still fire-blackened stubs and stumps on the mountain. Then he pointed out the spot where, within a year or so, due to an error in the signals two trains had met head-on at a curve of this single track. An engineer had been killed.

These catastrophic occurrences were belied by the wealth of wild flowers that lined the track. Fireweed, pearly everlasting, multitudes of wild asters, masses of goldenrod, joe-pye weed, meadowsweet, bunchberry, Canada hawkweed, vetch, mullein, wild daisies, blueberries—all these I listed as we passed along the short half mile of track before turning off again to our right into the woods.

On this part of the carry the going gets rough—a narrow trail abounding with hidden stones and the slippery surfaces of the moss-covered logs of ancient corduroy stretches.

Finally, at the end of the laborious clambering, we saw glinting through the leaves the blue surface of Clearwater—a deep, dark liquid eye in the depth of the forest.

I was reminded by this light, shining through the trees and indicating the approach to open water, of the exclamation of the Indians when they would come upon this welcome sight.

*Xsebem!*

Pronounce it if you can.

We made our passage across the pond in a small clinker-built craft that leaked villainously through the seams of its lap-streaked planking. A sudden move on the makeshift seat—a board picked up on the shore—would cause little spurts to come in on the other side. At length, an uneasy equilibrium reduced the leakage to a minimum, and our little argosy proceeded across the dark blue surface. As we rowed slowly across the placid surface, there was time aplenty to admire the asters that lined the shore and the clumps of green pickerelweed thrusting their deep purple spikes aloft.

It was shallow in the little cove where the carry over into Benjamin commences. Submerged and projecting rocks required skillful navigation to bring our craft to its haven. At length we disembarked and as we stepped ashore a large bird flashed in silent flight out of the cedars in the swamp to the left of the carry. Then another one appeared, only to disappear in the trees ahead. There were one or two soft calls—*whee-ah*—then silence. Now and again, as we proceeded along the portage, they were seen suddenly in flight out of one spruce and into another. They were large birds, and their silent flights gave an air of mystery to the dark spruce grove.

At length I got my glasses on one on a dead stick of a distant spruce. The squat head, the pure white patch on the forehead and crown, then the black patch at the back of the

head which runs forward on each side through the eyes—
this was unmistakable, albeit it had been a long long time
since I had seen one.

Moosebirds!

The meat bird of the lumberjack, the whisky-Jack, a cor-
ruption of the Indian name for this Canada jay—*wiskatjân*.
Silently, and in flight after flight through the dark tall
spruces, they ushered us on our way over the carry. Finally,
as the blue fillets of Benjamin began to shine through the
trees ahead, they departed through the silent forest, uttering
no cry, returning no doubt to their silent perches in the
cedar swamp. They are ghoulish birds, these camp robbers.

Overturned on the shore of Benjamin was a canoe, and
in jig time we were waterborne once again. What a glorious
day this was, with the white clouds sailing in the blue above
us as we glided on the surface of the blue below. The wind
had freshened. This called on muscles long unused for extra
effort as we slowly inched our way past the granite ledge
that marks the point of an island. There we encountered the
full force of the head wind.

In this pond of curiously combined sedges and ledges, we
disputed possession with a loon. We came upon him swimming between two pine-topped islands, watched his powerful mandibles go agape, and listened to the long broken cry
that poured forth and after a pause came back in a haunting
echo. Dropping the bow paddle, I responded to his cry and
for quite a piece the silence of Benjamin was broken by our
calls.

At the carry I swept the far shore of Benjamin with my
glass. First there was an expanse of blue, then an expanse
of unbroken green mounting in steady and majestic splendor
until it ceased at the bare granite ledges at the top of Sally
Mountain, where another blue began. I say an unbroken expanse of green. I am mistaken. There was one lone tree, a
tall white pine that towered in wild isolation above the green

tops of the other trees. There it spread its black plumes, and they were waving in the wind and flashing in the sunlight. This monarch stood in dramatic isolation on the side of the ridge, towering against the lighter green background of hardwood growth. In this corner of the Maine woods the white pine is once again growing to its former grandeur. From the lakes and ponds, as at Holeb and here from Benjamin, you can see them as men saw them a century ago, now one here, now one there, tall and stately, their spreading horizontal branches in dark outline against the sky. Lonely sentinels they are that thus lord it over the rest of the forest.

On the carry, I staggered along the rock-strewn and uneven ground, with the canoe bottom side up and balancing on its middle thwart on the nape of my neck, pausing now and again in my slow course to establish my balance before stepping up over a knee-high windfall athwart the path. This leads to concentration on the task at hand, and in such a posture the suggestions of others are unwelcome. I was reminded of the injunction of the Frenchman with whom I had cruised the waters of the St. John and the Allagash.

"When a man, he be bullin' on de portage, that's de time to leave him alone. Don't talk wid him."

The sweat pearled on my forehead. It trickled, tickling as it ran. Encircling my head was a buzzing that reverberated within the curved enclosure overhead. A mosquito was in orbit. I stopped, balanced the canoe with my left hand on the gunwale, and wiped my face with the other hand. Then I started up again, treading slowly. The mosquito's monotone continued—around and around and around. I cursed. Then my companion, the good samaritan, wiped my sweating face with a bandana, dabbed my neck and bare hands with fly dope, and I traveled on, mounting the slow incline.

Suddenly the carry shelved sharply toward Horseshoe. This far side of the ridge was steep, and I balanced back by letting the stern of the canoe in back of me drop toward the ground and allowing the bow to rise. In this fashion I edged my way in carefully felt steps down the side of the ridge, avoiding loose rocks and roots. At the bottom I slipped the thwart from my neck over my left shoulder and, turning, caught it as it slipped down, first with my right hand and then with my left. Then I lowered the canoe right side up on the surface of Horseshoe.

Now we had a problem. This canoe was only a fifteen-footer. Luckily, Horseshoe is narrow and there would be no long traverse across open water against a head wind, as there had been on Benjamin, a circumstance, indeed, that would have put an end to our excursion right there. We made a careful assessment of our weights, distributed our gear, not forgetting to sling cameras and binoculars around our necks, and then loaded the craft to achieve the best balance, neither down by the head nor stern-heavy.

At length, we were afloat on the waters of Horseshoe. The wooded shores slipped slowly by as we made for the point that marks the inner curve of the horseshoe. The banks are of granite, some of them high and falling sharply and sheer toward the water. From the crevices of others clumps of sheep laurel grow, and small pines, and here and there a birch sapling. The other shore, which makes the outer edge of the horseshoe, is low and lined with tall pines.

BUMP! GRATE!

We came to a sudden stop and I found that I, in the bow, was sitting on a submerged rock.

To get the heavily laden canoe off a submerged granite boulder was no easy task. We had no pole upon which I could take up some of the weight, and so it was by dint of considerable nudging and maneuvering, accompanied by a horrible grating under my feet, that we managed at length to slide her off.

Once this was achieved, we rounded the point at the apex of the horseshoe, and the other long pocket of Horseshoe Pond stretched before us. On the far outer shore, where a great granite ledge slopes in an easy incline to the water's edge, there is at the top, outlined against the woods, what the Maine woodsman fondly calls "a old set o' camp."

This curious term is met with on every hand in the north of Maine. It derives from the parlance of lumbering, in which the cluster of log huts, cookhouses, bunkhouses, lean-tos, stables, and other sheds necessary to the operation were known as a set of camps. By dint of constant usage, the phrase has come to have a generic tinge, and a single cabin in the woods—a trapper's cabin, as here on the shore of Horseshoe Pond—is often referred to as "a old set o' camp."

This was to be our lunch ground, and toward it we headed, bending on the paddles. Midway on our angling traverse across this second pocket of the pond, my attention was called from the stern to a great rugged outcropping of granite that stood out in bold gray outline amid the green of the trees in an almost direct line with our course. Then came the suggestion that after our nooning my companion and I go "cruising" and climb this ledge for a view of Horseshoe.

Thereupon he stopped paddling and took a bearing. Now this is all very shipshape, my friend being a scientific feller, but I planned to rely, as I always do, upon a God-given bump of direction which rarely fails me whenever I go "cruising."

In short order we reached the shelving ledge and there had our nooning. We seated ourselves beside fragrant bayberry bushes on a cushion of gray lichen-like moss that covered the bald brow of the ledge with tight curls. There were cold cuts, cold johnnycake, sinkers, and the woodsman's benison—plenty of good, hot, strong tea. Then we lazied for a bit by the side of Horseshoe, watching its dappled surface now entirely spangled with gold.

Finally my companion rose, dusted off the seat of his britches, cocked his felt hat over his eyes, and started off.

I followed, threading through the tangle of bayberry bushes at a distance calculated to keep me clear of the backlash of the branches he was shoving aside. Directly the ledge by the shore of Horseshoe shelved and we found ourselves at the edge of an alder swamp. We proceeded across this, stretching from tussock to tussock in an effort to keep our feet dry. But, as usual, it was in vain. Then having crossed the swamp, we came upon a narrow open space extending in both directions and paralleling the shore that we had just left. This was "the old tote road 'round Horseshoe."

On the other side of the tote road the terrain began to rise, and we mounted the side of a ridge through the thickest kind of growth—second-growth pine, balsam, spruce, all choking each other as they stretched toward light and air. The light in this dark, dusky grove was dim. We had to weave now one way, now another, to get around an impassable windfall or circle an impenetrable thicket. I soon lost sight of my companion. Then I noticed that he was steadily veering toward the eastward, whereas I tended to swing toward my left hand and the west. After a bit I hollered to him: "Hey, you're going too far to your right."

He called back from his now hidden course. "You're too far to your left."

Here was a contest, between his compass-directed course and my own sense of direction. And so we proceeded on our diverging routes.

Soon I could no longer hear the thrashing of his passage. Over the crest of the ridge the going became easier. I walked faster and in a straight line. Suddenly a granite ledge loomed ahead. This could not be it. It was too low. I clambered over the rounding boulders and reached the top of it. And there, directly in front of me at the far side of an open logan at my feet, rose high and bold the bare face of the ledge we had seen from the surface of Horseshoe Pond.

The logan was a wild cranberry bog that stretched its flat

tawny expanse to the wall of this next ledge. It was studded here and there with crazily tilted stubs of hackmatacks that had long ago died and dried. To my left it contained the blue of a small bog pond.

I realized that here on the shelving between the two ledges—the one on which I stood and the other higher one across the logan I was about to climb—I had chanced upon a hidden bog pond. A blue heron rose, laboriously pumping, out of the tall sedge by the shore. It sailed forth in lonely grandeur and disappeared on slowly undulating wings behind a clump of pines where the ledge touched the shore of the pond.

"Halloo!"

Faintly, from above and to my right, came the call of my companion. I looked but could see no sign of him. The ledge on which I was standing mounted in that direction, and I figured that he had climbed the high end of it and was now attempting to tell me that he had won the race.

So I followed along the ridge of the ledge toward the sound of his call. It is always easier traveling along the peak of a ledge or ridge. The brush is not so tall, there are few saplings, and the trees, mostly pine, are scattered. Still, it was a rugged climb and when I reached the top I found neither hide nor hair of him. But across a deep and narrow ravine rose the bold bald face of the ledge we had been seeking.

"Halloo!"

This time the hail was mine, and his answering call, coming from the depths of the woods in the narrow ravine, showed that at long last he, too, was trending to the left and toward the west. And so I started and was soon sweating my way through the thick and tangled dark growth in the ravine between the two ledges.

Then came the hardest climb yet—up over rounding granite, with nothing to hang on to save an old dried-out root or clumps of pine needles and moss lodged in the crevices which were treacherous and often gave way. It was the part of wisdom to take it easy and not put undue strain on an old pump. So, sweating and resting, I made a slow traverse and at long last came up with my companion at the crest.

Once I got my wind, there was a bit of dispute over the respective merits of his compass and my bump of direction. He pointed out that he had reached the top first, and I maintained as stoutly that I had come by the straightest line and had come upon the ledge before he had.

I was reminded of the ancient saw that in my family was supposed to settle all disputes between brother and brother. We would take our case to our grandfather. He would lay aside his newspaper, shove his spectacles up on his forehead, and listen patiently to both sides. Then he would take his pipe out of his mouth, wipe his mouth and beard with the back of his hand, and pronounce with all the magisterial dignity of a Bridlegoose: "Well, boys, it appears to me you're both right."

A noble prospect stretched before us as we sat at the edge of the shelving brow of this outcropping of bare gray granite. A light breeze was blowing and it soughed softly in the plumes of the pines overhead. This cooled and refreshed us as we sat in the shade amid fragrant bayberry bushes, lolling and taking our well-earned ease. At our back, wooded ridges stood in successive tiers until, at the skyline, the last one formed the crest of Burnt Jacket in a clear line against the blue sky.

And out in front, in unbroken expanse, were the tops of the trees that stretching in a vast pattern to the far distant horizon comprise this segment of the Maine woods. It was a woodland scene cupped by mountains—in the eastern quarter by the long high wall of bare granite that formed the top of Sally Mountain, beyond by the green shoulder of Attean

Mountain, and then over to the westward by the dark blue masses of the Boundary Mountains.

Across this panoply of forest, great dark patches were moving slowly—the shadows of the fleet of white clouds sailing across the blue sky. Close at hand we saw outlined in green the horseshoe of blue that gave its name to Horseshoe Pond. On its surface the sunlight sparkled and glanced from the fillets of water stirred by the successive dartings of the cat's-paws. The little "set o' camp" on the near shore, where we had lunch, was hidden by the trees. There was no sign of the human hand in all this wide wild woodland.

Instead, there was the work of the beaver. At our feet we looked down on the cranberry bog and logan. From this high vantage, its whole contour of blue was visible, and at the far end I could see the slanting alder stakes stretching across it that are the hallmark of the beaver.

This small span of blue water is marked on no map. It is a hidden pond that nestles between the ridges and is perhaps known to no other man. It is the lonely abode of the beaver, of the blue heron that in flight on ponderous wings utters its wild *frawnk* and alone hears its echo coming back out of the surrounding woods, and the summer home of the black duck —they and their brood scuttle in the surrounding sedge. To discover such a bright blue eye that looks up into the sky from the depth of the dark forest is the secret joy of the explorer.

At length, rested by our sojourn and with our spirits eased by long looking across the forest valley to the clear-cut crests of the far horizons, we prepared for the descent. I took a long last look down into the little blue pond, and suddenly observing that it hooked around the pine-crowned point where I had seen the blue heron disappear on slowly pumping pinions, I realized that it deserved the name of Little Horseshoe Pond.

Our descent was as easy as our climb had been arduous,

because it was all downhill, save for the short ascent of the near side of the next ridge. This time there was no talk of compass courses. We went in company and made a bee-line, not failing to skirt the copses where the growth was thickest. We soon arrived at the tote road, crossed it, entered and traversed the little alder swamp, through which, we now realized, there trickled the brook that was the outlet of Little Horseshoe Pond. Them we came up over the ridge at the shore. By now the sun was well past the zenith and its slanting angle warned us that it was time to backtrack.

First came the paddle across Horseshoe, up one reach, around the bend, and down the other reach to the carry on the far shore. Fortunately we were to leave the canoe in Horseshoe for the next party. Crossing Benjamin, I saw again the single dark pine that towered above the green tops of the surrounding poplar covering the side of Sally Mountain. Next there was the longer portage to Clearwater, where we refreshed ourselves at a cooling spring. And when at the far shore of Clearwater we hit the end of the long trail over to Attean, a good hour had passed.

This was the hard part, and I took note that my companion was plodding a little slower. The light in the woods was darkening, for the rays of the sun now hit the tops of the trees at an acute angle and the light that filtered through was somber. Now and again a single golden beam slanted through the tree trunks. In it motes were dancing. The short haul on the railroad ties—they are never far enough apart for a decent stride—was tough on tired feet, and at length, after another hour of tramping, we emerged on the shore of Attean.

We were tired.

There was little to say, and hence little was said. Each man looked to his own gear and we slid the heavy twenty-foot canoe into the water and clambered aboard. Slowly the canoe turned about. The ratchet of the starter sounded once, and with the second pull of the lanyard, the motor roared and the canoe surged ahead.

We moved along the upper end of the lake with Attean Mountain on our right hand and the slope of Sally Mountain on our left. Now the sky was overcast, but the far horizon was clear, so clear that with the glasses I could make out the shape of the trees that lined it. In the bow seat I settled back, looking forward to the restful half-hour ride before us.

Then came some scattered drops, dappling the surface. I reached back into a knapsack for ponchos and passed one back to my companion. To the eastward, the clouds had descended to the earth, blotting out the timbered slope of Attean Mountain. Then I glanced over into the west and saw the gray shades of the squall racing against the trees on the incline of Sally Mountain. Curiously, in the pocket in between, the squall had not yet struck us.

But not for long. A wall of rain now enveloped us from astern. Successive walls passed over us, to be succeeded by a steady downpouring that kept the rising seas down. The shores grew dim. Then they disappeared. We plowed on before the wind. It was the only thing to do. The distance began to lengthen out astern, and then the full force of the driving squall struck us.

The seas rose, and with them my apprehension. Before us was a run of nearly a mile, now that we were out of the upper pocket. The seas were cresting, and the spume torn from their crests blotted our course. The heavily laden canoe rode them sluggishly. My great fear was that if the bow should plunge down into a cresting wave too far, we would ship water. Once that might be all right, but twice! Water in heavily laden canoe makes her hard to handle, even unmanageable, and if we broached too, over we would roll. Twice, as the bow plunged down into the top of a cresting wave, I saw black water at the very level of the gunwale. I didn't want any more of that. I shouted above the gale, and the helmsman cut her speed.

By the time we reached the point of Birch Island, they were really rolling. In a matter of seconds, we were in the lee of the point, in the cove, and on the beach.

A few moments later, we had changed our wet clothing. There was a bottle handy, and it passed from hand to hand. Everybody shook hands with himself and his neighbor. Then we went to dinner, and as we stepped outside the cabin door, the rain had stopped, the wind had dropped, the lake was calm, and the sun was gleaming through the clouds in the west whence the squall had come.

I glanced at my watch. It was less than an hour since we had arrived at the beach. And that, my friends, is how it is when a squall catches you suddenly in a canoe out in the middle of a lake.

The next day is the day of departure. It is a gray day and the louring scud trends steadily overhead, eastward across the State of Maine. As the boat chugs slowly toward the landing where the course of the Moose River forms the thoroughfare leading into Big Wood Pond, I take a final look at the mountains and ridges that surround Attean Lake.

Over in the west I watch the mists that are rising slowly in scattered columns out of the dark green woods along the shore, mounting against the slope of the woods toward the crest of the hills. From the steep slope of Sally Mountain they rise, like gray wraiths appearing and disappearing, forming and reforming. Some assume weird shapes, drifting upward like a genie out of a bottle until the wind, blowing across the top of the mountain, catches them and tears them to shreds.

Toward the east, there is a long bank of scud, and at each end it is clear of the high ridges in that quarter. Below the scud, the sky is of a lighter gray. But in the middle, where the peak of a mountain rises, the scud dips down, covering the top of the mountain and draping a gray pall on its timbered slope.

We approach the landing. Time now to look to the gear, to heave it ashore, to start packing the car. But take it easy, not yet, not quite yet, not until nature has put on a parting show.

Off the lake now, in swift flight, comes a bird, a kingfisher making for the calm waters of the thoroughfare through the opening alders. Directly behind and just above it, in equally swift flight, is another bird, several times its size. In the flash of an eye the prey dives, straight down, and as the water splashes, the predator sweeps on past.

Then a second scene succeeds the first. The kingfisher, breaking water, mounts to flash into the thick of the alders. The hawk, soaring upward on tilted wings, comes to perch in a small maple hard by, and we have a long look at him—the curved predacious bill, the flat head, and the sharply streaked brown and white breast of a young red-tailed hawk. Now startled, he is launched in flight and disappears in silence through the woods. The only sound in this sudden drama had been the splash of the kingfisher's dive.

And so we take our leave of the Moose River country.

# Scarborough Beach

ALL DAY LONG, in our passage from the mountains in the north of Maine down to the sea, a northwest wind had pursued us, driving the low-lying scud on ahead. Now and again these louring clouds shrouded the eastern horizon, and intermittently we entered showers that became down-pours. Then, as we passed over another ridge, the weather would clear and a ring of light would lift the heavy cap of clouds above the western horizon behind us. When in our course down the Kennebec we reached Augusta, we caught up with and passed the rear guard of the storm, and there-after we swept swiftly on our way through an endless cur-tain of downpouring rain.

Then came the bustle of arrival, the confusion of unpack-ing, the greetings of old friends, the bending of the elbow in celebration of this anticipated event. Amid these pleasant-ries, I lost track of the weather and was quite unprepared for the scene that awaited me when I emerged out of doors after dinner.

The rain in which we had arrived proved to be the clear-ing shower. The retreating storm could still be seen out to the eastward and the southward, across the indistinct sur-face of the now calm sea. All about there was fog. I looked aloft and saw that it hung in the air in great formless gray masses. The trees, the shrubbery, and the sharp edges of structures that made the skyline all round were shrouded.

Then this indistinct world of gray became suffused with a warm light. Unsuspected shades of the familiar colors of this familiar scene came on to glow. The flat white of the paint on the clapboards was spectral white; the dark green of the line of white pines shone now a luminous blue-green; the brown of the now withering vegetation deepened to a dark lustrous brown; the blossoms of the gladioli, of the petunias, the begonias, the asters, of all the flowers in the formal gardens shone like jewels scattered in profusion.

The light waxed, then it waned. Never for a moment was the effect the same, the colors now deepening, now fading. Aloft I saw that the rounding heads of the great masses of gray fog were tinged with pink, and beyond their low height there was the deep blue of a clear sky. The cause of the evanescent, fleeting shades was the light of the afterglow flung down by the great vault of the sky, to be diffused through the tiny drops of mist that are the essence of fog.

Later the moon rose out of the sea. For a space it climbed slowly and seemed to hang in the gray eastern sky. Thus seen near the horizon, it was an orange moon, but after a bit, as it rose slowly, it emerged above the fog a bright white moon in a dark sky. Then it spilled its light down on the surface of the sea. The tide was high, very high, with this full moon. As the volute of an oncoming wave would rear and roll on its way shoreward, its crest would catch and reflect in a long wavering line a gleam of golden moonlight. Beyond these successively breaking waves, for a long distance out over the sea all was dark, but at the horizon the water glittered ceaselessly with golden coins.

As I watched wave after wave bearing for its short moment of life a wavering line of moonlight, and far in the distance the ceaseless tumbling of the coins, I heard out over the water in front of me as I stood on the beach the plaintive note of a lone shorebird winging past, unseen.

At daybreak the next morning, as I walked down to the beach the grass was strewn with dew that was cold to the foot. I luxuriated in its soft, cool, wet resilience underfoot, and the wet spears of the long grass on the dunes scored scars of chilled moisture on the bare calves of my legs. No bird chirped. The dunes were deserted. The bathhouses loomed in uncertain shadow, and beyond them lay the beach. Now, dimly seen through the early morning haze, the oncoming seas were surging. Overhead, three gulls were suddenly and silently in view, and as suddenly and silently they merged with the fog.

As I emerged from the dunes, I saw the tall angular form of my early morning companion, stalking the foreshore by the edge of the wash like an old man of the sea. For half a century and more he had walked these beaches just after sunup and had his before-breakfast plunge in the bracing water of this Western Ocean. We fell into step and walked in friendly converse to the westward, with the low sun shining through the haze, dispelling the chill and warming our backs.

Far ahead, where the crescent of yellow sand makes its sharpest curve, was the colony of gulls that congregated there every morning. In the distance they were brown and black and white spots on the sand. As we walked on, one made the short run and became airborne. Then another and another, and now all the rest were in the air, winging in scattered flight, some out over the placid sea, some along the beach, and some in over the low dunes—a pandemonium of flapping wings, soaring birds, screaming cries. When we reached the spot where they had been, there remained only scattered feathers and splotches of white lime.

Two seals, their long rounding black heads rising, dripping, out of the sea just beyond the breaking of the waves, their big eyes giving us a glassy stare, dove as we shouted and waved our towels.

Next came the plunge in the sea. We were far enough now from human habitation to go in stripped. The first few steps were torture, the blow of the broken surf amidships bringing forth a deep gasp, and then came the plunge into a breaking wave. The surf, unaccountably strong, turns, twists, and tosses me until, getting a footing, I make a dash for the certainty of the hard sand. And then comes the sparkling glow that follows a plunge in the surf.

After the long walk back, I passed up through the dunes, and there amid the alders I watched in bouncing flight a goldfinch, a spangle of black and gold, and heard with each bounce its *ti-dee-di-di*. The sun had commenced to burn through. The trees and the cottages came into clearer focus, and beyond, through the white of the thinning fog, was the blue of the open sky.

I am one who likes to investigate, in any locality where I find myself, the points that are linked with the past. And so after breakfast on this gorgeously clear morning, I took out along a path skirting a pine grove to where a turn led me to the edge of a field. Here, propped to face the field and the sea, is an ancient millstone with great curving scores still marking its granite face. It bears a bronze tablet, and from this I learned that I now stood upon "the western bastion of Scottow's Stockade Fort." Thus I was in touch with the days when the marauding scalping parties of French and Indians were the scourge of this countryside.

A granite bench provided a hard seat, and I looked out over a broad field decked with the white discs of Queen Anne's lace amid the rich yellow plumes of goldenrod. Just within sight, a single gladiolus raised its pink flowered spike above the edge of the field. At the other side, a stand of poplar fluttered. There is no tree like a "popple" in a small breeze. Each individual leaf dances, and the ensemble is a symphony of motion. Beyond lay the cattail rushes and the brackish waters of Massacre Pond. Legend has it that in the days of the French and Indian Wars, after a sudden ambuscade, the waters of this pond ran red.

Then the eye swept to the eastward. There the blue sea stretched to the skyline, and in the path of the sun it was all aglitter with fillets of flashing light. Here a long low brown contour of ledge and island with a single frame house is Richmond's Island, the site of one of the fishing stations that dotted the Maine Coast from Matinicus to the Isle of Shoals long before—centuries before, some say—the landing at Plymouth. Indeed, but for the supplies furnished by these down-east fishing stations, that overly famous colony of the Pilgrims would never have survived. On the charts of Sieur de Champlain this squat island bears the name *Ile de Bacchus*.

Later, in the library of the century-old hotel, I read what a local maritime historian has written:

"The largest of these stations was located at Richmond's Island off Cape Elizabeth. It is described in great detail in the letters of John Winter, the agent resident there, to his employer Robert Trelawney, a merchant in Plymouth, England. From them there may be reconstructed the daily life of the enterprise that was springing up all along the coast from Piscataqua to Matinicus at the foot of Penobscot Bay. We see the various buildings go up, the boats' crews arrive from England and go out with their lines and bait, returning with their fare, sometimes good, sometimes light. We hear of the making of cor-fish (whole cod pickled in brine) and the splitting and salting of the dry cod and trying out the fish oil or 'traine'. We read Winter's orders to his patron for clothing, strong waters, and fishing gear, or the iron work of a vessel he is building. We know the names of his workmen and his accounts with them, which show the amount of aqua vitae or 'cyder' demanded by each. He even tells how much of each man's wages are paid to his wife in England. Mrs. Winter comes to be with her husband and to feed the men. The quarrels about food and slothful servants enter the correspondence. Tragedy stalks when a favorite maid-servant is caught by the tide and drowns on the bar."

I read around, too, in the quaint notes of old Josselyn, who left for posterity a relation of his doings in the 1660's in the environs of Black Point, known in these latter days as Prouts Neck. Witness this account of how the Indians were wont to take lobsters:

"The *Lobsters* they take in large Bayes when it is low water, the wind still, going out in their *Birchen-Canows* with a staff two or three yards long, made small and sharpen'd at one end, and nick'd with deep nicks to take hold. When they spye the *Lobster* crawling upon the Sand in two fathom water, more or less, they stick him towards the head and bring him up. I have known thirty *Lobsters* taken by an *Indian* lad in an hour and a half."

Then my eye alights upon an almost contemporary note—of sanderlings and a peep pie:

"There are little Birds that frequent the Sea-shore in flocks called *Sanderlins*, they are about the bigness of a *Sparrow*, and in the fall of the leaf will be all fat; when I was first in the Countrie the *English* cut them into small pieces to put into their Puddings instead of suet, I have known twelve score and above kill'd at two shots."

And his remarks upon the fishermen of that day make a fitting gloss on the account of the maritime historian:

"These often get in one voyage Eight or Nine pound a man for their shares, but it doth some of them little good, for the Merchant to increase his gains by putting off his Commodity in the midst of their voyages, and at the end thereof comes in with a walking Tavern, a Bark laden with the Legitimate bloud of the rich grape, which they bring from *Phial, Madera, Canaries,* with *Brandy, Rhum,* the *Barbadoes strong-water* and *Tobacco,* coming ashore he gives them a Taster or two, which so charms them, that for no perswasions that their imployers can use will they go out to Sea, although fair and seasonable weather, for two or three days, nay sometimes a whole week till they are wearied with drinking, taking ashore two or three Hogsheads of *Wine* and *Rhum* to drink off when the Merchant is gone. If a man of quality chance to come where they are roystering and gulling in *Wine* with a dear felicity, he must be sociable and *Rolypoly* with them, taking off their liberal cups as freely, or else be gone, which is best for him, for when *Wine* in their guts is at full tide, they quarrel, fight and do one another mischief, which is the conclusion of their drunken compotations."

And so it went in these parts three centuries ago.

The next event of this first day at the shore was a noonday swim. I went up to dress, and for a space I sat looking out over the sea. My window on the top floor of the old hotel gave upon a wide prospect. The ocean was calm, as flat as a floor, and its broad expanse of blue on this summer morning was broken here and there by cat's-paws of wind that were etching patches of a deeper blue. Only along the crescent of yellow sand that forms the shore was the endless action of the sea to be seen. A streak of white here, another a bit farther on, and again a third, running in both directions along the cresting of the wave until, merging in an unbroken line of white, that wave crept ashore on the sand. The tide was at the ebb. These waves were small, and they made a little rasping that now waxed, then waned.

With my glass I swept the sea from west to east, and I was startled by the activity afloat. I made a count of the lobstermen's boats chugging in endless circles. There were twenty-one. Nearby I could make out the buoys, black specks that spotted the water. A roaring told of the presence of a plane, and then I saw it high in the western quarter. In the far distance I could see the slanting sails of a ketch, close-hauled. Scattered on the calm surface were rafts of coots.

This country was familiar, and I took notice of the changes. Over in the southwest, on Stratton Island, which has borne that name now for nearly three centuries, there had always been in my memory, sharp against the sky, a large hulking farmhouse. But this morning I could make out three tall stacks, and that was all. They were the chimneys that still stood, and later I heard the story hereabout—of small boys and a picnic and a fire that got out of hand.

A single house on an island is always a landfall. It stirs

the imagination. Is it deserted? Who built it? When? Why? Henceforth, these three gaunt stacks will tell their bleak tale. And so I swung my glass toward the eastward, where another long, low mound of an island—Richmond's Island— breaks the line of the sky and the sea. Here another lone farmhouse stood silhouetted against the sky, asking the same unanswerable questions.

Next I watched, broad off in front, the rise and fall of the small seas on the brown surface of a ledge that has long been known to mariners as the Old Proprietor. Here, on other days and in other states of the weather, there is ex- hibited with spectacular majesty the unbelievable turbulence of the sea as the waves pile in whitening fury on these ex- posed rocks.

For a few fleeting moments, all the way from the shore to the distant skyline, there danced fillets of reflected sun- light, and this was so widespread on either hand as almost to encompass the width of the bay. Scattered here and there in this reflected sunlight were the black hulls of the lobster- men's boats. Now and again the windshield of one flashed to my eye a brilliant shaft of light, a sudden signal, as it were. Near the horizon a small triangle of white told of a sloop on the port tack.

Finally I took note that the foreshore was becoming popu- lar and populated. It was time to go down on the beach. For soon its warm sands would be but the memory of one season and the haunting promise of the next.

After luncheon a breeze sprang up out of the southwest. The afternoons of late summer on the western coast of Maine are often distinguished by this phenomenon, which is known in alongshore parlance as a smoky sou'wester. This will start up at noon after a calm and brilliant morning. In the early afternoon it will freshen, capping with white the rolling waves that it has churned up and suffusing the air with the gray haze that gives it its name. Then the bays, coves, and the open sea will be spotted with triangles of white bent at variant angles, as sailing craft course on different reaches or tacks or run free before the wind. There is no better sailing breeze than a smoky sou'wester.

Thus it was until sundown all of this first afternoon at the shore. Then the wind died, and as I faced westward at the eastern end of the long slow curve of Scarborough Beach in the evening, I felt on my left cheek the gentle caress of a soft southerly. This brought clearly to ear the successive crashing of the cresting waves, and now and again, there mingled with this steady monotone a sharp concussion-like thump as the extended edge of a long wave thumped on the sand. This rote of the sea is a noise at once monotonous and yet never quite the same. It is the endless music of the restless sea.

As I walked, I watched the white crests of the successive waves come gleaming shoreward. It was very dark. There were few stars out, all of them overhead, and a moon, orange against a dark gray sky. This was the effect of the haze of the smoky sou'wester. Through it, the dark line of the dunes and the more distant broken skyline of the black pines were indistinct, shrouded with uncertainty, and on the distant shore of Prouts Neck there were scattered lights, dim and dulled. It was lonely on this deserted beach.

As I walked, I passed through successive layers of air of differing temperatures. This is a phenomenon I have experienced many times on this coast, and I believe the explanation is this. Often on a calm warm afternoon I have noticed the surface of the sea spotted by different cat's-paws. Often also, the long calm slicks and the riffled patches appear for a considerable space in the same locations. Thus it must have been on this beach on this night as I walked first through a calm and then in the midst of the light stirring of air that is known as a cat's-paw.

On the way back I had a new experience. Somewhere out

on the dim dark surface of the sea, those who order such things ordained a change of the wind. Suddenly, in contrast to the soft caresses of the warm cat's-paws, I felt the sharp damp chill of a down-east Labradorian breeze. This was an easterly, the harbinger of unsettled weather. The warm soft evening was over.

Then my solitude was broken. I heard the barking of a dog. He was way out ahead, close to the sea. I walked on, and the barking came closer. Then I saw him splashing through the shallow water of the foreshore, barking at the waves. Now he came bounding toward me, and wet and dripping with salt water, inspected me. He was an odd-looking crittur, broad and squat, with long dark ears and a single black spot on his white coat near his vociferously wagging tail. Later I learned that this hound of the Scarborough Beaches was the incongruous product of a basset hound and a St. Bernard. His sniffing soon satisfied his curiosity. Then he was off again, and when I left the beach, he had resumed his barking at the waves. That night the wind hung in the east, and by dawn the fog had rolled in.

Those mornings when little watery rivulets trickling down the mesh of the screen give notice of a thick fog outside are memorable ones. I looked out on a gray-shrouded world. The sea, the beach, the dunes, the rectangle of bathhouses that lined them were all obscured by the fog, and nearer at hand the clump of alders that marked one side of the formal garden was in indistinct outline, and its far edge was lost to sight.

When I emerged there was no one abroad, and after a walk of half a hundred yards, I too was hidden in the fog. This is the way I like it. Privacy, remoteness, detachment— all three are hard to come by, but a good thick fog provides them in abundant measure. And so alone I proceeded down to the beach, the white fog becoming thicker with every step.

The birds of the foreshore were my only companions. In a fog, birds in flight have a spectral aspect. They fly silently, and when first seen, they are a mere motion in the gray air. Then wings and body assume indistinct form. For a short moment the bird, a large herring gull, is overhead. Then silently it begins to merge with the fog. Once again it is a shadowy motion, and a moment later it is lost to sight.

I walked on. This scared up a couple of crows that were feeding amid some thick-strewn kelp. Their startled *cawings* sounded softly, for the fog mutes sound just as it obscures sight. And their soft *caws* ceased when the thick fog shut down between us.

A single shorebird flashed past, uttering as it passed within sudden sight of my alien presence in the fog a single, frightened *tirr-whitt*.

After a plunge into a greasy-looking gray wave, as I retraced my steps to the eastward I heard from behind and above a sharply whistled cry in a swift sequence of four:

*Whir-whir-whir-whir.*

Stopping but not turning, I whistled in reply. The bird answered. Then I saw it in toward the dunes, a large bird looming past out of the fog. It whistled. I whistled. Turning, it circled around me, responding to my calling. It did this twice and I saw arched, pointed wings, an oval body, a curved back.

Now with a flare of wide wings it was down, walking on the beach above the wrack of the tide line. An upright stance threw its down-curving beak into clear outline against the soft sand. It was in close, a bare thirty feet from where I stood. Now it was up again in swift flight. Again it circled. Again we exchanged calls in close succession.

*Whir-whir-whir-whir.*

It went winging out over the dunes. The wingbeats grew indistinct, and then it was lost in the depth of the fog. The event of the morning was this encounter with this lone curlew, *Numenius phoeopus hudsonicus.*

This foggy morning ushered in a gray day and a gray sea. In the early afternoon, as I sat before a small open fire, there came from it a low fluttering, interspersed with a faint chuckling. In the wet pine needles of the scrub pine just outside the door, I could hear the soft rustle of the southerly off the sea. The light rain that it was bringing pattered on the roof. A few moments of this, and the lassitude of the sea and the seaside overtook me, and dozing, I fell asleep in my chair.

Later I put on a poncho and walked the beach in the rain. As I emerged from the dunes, three great black crows that had been feeding on the husks and shells of an old clambake arose silently and departed flapping. The sea was steel gray, and broad off in front through the drisk I saw a short white gash that appearing, disappearing, and reappearing, showed that the Old Proprietor was awash. As I walked slowly by the side of the sea, its small surf gave off a low wet wash of sound.

Suddenly I was the lone witness of a piscatorial adventure. Close inshore and just beyond the cresting of the waves, a hell-diver was swimming. I observed the oval, rounding back, the thin reedy neck, and the small head that comes to a sharp point at the end of the beak—a singularly unattractive bird. Of a sudden, in a quick, rolling motion, it dove. Glimpsing this, a gull, hurrying, flew in. It dove and, resting on the surface, gulped up a sand eel. This attracted still another gull, which, gull-like, instead of fishing on its own, went after the prey of the first gull. A shag, scaling just above the water in long, low, curving flight, dropped in. Then out of nowhere three more gulls flew in.

All this time the surface of the glassy sea was being roiled by the swift passage here and there of the school of fish that was the center of this avian attention. After a bit, the school disappeared. The gulls flew off on long errands, the shag departed, and the hell-diver vanished in the volute of the next wave. The gray sea was again completely calm and deserted, and I walked on.

A mile up the beach I left it, passing in over the dunes. Here in the shelter from the sea, a few bedraggled pale pink and blue blossoms of the delicate beach pea were still in evidence. At the edge of the dune a small stand of scrub pine marks the upland, and beyond it lies the large fresh cattail pond known as Massacre Pond. Creeping through the cattails, I came to the edge of the open water and found there, swimming placidly, a pair of young black ducks. In another month's time, this small pond would be full of migrating waterfowl.

Later, in the shank of the afternoon at cocktails, the conversation turning to the great quantities of shorebirds to be seen in this early fall of the year, I listened while my neighbor and host remarked:

"I could swear I heard a curlew whistle in the fog this morning."

Then I gave an account of my lonely meeting with the lone curlew.

# Islands, Marshes, and a Bar

STRATTON'S ISLAND is a lonely island. It and its smaller neighbor, Bluff Island, front the Atlantic broad off the beaches that circle from Prouts Neck in the east to Wood Island in the west, thus forming the shoreline of white sand that enclasps within its great curve all of Saco Bay. The winds of the Western Ocean ceaselessly assault the bleak and bare ledges and rocky shores of these uninhabited islands, and in the air above them the wild cries of the sea-birds are never absent.

In the annals of man, Stratton's is an ancient island. By virtue of the mere existence of John Stratton of Shotley in Suffolk, it was known in England as early as 1631. The sum of our knowledge of John is that he lived for a time on his island and that, at the suit of one Godfrey, there was once attached in his hands a brass kettle. Beyond that, the record is as barren as the islands themselves. They are to-day, as they have been for centuries, a site of shipwreck and a haven for birds.

For many years the low rounding skyline of Stratton's Island was broken by the gable roof and high dormers of a substantial house. I never heard that anyone lived there, and the story was that it was built for the use of gunning parties who used to gun the small fresh-water pond on the island in the fall of the year. Then one day vandals fired the house. For a time the gaunt stacks of the chimneys remained, and when I first saw them I felt as if I had lost an old friend. Later, all but one fell into the cellar hole, and another ancient landmark was lost to the sight of man.

In my time I have visited Stratton's Island twice, the first time a quarter of a century ago. Our point of departure was the creek behind Pine Point, our craft a lobsterman's boat, and our cargo a picnic lunch. This faraway August day was a memorable occasion.

There was the swim of one of the company out to a ledge in the channel between the islands. Here the tides run swift and strong. He was a powerful man, a strong swimmer, and I can see him now as he reached the distant ledge. Again and again the white surf flung him up against it, and then washed him from it. He could not hang on. The sea was running too strong.

Alarmed, I attempted a rescue, putting off in a clam boat and rowing it back-to, fisherman-fashion, to keep him in sight. Despairing of mounting the ledge, he had turned and started swimming back. I met him in mid-channel, and my proffered rescue was declined. But, in old maritime lingo, I kept him in company until we both went ashore on Bluff Island. There, seated on the sparse grass, with the vast gull population our landing had put up into the air screaming and white-flashing in circles over our heads, we celebrated the occasion with a round of martinis that I had brought along for the now fruitless purpose of resuscitation.

Then he swam the channel back to Stratton's Island. Here the tarpaulin was being ripped off the rockweed, and the rockweed was being tossed aside to reveal the red bodies of the finest mess of short lobsters ever steamed in a clambake. Again the shaker passed.

What a day that was, in August a quarter century ago.

Today a west wind is blowing, cool, strong, and steady. Before it, racing mounds of white cumulus move steadily across the sky. Both wind and tide slow our course in the channel between the islands to the pace of a slow snail. In a small cove the anchor is dropped, the throttled motor conks out with a cough, the clamboat that serves as tender is hauled alongside, and for a space there are successive trips ashore before all of the party are disembarked. This activity disturbs the birds in the pond ashore, and five black-crowned herons are counted as they mount out of the cattails into the sky.

Ashore, people start walking without plan or concert, everybody on an exploration of his or her own. For myself, I sit for a while on the bank and take in the scene. Across the channel lies Bluff Island, brown, bare, rounding in contour, and windblown. Its ledges extend into the sea, and they seem to be covered with long spikes that stand out against the background of the sea. The glass discloses that these are the necks of the shags that populate them in thick array. Beyond, across the broad sweep of the blue bay, I see the encircling beaches in a long crescent of white, and their names come back to me—Ferry, Old Orchard, Grand, and the Pine Point Beaches. I take notice that the amusement pier at Old Orchard still stands on its iron pilings out beyond the breakers and over the open water.

On Stratton's Island there is no amusement park, and I am suddenly alone. My companions have all departed on their explorations. The dominant theme of this lonely island is the incessant crying of its birds. Never for an instant is the air silent—always a wild cry or mewing. From up above me comes a series of sharp shrill notes not unlike a harsh laugh. I look aloft and see poised in flight into the eye of the wind a single gull. The cry and its sharply defined black head mark it as the laughing gull. In these parts, *Larus atricilla* is nowadays a rarity, because, it is said, of the savage competition of the vaster quantities of herring gulls.

When I commence my walk, I come upon many evidences of the great gull population of Stratton's Island. Its ledges and shores are spotted with the white lime of their droppings and littered thick with the broken shells of mussels, crabs, and the like. These have been dropped by flying gulls to break the shells, whereupon they descend and feed. Again and again in the thick wiry grass I kick up the drying feathered carcass and half skeleton of a dead gull. Assuredly life is rugged and cruel on this bleak and lonely island. Yet it is abundant, as I am constantly reminded by the incessantly uttered cries and sweeping shadows of these great birds.

Now up comes one of the party bearing in his hand a great horse mushroom—at least eight inches in diameter—

and after proclaiming his intent to consume it for lunch, he tells a tale of two strange duck to be seen off the most easterly ledge. Two of us set off across the intervening shingle beaches, ledges, and rockweed pastures, creep up behind an outcropping of rock, and put our binoculars on the scene. In the wash flowing in and out over a dripping weed-covered rock they swim. They are new to me, but my companion identifies them as a pair of eiders—*Somateria mollissima.*

Leaving the eider ducks paddling and diving in the surging and washing of the waves on the rocks, and continuing my walk around the shore of the island, I come upon evidences of the hand of man—a dry stone wall buttressing the seaward side of the cattail pond, the crumbling foundations of a barn, a rusting pump, the well, and finally the cellar hole of the once substantial house that for years broke the skyline of Stratton's Island. I am struck by the Druid-like remains of the huge chimney and the wide stone mantel beneath which a great fireplace, now bare and empty, yawns toward the eastern sky.

What fires once burned here! What tales have been told before its out-thrown warmth! What toasts drunk! All gone —gone with the wind and the carriage trade.

On returning to the cove where the boat lay, I hear tales of the cattail pond—how the young and rugged had dragged the clamboat up the steep shingle beach, over the bank, through the thick grass and reeds, and then "lanched" her in the dark red waters of the pond. From here, on their first voyage, they flushed a pair of blue-wing teal and a rare kind of rail, the yellow *Coturnicops noveboracensis*. But when I row the boat through the narrow passage between the thick cattails that tower above me on either side, I see only a lonely muskrat. When I return and express my wonder as to how it got there, I am told that old-timers in these parts have seen them swimming out to the island in a very calm sea. And so indeed it may be.

One of the party has been compiling a list of the flora to be found on the island. As we stand near the shore of the pond, he points out, within sight, nearly a dozen different plants—chicory, asters, beach pea, goldenrod, jointed charlock, purple nightshade, and also the white, which is the poisonous kind, two kinds of cattails, and so on. And he tells me that his list now contains close to a hundred different plants, flowers, and grasses.

This is the advantage of an island. A man can make himself the master of one aspect of it. Perhaps he will one day publish a learned paper on its flora and fauna, including the birds that will soon now be making Stratton's Island a port of call on their fall migrations. The island lies right in the middle of the Atlantic flyway, and is dedicated as the Phineas W. Sprague Memorial Sanctuary.

While I eat my lunch and take my ease on a bleached and windblown spar, a beetlehead comes circling over the cove, uttering its cheery whistles, and there come to ear the shouts of a group of hardy young swimmers who dive and dive again from a wave-washed ledge and are disporting in the green water. In the afternoon I walk to the western end of the island. Here lie the bare bones of the *Washington B. Thomas,* a large coastwise schooner. I remember the year she came ashore, upwards of half a century ago. I used to see her high sides through a telescope from a cottage on the distant beach at Pine Point. Now she lies supine on the rocks, and who knows when her great oaken timbers will disintegrate and disappear?

In the late afternoon we depart, and as the bald contour of Stratton's Island recedes into the distance toward a sunset sky, the weird, wild cries of the gulls make an incessant chorus, while they circle in the sky above it, now departing on, now arriving from their mysterious errands over the surrounding seas.

· · ·

## Islands, Marshes, and a Bar

The excursion to the Scarborough Marshes is made by canoe. As we put her in the water at the head of a small cove, shove off, weather an exposed ledge, and then leave the rocky shore of Prouts Neck behind, the steady southwest breeze that is blowing across the blue and green bay helps us on our way. Threading our way through the buoys of the Yacht Club anchorage, which are tugging shoreward with the sweep of the incoming tide, we head for the mouth of the River and the Scarborough Marshes.

The River is a generic term. Actually there are six streams, each one of them a small tidal river, or "salt crick," as is often said hereabouts. They wind slowly in unimaginable hidden curvings between pine-covered necks of land to form and drain the wide Scarborough Marshes. Their names, listing them counterclockwise—Libby's, the None-such, Mill Creek, Dunstans, the Scarborough, and Little River—bear ample evidence of their usage from the early 1600's by men of the west country of England.

As we pass on our left hand the long lonely spit of sand and dune that lies to the west of the River, I am reminded of an old lady, one of the old-timers of these parts, who once told me that in her girlhood this point of now bare sand had been covered with towering pines. From these perchance the name Pine Point derived, albeit claim is made by some for one Charles Pine, a redoubtable Indian fighter in his time. Opposite, to the right on the east shore, is Ferry Rock. This name marks the site of a ferry in early colonial times.

Here we are greeted by a flight of roseate terns. As we approach the end of a bar, they spot it thickly, all facing into the wind. Waiting until we are almost abreast of them, they then clamber aloft. The air above the bar is filled with a great flashing of their black and white markings, and with the clangor of their high-pitched cries. Then we pass on our separate ways.

Here the River has carved a cove out of the eastern

bank. Ahead to the westward I see a thick clustering of fishing boats, mostly high-sided and bluff-bowed lobstermen's boats. On the east side, at the far end of this cove, Black Point makes out. This is a site of early settlement. For me it is a site of remembrance, and I see again the superb stand of beach plum bushes nestling against a grove of black pine that was once the scene of many a stealthy raid by small boys.

Here gulls and terns spot the brown rockweed, and my companion, an expert ornithologist, points out an Arctic tern, distinguishable from its companions by its blood-red beak. These, too, clamber up into flight, and again we pass on our respective ways.

Now the great broad yellow marshes lie ahead, interlaced with the blue water of the inflowing tide, and a flight of four summer yellowleg with their shrill-whistled cries warns its denizens of our alien approach.

The course of Libby's River is like an augur. As we enter its mouth, the canoe glides swiftly and silently before the steady southwest breeze. But soon, when rounding its successive hairpin turns, we now and again bend to our paddles and claw a passage upwind. So, we slowly twist our winding course upstream. Stretching on ahead like the converging arms of a great V, the shores of the marsh are wooded mostly with the black of pine, save where an occasional meadow merges with the marsh, or a white house stands alone, or the Black Point Road traverses its upper range. The tide is approaching its peak. The marsh is flooding and the blue water seems to support the golden spears of the salt hay.

I well remember the day when what caught and held the eye as it ranged across these golden marshes were the conical mounds of salt hay. Today salt hay is no longer an annual crop of the Scarborough Marshes, and the mounds are missing. But spotting the marsh here and there, I still see the clumps of gray-black staddles on which they rested. Today what arrests the eye as we pass slowly along are the gunners' blinds, carefully contrived to face away from the prevailing winds and out over a broad reach of open water. This is so that the duck will pitch to the decoys when coming upwind toward the blind.

But it is too early for ducks. I see only a brace or two of high-flying teal. Instead, I catch in the field of the glass, atop a blind, a green heron, see its crest aroused in alarm, watch its flight until it drops down into the marsh, where its head and crest alone remain visible.

There are many blue herons. Standing motionless in the marsh grass, they elude the eye. But then comes the clumsy ascent—and once, when this is close at hand, there is a sight of the orange patch on the wings—the laborious pumping of the great sweeps, the hoarse cry, then afar at the end of flight the long slow glide, the dropping of the long legs, the abrupt alighting on the marsh, and the folding of the wings. We count twelve of these great blues.

We leave the course of the river, paddle through the grass, and sit to watch a myriad plover feeding along the dark brown shores of a pothole. We put up a great flight of herring gulls who are resting in the marsh over the high tide. They make a startling spectacle of circling and flashing white patches up over the marsh before scaling downwind to settle again.

For me, the event of the afternoon is the flight of the kingfisher. At first I do not see him. Instead, I hear his long chattering cry. Then I see the bouncing flight. But wait, now! He is hovering on fluttering wings, transfixed in space against the blue sky. Like a plummet he drops. Where he has disappeared, there is a splash of clear water above the top of the yellow grass. And now he rises dripping out of the marsh.

I have been on these Scarborough Marshes in the fall of the year. This is an especial privilege. The dun brown salt hay with the ribbons of blue winding through it forms a flat foreground for the blazing brush and the crimson maple sprouts that rise at the far edges of the marsh. They are a rim of fire at the base of the pine-covered spurs that jut out into the marsh on either hand. Thus from the vantage of the marsh there are presented to the eye vistas of blazing color.

And in the late afternoon, if you stand at the edge of the marsh with the falling sun at your back, its rays will come slanting through the tinted trees, filling the air with the autumnal twilight. It is a premature twilight, for the sun still hangs in the sky. Yet the light thus filtered through the crimsons, the reds, and the yellows of the leaves is of a rare and special quality. In such a light there is a sadness, an ineffable regret that such beauty will be of so short a duration. The melancholy of the fall of the year is distilled from this fading daylight that floods the Scarborough Marshes through the painted leaves of October.

On this next excursion we are headed for Ferry Rock. This is a barnacle-encrusted ledge at the mouth of the River formed by the six salt creeks that drain the Scarborough Marshes. Jutting out from the east bank, it supports a high red spindle, a warning to the fishermen whose bluff-bowed craft lie moored in the winding turns of the little creeks.

This is its latter-day function. Anciently, as its name implies, Ferry Rock was the site of a ferry. Here the colonial traveler heading westward or bound down east on the only coastal road there was would at this point be ferried across the River.

Here the tides run with the swift coursing of a millrace, and the wide-spreading marshes and the flats and bars that are laid bare with each ebb have long been renowned as a rendezvous for great varieties of shorebirds.

A sight of these, now at the peak of their migration, is

the purpose of our excursion. As we round the point, clambering over the ledges, I am startled as always by the present prospect from this point. A generation and more ago, when I used to whistle down yellowleg from this Ferry Rock, the River made in close to the easterly shore and followed it to run alongside Prouts Neck and out into the sea. Not so today. With the working of some titanic storm and tide, or a series of them perchance, the River now trends in a southwesterly direction out into Saco Bay. The result is that today along this easterly shore there is a long low wide flat, brown with mud and in patches black with great mussel beds. Indeed, mussels are so plentiful that this might well be called Mussel Cove, since the high sandbar, the white crest of which is dry at high tide, now runs out from the shore of Prouts Neck to form this cove and shelter it from the bay and sea.

On this clear August morning, with the tide at its ebb, Ferry Rock is alive with small birds that scatter here and scutter there, up and down, and over and around the brown rockweed. I put the glasses on them and make out the fantastic face pattern of the ruddy turnstone, *Arenaria interpres morinella*. The black and white marking is like the makeup of a clown, an effect that is heightened when they leap off into low flight, displaying a harlequin pattern of white patches amid their bronzed and ruddy backs. Sea chickens, my companion calls them as they peel off the ledge, uttering their chuckled *ket-a-keks*.

Across the River, lining the side of a spit stands a clustered colony of terns, their white bodies and black caps all facing into the southwest wind. At the head of the spit, alone on the sand, is a great black-backed gull. Mounting clumsily into flight, he is then seen to be black from wingtop to wingtip, with his head and tail in snow-white contrast.

We wade across the little run at the mouth of the cove and walk along the curving edge of the bar. On our right hand is the high sandbar, its sea side populated by gulls, its cove side by shorebirds. Ahead of us lies the long low line of Prouts Neck. Across the cove to our left and beyond its beach lies the green expanse of a golf links. At our feet stretch the mud flats of Mussel Cove, alive with shorebirds. The soft air of early morning is filled with their whistles and calls, peeps, and chuckles.

The sharp double whistle, repeated in pairs, of the summer or lesser yellowleg, *Totanus flavipes*, comes familiarly to ear. Then I see what I take to be one wading in a pool. He has the white rump, black bill, and he puts on a considerable show. He dashes on nimble twinkling legs this way and that through the shallow water of the pool, plunging his bill into it as he runs. Now and again he spins around in a circle, dabbling all around him. On balance, I have concluded from his peculiar actions that he was not a summer yellowleg at all, but a Wilson's phalarope, *Steganopus tricolor*. I can see him now as I write, spinning in a tight circle and stabbing the water with his bill. Yellowleg do not act that way, and the manual tells me that at this time of the year the similarly marked phalarope does.

"There he is."

I raise my glasses and follow the directions of my companion—out there past the middle of the cove, to the left of those slats of the old wrecked lobster pot, now a little farther out, right on that tussock of black mussel shells. I focus and bring into clear outline the beautifully mottled oval body and the delicate down-curving bill of the lone curlew, *Numenius phaeopus hudsonicus,* of that morning on the beach in the fog.

Soon he is up. The familiar quadruplet of whistled cries resounds, and he glides in curving flight across the cove to alight on the shore of the bar. From there, in a few moments he takes off again to disappear in high flight out over the Scarborough Marshes.

*Whee-ur-eee. Whee-ur-eee.*

The air is filled with these small plaintive whistles that come wavering, first up, then down, then up again. I sight them—a large flight—there must be thirty of them—bunched like pigeons, now turning from the course of the River in toward Mussel Cove. Their line of flight inclines, and as they drop, their wings cease their irregular beating, and on poised pinions they glide, their speed slackening, above the surface of the cove. Their oval bodies are seen to pass in reflection in the calm water. At a spot where the sandbar opposite us shelves sharply and merges with a mussel bed, stands a welcoming group, all facing in the same direction. Wings flare. Feet drop. They are down.

Such is the flight of the beetlehead.

*Whee-ur-ee. Whee-ur-eee.*

This time the whistle is that of my companion, and *he* tells me that the call of the beetlehead plover, *Squatarola squatarola*, has for many years been a kind of tribal salutation in his family.

I look out on the mussel bed, where they have scattered to feed, and curiously, to the naked eye they are lost to sight. Then through the glass I make them out and see why they had disappeared. They are a miracle of protective coloring, these chunky, stocky birds on long, wading legs. The throat and the belly are jet black, like a bib and tucker, set off against the white sides of the neck, the shoulders, and the rump. This, coupled with the speckled black and gray back, renders them indistinguishable from the mussel bed on which they feed.

On the muddy margins of the little pools there is a multitude of snipe. They cluster close together and feed in apparent great haste, stabbing into the mud about them with repeated swift jabs of their sharp black bills. In their short fluttering flights, as the tide wells up in the pools and erases the shores, they display a striking white triangle that extends well up into their backs. From this prominent characteristic my companion identifies them as dowitchers, *Limnodromus griseus.*

And, to my surprise, I make out a pair of chunky little jacksnipes, *Capella gallinago delicata;* I had not expected to find Wilson's snipe on a mud flat so near the sea.

We are not alone, for ahead on the bar we see a man and a woman approaching, and they appear to be watching too. There is the short walk, a sudden halt, and then the binoculars come up. Soon we are in converse and exchanging information. The gentleman is an expert. He keeps a list of the birds he has identified each year. He has 187 species and expects to top two hundred before the year is out.

As we talk, the terns come fishing with the turning of the tide, and he stops to put his glasses on them. Then after a moment of silence there is a pleased chuckle of confirmation. He has spotted an Arctic tern, *Sterna paradisaea,* by virtue of the infallible sign—the blood-red bill that is red to the very tip, that of other terns being black. He marks the tern down as number 188. Then we all have a look. It has landed amid a multitude of terns and plovers, which form a horizon of birds as they stand on the crest of the bar in outline against the sky. It is a spectacular sight.

Now amid a parcel of peeps and plovers beside a small pool, he picks out three knots—small chunky birds, almost pure gray—*Calidris canutus rufus.* These, too, our friend adds to his list.

Suddenly, in from the direction of the marshes, there comes, sweeping above the cove in strong vibrant flight, a large bird. Descending sharply in a beautiful down-curve, it alights on a mussel bed, where it stands in profile. It is predominantly brown in color. Instantly, and before it has alighted, our expert identifies it—a Hudsonian godwit, *Limosa haemastica.* It reminds me of the lone curlew of the morning of the fog, seen again in this cove. Yet it is sharply differentiated by its long slender bill, which, instead of curving delicately downward, is turned just as delicately upward.

These shorebirds are in migration. The winter months will find the ruddy turnstones and the beetlehead plover on the faraway beaches of the Carolinas—and in South America the little knots, the curlew, godwit, phalarope, dowitchers, and the summer yellowleg. All the birds we have seen will soon be gone to their winter quarters in warmer climes, all save the Arctic tern, who will disappear into the wild wastes of the Atlantic, the Western Ocean of Columbus.

A swim before lunch is the aim of my companion, and we take our leave of Scarborough Bar and the whistling beetlehead plovers. It is a drive of only a few minutes across the neck to the beach that fronts the wide Atlantic. On the way I take note of a swamp maple that has turned blood red by the side of the road, and the yellow of a poplar touched by the frost, high on a hillside amid the green. These are the portents of an early fall.

# Shy Beaver Pond

A TRIP to Shy Beaver Pond for a bit of fly-fishing was always
a pleasant interlude in a stay at Scarborough Beach, and
the instructions on how to get there have stuck in my mind.

"I tell you what you do. You take right out through the

sand plains to Buxton. Then you take out on the road to West Buxton and go acrost the Saco. From there its only a mite of a step right down into Shy Beaver Pond."

So here we were, rolling across the hot "sand plains," which is what the lower valley of the Saco River was anciently called. A mixture of loam and sand atop a deep foundation of clay, these plains support the greenest of meadows where, at the moment of our passing, a flock of white-faced sheep were steadily cropping. On either hand there are rolling ridges covered with stands of white pine, whose green plumes gave off a bright sheen as they tossed and swayed in the steady northwest breeze. Now and again, we passed the traditional Maine farm—the story and a half frame house with the low woodshed, and then the big barn beyond, marked always by elms that tower aloft to droop with spreading foliage. Swiftly and pleasantly the miles rolled by as we sped over this route, which in the old days meant a long day's excursion in a buggy behind a plodding mare.

As we approached an old family burying ground, my companion pulled over to the side of the road and stopped. He pointed to the top of the bank opposite, and following his pointed finger, I saw what had caught his eye. There, atop two granite posts, carved in marble, reposed a pair of lambs.

Now this friend of mine was in the wool trade. He had already saluted with a toot of the horn the flock of sheep we had passed down the road, and here we must stop and have a look. We clambered up the sandy bank and came upon a gravestone the like of which I had never before encountered. A long cylindrical block of marble cut with eight sides had been hung horizontally between the two posts supporting the recumbent lambs by means of an iron rod running through the block parallel with its eight facets.

Laboriously we rolled this heavy stone on its axle, and then spelled out, by name, birth, and death, the humble history of a family that had its roots hereabout in the eighteenth century. Where, under the sod now thick with the waving plumes of goldenrod and wild asters, their bodies repose was anybody's guess. Yet, for their necrology, we two, passing strangers in the twentieth century, had only to turn this octagonal gravestone upon its creaking axle.

We went on, and descending a hill that curved down through a tree-sheltered village, we came upon the Saco River, a ribbon of blue hidden from view by overhanging foliage until you come upon it. With the planks rumbling, the car passed over the old bridge, climbed the curving rise on the other side, and lined out across the flat sand plains again.

A sandy side road beckoned us off at a tangent to the right. Suddenly, in front of the car a chipmunk hightailed it across the road, and the swift brown flash of his passage, with his tail on high like a warning flag, was startling. We passed through a grove of white pines. The road dipped and we dropped down slowly over its needle-matted surface. Through the thick branches there came glints of blue water.

Shy Beaver Pond now lay before us. Cupped in this depression by low ridges, it was a limpid eye amid the green. A small pond it is and spring-fed. The water is so extraordinarily cold that a drink of it is a rare experience. The shores, covered with water willows, recede easily toward the pine-covered ridges, and at the outlet there are hackmatack, with their clinging shreds of gray moss.

Shy Beaver is a quiet, peaceful spot. Swallows in continuous flight dart toward the surface, sometimes kissing it, sometimes not. Here and there a widening dimple bespeaks the rising trout. There are cedar waxwings galore that circle out in unceasing forays after insects and then return to a perch. Never have I seen so great a quantity of these curious birds with their solemn chieftain-like aspects.

A sound of the horn on a truck by the landing brings an answering hail. Then rods are assembled, reels adjusted, lines rove, leaders tied on, flies chosen. We each step into a little double-ended flat-bottomed boat and row out. Soon the silence is broken only by the swish of the casts.

Two hours of excellent fly-fishing follow, for Shy Beaver Pond is literally alive with fighting trout—the native square-tail or brook trout, in abundance, and now and again a rainbow. I stand in my skiff, and when I pull the line taut, the fly whirls in back of me with the back cast and then flies forward with the snap of the wrist and the cast, and, following the line into the water, it kisses a dimple as it falls.

In the next instant the rod snaps up, then bends—an alluring curve. The fight is on. The reel crackles. There is the whipping, back and forth. Then the net is overside, and a dripping trout is encurved in its mesh. Soon the bottom of my box is covered with shining beauties.

This was it—what we had come for.

Later, reclining lazily on the soft brown needles that carpet the ground beneath the white pines, we ate a leisurely lunch. Thin sandwiches of rare beef, deviled eggs, and cheese constituted our fare. These were well washed down with ice-cold cream ale that had been kept chilled in the spring in the hatchery by the side of the pond.

A bit of history goes with Shy Beaver Pond. Not far from where we were taking our ease in the cool shade of the whispering white pines, there was an old camp. Above the door a weather-beaten sign still proclaimed "La Jolla." This dated from a day when this pond was the property of a family by the name of Hale, a name famed in the State of Maine. But that was long ago. Later I walked beside fish pools that had been constructed in those earlier days.

The hatchery, a low, pitch-roofed frame building, stands hard by the pond. Within is a long, dank, dark interior where in vague outline I saw a number of long narrow tanks. Outside, the air was warm and muggy. Inside, it was chill and clouds of white condensation were rising from the surface of the cold spring water in the tanks. Here the eggs are laid and fertilized. Here the fry is hatched. And, I am told, selective breeding is practiced with remarkable results in size and beauty.

In each direction, running nearly around the pond to its outlet, are a series of pools, some circular, others long and narrow. As I walked beside and between these pools, dark shadows flashed in the clear waters. These were fish swimming toward me. They were expectant, and I did not fail them. Reaching into a pocket, I pull out fistfuls of Purina Trout Chow and cast the square brown pellets out onto the surface of the water. Instantly the surface churned violently as a multitude of fish rushed toward the pellets, voraciously snapped at the morsels, turned in a flash, and with a flick of the tail sped away.

From time to time, as I made a leisurely peregrination around the shores, the sedge, the cattails, and the alders parted, providing me with a vista out over the pond, where my companion in his flat-bottomed boat was endlessly casting. I was struck by the prodigality of nature in this spot. I walked beside pools that contain thousands upon thousands of trout. Out over the pond, the air was alive with a myriad invisible insects. This was evidenced by the continuous dartings of the cedar waxwings, in incessant flight, and by the widening circles on the surface where the trout were rising.

Shy Beaver is a place for visiting and revisiting. On my second visit I went alone, arriving in the middle of the morning. There ensued for a space a comfortable conversation with the proprietor, leathery-countenanced and of uncertain age. Former visits were recalled, the present occasion canvassed, future visits anticipated. The while I was jointing my rod, adjusting the reel, threading the line, and indulging in pro and con over the content of my fly book. At length I took my place in the familiar double-ended boat and ran out the short oars. Then dark water opened up between me and the float. I rowed slowly and with a minimum of effort to the post that had been recommended, and there slipped the painter over the butt of the small pole. A small westerly breeze that was sending gusts across the surface of the pond quickly tautened the mooring line.

I was alone on the surface of Shy Beaver Pond, save for the birds—swallows that sailed past, dipping to make dimples on the surface; cedar waxwings making circular forays out of the alders on the near low shore, the soft metallic snap of their bills certifying the success of these ventures.

And then there was that gull. Like myself, he was alone; like myself, he was fishing. He was a great white herring gull with a predaciously curved yellow beak, and he sat quietly on the top of another mooring pole that was just awash, perhaps fifty feet distant.

First I tried a Coachman and many a cast I made and never a strike ensued. So after a bit I looked aloft and deduced from the haze of this August dog day that a bit of color was what was wanted. I reeled in, selected the bit of flaming crimson feathers known as the Red Ibis, and went afishing again. And as before, I had no luck.

Then of a sudden I heard a great thrashing and splashing. I turned. There was that herring gull, off the post now and in the water, its curved yellow beak under the surface. With its great wings whipping and its powerful neck stretching back, it pulled clear of the water the tail of a trout. There was a voracious snap, lightning quick, and the beak went back under the surface. This was repeated several times, the gull swimming, or floating, or being towed downwind with its tail high and its head down, like a miniature high-pooped galleon.

Twice, with powerful sweeps of its wings it tried to rise out of the water with the trout in its beak. Both times it failed. It was out of balance, nose-heavy. Then the tactics changed. The gull began to consume the trout, encroaching upon it with quick gulps. By now I had the glasses on this piscatorial adventure. With the beak high and wide agape, the muscles of the throat rippled under the white feathers, and a bulge formed and then receded. The swallowing completed, the wings arched wide, and the gull was airborne.

I watched it mount and circle against the green of the pines and then line out over the tops of the trees. Its day's fishing in Shy Beaver Pond was over.

I turned to my own fishing, choosing this time a little Black Gnat. Without doubt the gull was the patron saint of Shy Beaver Pond, for now came the familiar tug—a strike —and the wrist snapped, the rod bending in that ever alluring curve. Slowly I wound in the reel and soon had a fat squaretail flapping on the bottom of the boat.

That afternoon the air grew heavy and humid, the western sky became a pall of dark gray, and the weather, dour and threatening. Occasionally, from afar came the rumbling of distant thunder. Out in my little boat, I soon felt the scattering drops. And hardly had I slipped into a light oilskin when the downpour began its steady march across the surface of the pond.

A watery roar arose. This was from the pelting of the drops on the surface, each one raising a circular cup of water as it struck. What a few moments before had been a calm and placid surface broken only by the ripples caused by rising trout now presented a mottled turbulence that stretched from shore to shore. Through the barrage of rain, falling straight down out of now low overhanging clouds, the white pines and timbered shores grew vague and indistinct.

Fishing was at a standstill. There was naught to do save to sit out the passing of this shower. The force of it now waxed, with the roar increasing in intensity, and the watery cups mounting—and now waned, with the noise dying away almost to a pattering, only to surge up again. Soon I was sloshing around in a puddle in the bottom of the boat.

Then, as suddenly as it had come, the shower departed. I could see the full force of the falling rain moving slowly across the pond and out over the trees to the eastward, in the direction of the Saco River. Soon the surface of the pond had subsided, and its former placidity was broken only by the circles of the scattered drops that were still falling. In a few moments, other circular ripples were widening, bespeaking the rise of the trout. It was time to go fishing again.

I was ashore when the catch of the day came in. Indeed, in this instance one might apply to trout fishing the phrase of the longshore fisherman—a full fare. The fisherman—he was a mere stripling—kept lifting trout out of his box. Sleek, shining beauties they were, both squaretail and rainbow, to a total of thirty-one. An indulgent father was footing the bill, and it was a good one, when you figured in the time on the rod, on the boat, and the poundage, which came to fifteen and a half.

I had been watching this youngster, already an accomplished fly-fisherman. Is there any other activity that combines grace, skill, and timing in so pleasing a blend for the onlooker? This young boy in action was a superb sight. There was no extra, no ungainly effort—only the forearm and the wrist rising up with the line taut, and then breaking water, and then they stood steady in the perfection of his timing, while the bight swung in its wide sweep behind him, finally to come forward, as the lad completed his cast, with the fly flicking the water again, and there came to ear in the still air the slight whipping *swish* of the cast.

Later in the afternoon I was joined by friends who came

to picnic at sundown. We settled down on the soft sand amid the low huckle and blueberry bushes on the crest of the easterly ridge, where the long horizontal branches of the white pines overhead framed an unforgettable picture. The far shores are low and for a fair distance from the shore sedge and alder grow. Then the land is higher and there are stands of hardwood. Here too the pine and the balsam and the hackmatack spot the edges of the woods.

The sun was dropping below the skyline and its horizontal rays extended a path of warm light across and above the darkening surface of Shy Beaver Pond. It was thus only for the short moment of sunset. The darkness over the pond deepened and slowly rose with the setting of the sun.

The cloudless western sky was now a sea of golden light, and out on the placid surface of the pond the fish were rising. In the ever-widening circles thus made, the reflection of the trees and the shores shimmered. Swallows wheeled and skimmed, dipping to flick the surface of the water, and the circular trips from the tops of the alders told of the flight of the cedar waxwings amid the myriad insects hovering over the pond. Bats were circling out from the pines and then returning.

Afar in the western sky, we saw a brace of duck, and we watched their swift approach until, out over the pond, they braked their flight, dropped, and then settled on balanced wings down onto the darkening pond, to break the surface with little plashes and to swim about, black forms in the gathering darkness. Then man added his bit to these scenes of sundown flight. In the deepening glow of the western sky there was etched swiftly upward in a long arc a slender line of pink. Then, when it ceased, a black speck—a jet plane became visible.

Thus it was as we sat and supped on this pine-clad ridge looking out over Shy Beaver Pond. A thermos of martinis passed from hand to hand and one of the group with a twist of the macabre that characterizes his tough mind proposed a toast to the survivor. And as the darkness gathered and the stars began to glint in the dark blue above pond and trees, we pledged this dubious honor to him.

# Labor Day Weekend

SINCE THE COAST of Maine runs almost due east and west,
the sun in late summer rises not out of the sea but out of the
never-never land known as down east. At Scarborough
Beach a striking aspect of this is that the rise of the sun can

be seen in the west before it is visible in the east. The upper windows of a distant house high on the bluff of Prouts Neck will catch the first rays and transmit them to me in a flash of golden fire as I walk westward on the beach. Then for the short moment before the arm of the sun illumines the tops of the pines on the eastern skyline, the calm surface of the sea and the wet foreshore will still be reflecting the muted pre-dawn tints of mauve and olive, magenta and pearly gray, as if they were the surfaces of a great kaleidoscope. At such a time the hue and cry of the gulls in the small cove formed at ebb tide by the uncovered rocks off the easterly point of the beach has a lonely and poignant quality.

The first day, I awoke to find my room suffused with the pink light of the false dawn. Outside, the deep green of the wide lawn was spotted by snow-white gulls. Half a hundred of them were walking about. I made a single *clop* with my hands. Instantly there rose in flight below me a pattern of flashing white, with the wing tips flashing black. Silently they circled out over the dunes. From there they came in again on poised wings, settling to alight and fold their wide wings, fitting them neatly to their backs. The lawn was as before, with the gleaming white bodies walking about on the green, now in a widening, now in a concentrating pattern.

I was fully awake. The opportunity was not to be missed. I emerged, and with my emergence the gulls left again in silent flight, this time for good, as I passed on down through the dunes to the beach.

The sky was overcast, and the light of the still-hidden sun striking against it was deflected as from the vault of a great arch. The placid sea was wine-colored, the beach of a brown that glowed, the dunes touched with roseate light; and beyond them, on the horizon, rose the dark plumes of the pines. These colors came on to glow, and to fade, and to glow again as the path made by my bare feet stretched steadily westward. The recurrent rasp on the sand of the small surf at half tide was the only noise save for the repeated *cheer-eep, cheer-eep* of some shorebirds hurrying past out over the flowing wash of the tide. A coot floated motionless, lifting and dropping with the swells. A black head withdrew beneath the surface, and then at a distance it rose again dripping. It was a seal. Out where a line of broken water marked the Old Proprietor, floated the boats of three lobster fishermen.

The sun was still down under, but when I turned to look, the open eyebrow of light in the east was glowing with golden light. Overhead, and coming on down into the west, the cloud-vaulted sky was bathed in a pink that deepened at the horizon. And just above the narrow height of land at Prouts Neck, I noticed what I took to be an unusual cloud formation—a great pink cross with a vertical stand and horizontal arms most perfectly marked.

Now a flash of golden light in that high window ahead announced the coming rise of the sun. I walked on, my eyes fixed on the curious cross of now almost red light.

With the rise of the sun behind me, I was witness to a miracle. This was no cross that I saw in the western sky. Rising high into the sky, it was the foot of a bow of light that with the rise of the sun commenced to glow, and to extend up and up, and around until it reached down to the northeast horizon in a vast and perfect curving. And curiously, it was red to yellow to green from its southern to its northern edge; the usual purple of the spectrum seen in a rainbow was missing. At my feet, I could see this great colored bow in the sky reflected in the wet wash of the tide.

For a short quarter hour I alone on Scarborough Beach was witness to this rare spectacle.

The sun was by now above the skyline. As I returned walking eastward, I watched with the flowing of each wave the sides of tiny bubbles catching and reflecting its light. Their flashing was like that of diamonds being washed up by the sea.

A weather-breeding sky this was. For later, when the sun climbed above the overcast, there came a gentle rain. But it did not last. By noontime the rain had ceased. Then the sun burned its way through, ushering in an afternoon of almost preternatural calm.

It was as if time and space and life hung in a balance. As I sat on the dunes on this late afternoon, the sea was a great flat floor, motionless and serene. It was like a vast stage set with scattered props. To the eastward, where the line of the horizon was shrouded with haze, it was broken by the low curving of Richmond's Island. In its turn, the island was broken by the single house that stood midway against the sky and by a grove of dark pine at its southerly end. Broad off in front, the brown weed-covered bones of the Old Proprietor lay bare and bleaching in the sun. Over in the western quarter, a longer and larger ledge rose above the surface, fronting eastward. On the line of its edge against the sky stood the silent forms and long necks of the cormorants that are never absent.

Gray-white mare's tails decorated the sky. There was no sound save for the recurrent seep on the sand made by the ebbing tide. The waves were so reduced in size as not to be noticeable. On this broad painted set there were evidences of activity—the scattered white stakes of the buoys of lobster fishermen, the still forms of silent gulls floating, scattered cat's-paws, and long smooth slicks of still water winding between them. Here and there on the surface of the bay were small boats, motionless. They reminded me of the line in *The Ancient Mariner*—"as idle as a painted ship upon a painted ocean."

For a long time I sat in the warm sun, lazying and watching this idle scene.

At first the only actors on this stage were some black coots off the long low ledge running out from the easterly end of the beach. They were swimming slowly in disorderly array from there across the front of the beach. When they reached a certain point, they would turn about and swim as slowly back to the point, then turn around and come back again.

In the van a well-bunched group of five was proceeding slowly. All of a sudden, they split apart as if erupting from an explosion, scattering in different directions on wings and feet that flailed the water violently. Then in the next instant they were as they had been before—black forms moving slowly.

A sweep with the binoculars from east to west revealed many a scene. Out in front there was an old squaw riding the rolling waves so nonchalantly. For one moment he was visible, his long needle-like tail sticking out aft like a miniature boom, and in the next he would be lost to sight in the trough between two waves. For as long as I wanted to watch him, he would flick on and flick off in the field of my glass.

The ocean was spotted with birds. The white breasts of gulls flashed as they swam to wind and wave. A bit to the eastward of the old squaw were coots. Commonly they are chunky blocks of black, but as they fell and rose on the incoming seas, I could see flashes of white. They were skunkheads—the coot of the longshore gunner.

A flock of them passed—a V of black-bodied birds perhaps twenty feet above the surface of the water in perfectly even flight, toward a long ledge, running east and west and coming to a peaked point at its easterly end. Here, way back in the past, gunners used to perch—it is known on the old charts as Shooting Rock. Crouched there, they would await such a flight as this to veer toward the line of their black-silhouetted decoys, tossing to wind and wave off the point of the rock.

Out over the surf, the terns were fishing, slowly, with slow, measured beats of their wings, their sharp beaks and sharp eyes pointing downward. I watched one dive—saw the splash and the ascent, with a wiggling minnow in the beak.

A flight of peep swept up off the beach, wheeled out over the wash, and flew down along the water's edge, seen now and again against the curve of a wave. On and on they went, until at length, swinging in flaring flight shoreward, they descended suddenly to join a few others on the beach. There they raced, now shoreward in the sweep of a wave, then seaward in pursuit of its wash, their little black legs atwinkle, and feeding steadily on the run.

Away out, in front of the Old Proprietor, there was a loon. As I watched, it rose full length out of the water and beat its powerful wings. Again and again and again it did this, and it was as if by this desperate flailing of its wings it was trying to escape from some clutch hidden beneath the surface of the sea.

The next two days were weather-breeders. The sea was a great level expanse of gray, running flat and untroubled to the southern horizon, where a taut line marked the foot of the lighter gray of the canopy of the sky. The winds were variable. Now and again the sun burned off a patch of the sky and for a bit shone feebly. The air was soft and expectant.

This grayness of sea and sky was like a mood. The only motion, the only irregularity that intruded upon it, was the slow and easy motion of the little waves rolling slowly ashore, to break in muted rasps. Just beyond their breaking, and inshore from where their visible rolling commenced, there swam, as if in formation, the usual large fleet of coot. Occasionally, a single one of these waterfowl would rear from the crest of a wave and beat its wings as in a gesture of defiance toward the all-enveloping grayness of flat sea and vaulted sky.

Often there was no skyline. Out there the fog would shut down, and seen dimly through it, an occasional white line of surf showed the seas breaking over the Old Proprietor. So, too, gleamings of white marked the shrouded contour of Seal Rock, and beyond there the wall of gray fog all but blotted Prouts Neck from sight. All along the curving crescents of the beaches, as the waves rolled ashore, recurrent foamings flashed and reflashed.

The year was turning. The only reminder of summer was a bedraggled beach umbrella that stood collapsed in the sand. Here, where vacationers had lolled on the beach and bathed in multicolored dress, there was now but a single figure in a yellow oilskin plodding steadily along the foreshore. This morning early, I saw in the bushes a great collection of small birds, all of a kind, busy with their feeding. Two hours later, not one was to be found. Thus, as the Labor Day weekend approached, migration in more senses than one had begun.

For some, this gray day was a day to sit inside, to hug the hearth, to feel the warmth of the fire at one's back and listen to its faint crackle as you gazed through the picture window, watching the mounting surf. But somehow or other I knew that shortly I too would put on oilskins and be pounding the beach along the foreshore.

At the end of the day, a cold offshore wind lifted the overcast, leaving in the western quarter a long oval of clear sky. Then the sun dropped below the long line of dark cloud. In an instant the whole scene was illumined with golden light—the black pines that formed the skyline, the rolling dunes, the broad flat stretch of the beach and sea.

Seen from the edge of the dunes, this flood of light encompassed both horizons and lit up all that lay between. Out where sky and sea met and merged there was on the surface a broad band of greenish-purple. The wind had dropped, and in the middle distance the breasts of a thousand birds were like pearls scattered on the gray and placid sea.

This great alighting was succeeded by a phase of colors. The underbelly of the overcast was tinged with gold. This was mirrored in the wet wash of the waves on the foreshore. The pools left by the tide became pools of pink. The breasts of the floating birds gleamed. In the west, detached here and there from the overcast, were clouds with hidden fires gilding their edges.

Twilight came slowly, as with the sinking of the sun the line of light rose and left first the beach and then the sea in shadow. Then with the sun gone, its upward shafts of light assaulted the overcast, and from there the afterglow was cast over the whole scene by the now glowing clouds. The breasts of the birds turned pink.

In the end there was darkness, the gilded crescent of a new moon, the evening star almost molten in its brilliance, and later the great dipper hanging low in the dark northwest sky.

All the next day the sun shone fitfully. The wind was easterly, except that it kept veering up into the northeast. The fog would scale in, and for a piece all would be gray. Then it would scale out again, and the sun would shine through, at first a pale orb through the low overcast, later shining down through patches of blue sky. In down-east parlance this is known as burning off. When the sunlight was burning through the mist, the light on the waves below would be not golden but a silvery cast, almost a pale green in hue. After a bit the overcast would shut down, the horizons would become hazy, and the booming of the foghorn at Two Lights could be heard over to the eastward. Then the fog would start moving in again.

. . .

Late that night it rained hard and long. This woke me up, and for a long time I lay listening to the driving drops pelting the panes, drumming a tattoo on the shingles over my head, and dripping from the pine needles in the woods beside the cottage. This was the beginning of a northeast storm—a no'the-easter in down-east parlance.

In the morning, early, the rain let up. Then it stopped. The air was warm. It caressed the cheek. But in short order a squall came down out of the northeast. With its coming, the air chilled suddenly, and heavy rain was driven slanting before the cold wind. Aloft, the low-lying furbelowed scud traveled swiftly seaward, and in a few moments what had been a great band of open sky out over the sea from the eastern to the southern horizon became a dark gray pall.

This pattern was repeated throughout the day—squall after squall, with periods of soft, warm, benign air, and the horizon lightening in between. It was as if this storm were a succession of furies, driven across this segment of the sphere by the wind. That is the way of a no'the-easter.

I went down to the beach to watch the sea. In the dunes I could hear the roar of the surf, a roaring punctuated by the thumps of crashing waves. At the crest of the dunes a scene of unbelievable turbulence met my eye. Successive seas came rearing, cresting, creaming, and cascading into tumbling foam. In their rushing shoreward, I counted four and sometimes five tiers of white, foaming surf speeding toward the dunes to spend their fury on the sand.

Broad off in front, where the Old Proprietor rears its ancient head above the waves, there was a maelstrom of seething foam and spray being tossed aloft to be shredded by the gale. As I watched this white spectacle out there in the darkness it slowly receded from sight, blanketed by the squall that was being driven out to sea. Then in that quarter all was hidden again.

Over to the eastward and close inshore, there was a sudden white gleaming of cresting foam. This occurred but once, and it told of the breaking of a ground swell there.

I saw the black slats of a wrecked lobster pot thrust for a moment above the white surf of a sea. The terns were fishing endlessly and silently, gulls were flying downwind low over the surface, now and again lost to sight in the troughs of the sea. And once, for a split second, I glimpsed a pair of flared wings spread against the rearing volute of a dark wave.

Off the headland to the eastward, where the beach ends and the point makes out in successive ledges, the surf was stupendous. It was half tide, and wave after wave came racing shoreward to stage its final assault on the rocks. I watched one that with reared crest came rolling on until, toppling, it struck the base of the outermost ledge with concussive force. I heard the *smack* and felt the jar as a cloud of white spray erupted, seeming for a split instant to hang in the air, then falling away almost gradually, and subsiding until the watery deluge was seen pouring in silvery rills off the weed-covered rocks. In fancy I half expected to see the ledge shake its mane of brown rockweed like a strong swimmer in the surf.

With the breaking of each wave the scene was subtly different, and this is why, I think, that the spouting surf of a northeast storm casts such a spell on those who watch it. There is a compulsion to wait and watch the next wave, and then the one following, and the one after that, and on and on, until all sense of time is lost and the watcher becomes a part of the tumultuous scene, attuned to the rhythm of the sea.

And so it was all along the coast. On distant rocks on distant points I could see the gleamings of white signaling the successive assaults of the turbulent seas.

At night I went again to the beach. The wind was strong and steady, and still out of the northeast. Overhead, the scud raced seaward, driven by the fury of the wind. No stars were visible, but nonetheless it was clearing. As I crossed the dunes, out of the inky darkness of the sea there flashed gleamings of brilliant white. These were the crestings of the waves.

On the beach I stood in the soft sand above the tide line. The surf was pounding out a roaring that receded into a rasping as each wave spent itself, sweeping up over the hard wet sand. Now and again there was a prolonged thunderous thump as the broad front of a long wave crashed from its reared height. Occasionally there was a moment of near stillness, a pause in the sea's outroaring. This was succeeded by the roaring, thumping, and rasping that merges in what is called alongshore the rote of the sea.

Far out in the blackness, a white cresting would gleam and then start spreading in each direction along the top of the wave. There were always at least four such lines of white foam rushing in toward the beach, and as the foremost was spending its utmost force up on the beach, another was forming and gleaming in the outer darkness.

Out over this wild tumultuous heaving of the sea there swept now and again a beam of baleful light. It came out of the northwest in back of me, then swept out over the sea in front of me, and receded toward the southwest until for a few moments it was lost to sight. Then it would reappear and its sweeping would recur. This was the occulting ray of Wood Island Light, casting its far flung beam out over this wild dark drama of the sea.

It was a sequence that would end only with the dawn.

The morning after the storm saw the weather clearing and colder, and the wind was still chill and still out of the northeast. It was, in the colorful phrase of the waterfront, trying to back around into the west, counter-clockwise. To the weather-wise this is a sign of unsettled weather. And sure enough, by ten o'clock the sunlight had been eclipsed by a vault of gray, and the rest of the day was overcast.

Thus was the fall of the year ushered in by this equinoctial storm.

Thick o' fog—heavy seas running. So read my notes of the day following the storm. Of this there were other signs. There was the wrack cast up by the waves, in disordered array, its upper edge marking the line, high on the beach, of last night's flood tide. Here, dotting the brown rockweed and kelp, were a myriad shorebirds—sanderlings and ringnecks —scuttering about, feeding busily on the wealth of seaweed. The soft sand had been encrusted by the rain, and when I walked through it, I made a perfect trail, the dry sand marking my steps.

There was the rote of the sea, waxing and waning, as wave after wave advanced toward the shore with reared volute, to crest with white, and then crash in successive pounding concussions on the hard-packed sand. Out over the turbulent surface, white gleamings dimly seen in the gray fog marked the jagged ledge of the Old Proprietor. To the eastward and in the west, similar gleamings told their tale of high surf on Richmond's Island and the rockbound shores of Prouts Neck.

Then the fog shut down, and I was alone in a gray world encompassed by the dark line of the dunes at my back, the dim curve of the fourth advancing comber out in front, and a gray wall on either hand. This was good. Now I could safely plunge into the gray sea *sans* suit. But my timing was bad.

I chose the moment of the ninth wave, which bore out its tradition of being the largest. Its surging surf rose above my head, and I got a mouthful of salt water. I turned for the beach. Great God! The speed with which that wave was sweeping shoreward! There was a race, and in the nick of time I snatched my towel and bath wrap from in front of its engulfing sweep.

All day long the deserted beach was a magnet. As I walked its length and back, I found memorabilia of the storm. There were lobster pots that had been lifted by the ground swell and washed ashore. I came upon eight of them, spotting them one at a time and at a distance, the slatted shape standing out of the dark sand against the gray fog. It told its own short tale of wreck and disaster. The excitement of the beachcomber was mine when in one of them I found four lobsters.

At the end of the day I stood on the high point that juts a ledge-lined shore out into the sea. There the waves could be watched as they broke, from three angles—out in front on the bare ledges, and rushing shoreward on either hand. The contrast was striking. Coming at me from the sea were ceaseless assaultings. Smacking against the exposed ledges, these waves spouted white and then boiled up over the brown tresses of the rockweed. But the waves racing toward the beaches on either hand came on rolling, cresting, and sweeping out of the sea and up on the shore.

Suddenly a woman appeared. Her apron was filled with crusts. As she tossed them forth, the shore and waves were dominated by the flashing, wheeling, soaring, skimming, and alighting of a multitude of great wide-winged gulls. A few moments later, the wind having hauled round by the south into the west, there followed a memorable moment of sunset. Although the sun had disappeared below the pines on the western horizon, I saw its light still pinkly reflected on the breasts of the gulls now floating, silently, high in the air.

In this hauling of the wind, we sojourners over Labor Day were fortunate. Had the wind "backed round" by the east into the north, as they say hereabouts, a continued "spell o' weather," that is to say, more rain and fog, would have been our lot. Instead, the soft westerly breeze brought on a clearing shower—a thunder gust punctuated by vivid flashes. By midnight the great black vault was studded with stars, and the next morning saw the dawn of a gorgeous blue and gold Labor Day.

The cove that lies at the easterly end of Scarborough Beach forms slowly. At high tide no vestige of it can be seen. It lies beneath the blue sea that enfolds this rocky point and curves away on either hand along crescent-shaped beaches. Out beyond the point a small fleet of black scoters can generally be seen swimming, riding the shore side of a wave and disappearing in the trough as it rolls, to reappear in a disordered array on the crest of the next wave. As the tide ebbs, there emerge the weed-covered ledges that make out into the sea. Over them the water sucks and gurgles through the rockweed as the waves of the ebbing tide slowly recede.

With the falling of the tide, a change of interest becomes evident among the frequenters of the point, the ledge, and the cove. A small boy will be seen proceeding shoreward slowly through the field, pole in hand. Come the ebb, and more particularly with the change of the tide, he will be seen perched atop the outermost rock, testing his skill with harbor pollock and hungry cunners. As the rocks, the rockweed, and the crenelated ledges appear, pools are formed and left by the receding tide. The gulls take an interest in these—great fat white creatures with yellow legs and yellow bills, and a spot of red on their bills as if they had just been withdrawn from the entrails of a cod. In equal numbers, the somber gray gulls assemble, and black-capped terns—the mackerel gull of the fisherman—wing across, occasionally falling in a swift dive to pluck up some hapless sand eel.

The afternoon of Labor Day, as the tide was ebbing I settled myself with a pair of glasses on the high bank that fronts the sea at this point. In a declivity behind a low ridge of rock there was a lone gull. I could not see its body, only its head outlined against the blue water just above the edge of the ledge. This scene was extraordinarily familiar. Then I suddenly realized that in effect Kilroy was there. Other gulls stood about, startlingly white against the brown rockweed, or squatted, facing seaward, lazily watching the heaving seas.

Now the half-hidden gull lumbered up from behind the ledge. From his beak there was dangling by a claw the body of a fair-sized, frantically clawing crab. The gull dropped the crab on its back in the rockweed and then plunged his curving, predacious yellow beak into its guts in short lunging thrusts. Curiously, the other gulls simply stood by and watched this glutton at his work. From this I deduced that they themselves were already well fed.

With the tide at full ebb and the ledges laid bare, the shorebirds assembled. I saw the white collar of the ring-necked plover, the tilting tails of teeter-rails, the long stilted legs of the yellowleg. There were also golden plover, the harlequin-like ruddy turnstones, an occasional phalarope, and the rare curlew. All of these were wading and teetering and feasting in the small pools.

Now a low black reef stretches out from the point to enclose between it and the beach a wide shallow pool. For the period of the ebb, this is a cove. Here, at this as at every ebb tide, small children wade, pick up starfish or sand dollars, and come running to seek parental elucidation. Gulls stalk solemnly and awkwardly on the rockweed. Shorebirds run hither and yon, busily feeding. On the surface there swims a small flock of sheldrake—the *shecorway* of the Indian. Startled, they scutter along over the water in formation, wings beating the surface, like a fleet of miniature airplanes trying to get underway. But they do not rise.

Once they are out of danger, the wings stop beating. They settle back into the water and go back to feeding.

Beyond the outermost edge of the ledge, the water was dotted with aquatic performers. In the deeper water a scant couple of hundred yards distant, a lobsterman's boat was churning slowly in successive circles as he ran down his line of pots. Astern on the quarter stood a large gull that gobbled up the gobbets of used bait the lobsterman pulled from his traps and tossed to him. This leisurely activity caused a congestion of the birds that were swimming in the narrow sea between the ledge and the circling boat.

Two flocks were converging and, counting quickly by groups of threes and fours, I reached a total of seventy-five birds before they merged. A considerable variety of swimming birds were congregated here. There were little grebes that dive with the speed of a flash and are known as helldivers. Here and there was the large black cormorant. A long slender bill that seemed to elongate at the back of a sleek head into a swept-back crest denoted a merganser. Mingled with these were scoters—the white-winged, the American with its orange spot, and the skunkhead coot with its black head and white face patches. Now and again one of these would rise from the water and beat its wings. All of these fellows are fish and shellfish eaters, and they will float and swim for hours, moving back and forth over the same expanse of water.

I was not the only watcher of this scene. Once in a while, between myself and the birds, the black round dome and bewhiskered snout of a seal would emerge. The head would twist for a leisurely round-about look and then, its curiosity apparently satisfied, it would sink silently from sight in the top of a wave.

Later, when the tide was making, these weed-strewn rocks that stretched out from the headland at low tide were soon awash. The gulls for the most part departed, though a few still spotted with white the unsubmerged crests of the higher rocks. And the little ruddy turnstones all retreated before the oncoming waves. On the sand at the water's edge, as they now pursued and then retreated from the pulsing surges of the surf, their curious harlequin-like appearance was even more distinctive than it had been when they were pecking at the barnacles amid the thick brown rockweed out on the now submerged ledges.

At half tide on the flood, the cove was submerged again. This was the best time to walk the beach in search of the varied views of the shorebirds. For this was their feeding time—when the oncoming waves with each surge would fetch ashore a myriad forms of microscopic plankton. It was not very long before I came upon a flock of peep I had marked from afar. It was fun to watch them on the run, their slender legs going it a-twinkle, bearing their small bodies swiftly over the level plane of the beach. The running of one became almost imperceptibly a take-off into flight. Then another peeled off, and another and another, until the whole flock of fifty-odd was wheeling out over the surf—a living constellation against the curving of a wave.

As the flock swung in a wide arc to avoid me, I heard their faint peeping, and I caught them in the field of the glass and followed their precision flight. Sweeping low over the on-coming surf, with a tilting of their wings they alighted on the sand, and again the black legs were a-twinkle, carrying them swiftly this way and that, with their heads bobbing and their beaks pecking at the particles of plankton. Again and again, with endless variations, this scene was repeated. The black collars of some and the flashing white stripes on the wings of others indicated that these were ringnecks—the semipalmated plover—and sanderlings.

Out beyond the line of the lazily breaking waves a gull was proceeding slowly upwind into the westerly breeze. So slowly did he fly that it seemed as if he would lose his flying speed and fall into the sea. And now he did—only it was a dive, for he was fishing. Unlike a tern, he did not dive into the water but alighted for the short moment of the catch on the surface. Then, as he rose, minnow in mouth, I fixed him in the field of the glass and I saw the soft gray, the dark spot on the side of the head, and the white wedge on the outer wing. This fellow was a Bonaparte's gull—*Larus philadelphia*— the smallest of the gulls.

In the next instant I witnessed a rare occurrence. The gull was again on its slow course upwind. Downwind there came sailing in swift flight a black-capped tern. The two collided, their left wings striking, and for a moment each was thrown off the even tenor of its flight.

At this point I was hailed in passing by two lanky forms, one of them trundling a wheelbarrow, the other bearing a long-handled rake. They were after a load of rockweed from the ledges behind me. This was in preparation for the annual feast of this day—the communal clambake that is always the climax of the Labor Day weekend. And thereby hangs a tale.

As regards clams, there are two schools of thought. There are those who pass them by and up with curling nostril and disdainful eye, and there are those who regard them as the most succulent of all the provender the coast of the Main affords. Of late years, that peak of Nature's perfection—the Pine Point clam—which once flourished in prodigal abundance in the Scarborough Marshes, has been in short supply. There are many theories to account for this. Some say the shipyard workers from South Portland dug all the flats clean during the war. Others blame the canning companies. Then there is the green crab. Be the cause what it may, the famous Pine Point clam exists only in the sharp nostalgic gleam in the pale blue eye of some old-timer when it is mentioned in his presence.

But this year it was different. There was a rumor afloat that they were back.

"They tell me," said one old lady, "that you can get some real nice steamers over't the Point. Something come and et the green crabs that was eating all the clams."

This had called for an excursion. And after we had rolled down across the marshes from Dunstan's Corner, we paused, just as we always used to pause, at the crest of Blue Hill, to admire, the tide being at flood, the ribbons of blue water winding through the broad gold expanse of the marshes which stretch away to the dark line of pine and fir. Then descending and crossing another stretch of marsh where Little River runs twisting through the marsh grass, we came to Pine Point.

Despite a modern complication of approaching turns for the accommodation of those who prefer to turn on two wheels, there is, as there always has been, one road in and one road out. The terminus is at what is always called "the crick." Here, clustered in close proximity, are the small frame houses of the lobster fishermen and clam diggers who make up the population of Pine Point. In short order, in response to a familiar hand-painted sign nailed to a picket fence, we were on a back porch that faced the golden marsh, bargaining for a good "mess o' steamers." This also was just as it always had been and just as it should be—all except the price, or, as they said hereabout—"the haahd paaht." Its ascent from the level of yesteryear had been astronomical.

Mid-afternoon, with the sun commencing its long slant toward the western pines, saw the beach active with the comrades of this communal adventure. Up and down the beach in the morning, scattered stones had been gathered and a fire built. Down off the point, where the tide was washing the thick tresses of rockweed, there was a wheelbarrow and two tall men were bending to the task of gathering seaweed. Now up the beach came one, now another, and now a third, laden with driftwood which was heaved on the flat, squared level of stones where for hours a fire had been crackling. Soon the embers were cleared away and great armfuls of wet rockweed were being tossed on the white-hot stones. Then the lobsters were for an instant to be seen on their backs, their claws and feelers waving in agonized gestures before they were buried by another armful of rockweed. Next came the clams, their gray shells streaked with the familiar oval dark lines, and of a proper size, neither too small nor too large—"steamers" in longshore parlance. And then the unhusked corn. Finally the tarpaulin was snugged down close on the rounding mound and secured by heavy stones.

There was time now for leisure, to rest the aching muscles, to repair up ashore for the bending of elbows, and to watch out across the marsh to the westward the western sky in red flame, traversed by long horizontal striations of black cloud. There was talk of an impending hurricane. There were storm warnings up and down the coast, which always coincide with remarkable sunsets. Then I heard the single call of a whippoorwill from a distant darkening thicket, and I watched the light of the afterglow fade slowly in the pools of the marsh. They were like dying eyes.

Then to the beach again, with appetites whetted. The clams were steaming, and the salt aroma permeated the cool evening air. Fond memories were evoked and ancient tales told, like the one about the old clam digger who "wouldn't eat a clam in a restaurant no more'n he eat a to'd."

Ah, the broth—hot, steaming, salty, and tinctured with the essence of the clam. And the succulence of their soft white bellies.

Now to tear into a lobster. Hot, almost too hot to handle, tender, and juicy they were, and seasoned with the subtle blending of salt, smoke, and steam that results from their imprisonment in steaming rockweed.

With the deepening of dusk, the September air was suddenly chill. A southerly sprang up from off the sea. It freshened. The small fire was boughed up and the rising wind chased the sparks away down the beach and in over the dunes—dancing glintings of yellow light that died in the distance.

Then came an immortal moment when the curve of the moon cleared the horizon, and all hands stood in silence as it mounted slowly, a great red orb, to take its place in the gray sky above the bar that runs shoreward from Richmond's Island. There followed the good cheer of the lifted cup, the warmth of the open fire of driftwood on the beach, and the singing of ancient songs while the moon sailed on its ancient course through the dark sky.

Later, in response to how she had liked the beach party, my companion, who is of the other school vis-à-vis clams, responded:

"Well, I'd just as soon nobody had put a clam in my knitting bag."

# Tales of the State of Maine

ONCE UPON A LONG TIME AGO in a Boston club I listened with no small amusement to an expert in the art of recounting tales of the State of Maine. He was using the dialect known in the purlieus of Boston, and west of that port, as down east. This man was a gifted raconteur and his diction had a ring of authenticity. For example, he knew when to drawl and when not to. The distinction is an essential part of the business.

But there was one thing that had me puzzled. His stories were of the coastal variety, but I could not pin down where his protagonist came from. And so, at the end of the evening I sought out the storyteller and taxed him with this small problem. He grinned good-naturedly.

"No wonder," he said. "I come from New Hampshire."

My point is both valid and important. Speech in the State of Maine is infinitely various. So is humor. And this can be demonstrated beyond peradventure of doubt.

Once upon an even longer time ago, on a hot July noonday, the stage that used to run out of Sebago Lake Station was moving at a slow pace up the long last hill to Standish Village. At the side of the road there approached a youth, straw-hatted and barefooted. The driver sung out to him. Then came the response.

"Haow-be-yeh?"

Whereupon my mother, whose ear for the nice gradations of diction was equalled by her power of their mimicry, leaned over the rail and sung out:

"When'd' jew cum over from Lim—rick?"

"Haow'd-jew-know?"

Years later I had a similar experience. Something in the speech of a pleasing young blonde librarian had a familiar ring, and so ensued a colloquy that ran thus:

"I reckon you must be from New England."

"A—yer"

" 'T 'wouldn't be Boston?"

"No. It ain't Boston."

"Nor Salem?"

"No."

"Nor Portsmouth?"

"That's right."

"Must be South Portland?"

"How'd-you *know!*"

Those identically phrased questions—how did you know? They were miles apart geographically and poles apart in inflection, phonetically and in import. The response of the up-country youth from Limerick, with the stress of his drawl laid on the *Haow,* evinced a state of shocked incredulity, whereas that of the along-shore lass from South Portland, with the emphasis on the *know,* was a token of genuine curiosity.

The spoken word in the State of Maine is a tender plant. Whether it is the enunciation of up-country, along shore, in the backwoods, or wherever you encounter it in Maine's sixteen spacious counties, it tends to wither on the vine when the attempt is made to transplant it. In print, any amount of it soon becomes unreadable; the reader gets lost in a bog of ill-spelt words that fail to evoke the tinkle of the genuine coin. Other modes of communication are equally disastrous. Of late, the tape recorder has produced a vast amount of mimicry, most of it bogus, which to one who knows the genu-*ine* article is positive torture.

There is only one true faith. Go there and listen. Don't, for God's sake, try to do it yourself. Just listen. Then the infinite variety, richness, realness, and humor will enchant you.

Take, for example, this anecdote of Uncle Ira, the past master of clambakes, whose function it was also to preside as master of ceremonies at celebrations in Portland's Cumberland Club. On the occasion in question, Uncle Ira is standing on one side of the capacious and brimming punch bowl. On the other side—there being a British man-of-war in port—there stands an admiral of the fleet, resplendent in full regalia.

Just beyond the bight of the circle around them are the Ricker boys, Jim and Ed, who have dropped down from Poland Springs, laying aside for this occasion their duties of bottling the only water that, in the day and eyes of the carriage trade, was potable outside these United States. What particularly distinguished the Ricker boys were their beards. They were iron-gray and of a prodigious breadth and length. Literally and without exaggeration, these splendid hairy appendages descended to dust their thighs. I who speak, once saw them.

Uncle Ira's keen eye catches them in the crowd:

"Jim! Ed! Come over here! Admiral—meet the Ricker boys. They've just swallered a pair of hosses, all 'cept their tails."

Then there are those whose use of words is an act of pure creation—like the old lady at Pine Point the night the schoolhouse burned. Said she:

"I ups and I ons with me boots, and I downs and I outs and I'm over there afore the flagpole fell."

In the same vein is the invention of her neighbor Bert Skillins of the verb "jellicks." Speaking once of the potent power of Scotch whiskey, he remarked to me:

"A feller's likely to jellicks it up and get drunk all over again."

Bert is a man who bulks large in my recollection. There was the greeting he would bellow at you, when on a hot August dog day, you appeared in the doorway to his kitchen:

"Set down and make your miserable life more comfortable."

Nor can I forget the explanation of his absence upon the occasion of one of these visits. He had gone, he later said, "up to Biddeford to doctor with a feller."

Then there was his response to my half-hearted apology for taking so much of his time:

"Se'still. My time is like that of a settin' hen."

His brawls with bureaucracy were epic. I once remarked

on the absence from the kitchen of a telephone. Perhaps now that he had retired from the business of hauling folks to the depot, he no longer had need of one—this was my suggestion. Well, no, that wasn't it. One day, it seemed, a repairman had appeared, and he would not tell Bert what he was up to.

"He set right here in my kitchen and he says to me: 'Mister, I'm getting my orders from headquarters.' Then he goes outside to his truck.

"Well, that fixed me. I goes up to that goddamned old box and I grabbed her. I give her a good yank and she come adrift from the wall with all her wires hanging. Then I marched right outdoors and hove her into his truck.

" 'There Mister,' I says, 'you're getting your orders from headquarters, right now.'

"And I ain't seen him nor his company since."

Then he would lean back in his old cane rocker with his eyes half closed, and you could see that in retrospect he was reliving that pleasurable moment.

Even better was his affair with the water company. Its side effects were more lasting and more visible. Bert had a lovely flower garden—nasturtiums that grew in a dory, tumbling their golden and orange blossoms out over the gunwales, hordes of red poppies, and a lovely stand of fragrant sweet peas. Come the dry spells of summer, they required watering. One day, the ubiquitous company man chanced by and espied Bert's hose. Then came the ultimate degradation—the installation of a meter.

Bert countered to this invasion of what he deemed his prerogative in character. Thenceforth, all around the little frame house, at the end of every gutter, at the foot of every downspout, there was to be seen a collection of hogsheads, barrels, buckets, wash and dishpans. To the end of his days, Bert watered his flowers with rain water and he never paid a nickel for the privilege to any goddamned water company.

I recall once a discussion with Bert during the days of the depression, on that perennial topic, the state of the economy. We were suddenly interrupted by an irrelevant, yet apt query on the part of my young son, who broke in with the question whether Prouts Neck was an island.

Bert rose nicely to this:

"T 'wunt be long before 'tis," he said, "if this administration stays in."

Then, turning to me, he asked:

"Where they going to git all the money to pay for all this?"

"Taxation," I said. "Right out of your pocket and mine."

"Well," says Bert, "they'll have to dredge awful deep down into my paw-kit and they won't fetch up nawthin' but a clam."

Bert had a neighbor who in his view was a mean man— "the meanest man" he had ever known. In the idiom of the State of Maine, this phrase carries a special connotation. Coupled with the characteristics commonly associated with the word is a degree of obstinacy that calls into use the words ornery and cross-grained.

"Why, you take it on cold nights. He'll come over and set in my kitchen to keep warm so as not to have to burn his own wood. He's a great hand to knit and he always brings his knitting. T'other night he was knittin' away and he run out of wool. Do you think that feller went and got him some more wool? No, sir! He jest kept right on knittin'."

Here Bert would simulate the act with his fingers, and you could almost hear the steel needles click.

"I was up to Bath the other morning . . ."

A friend of mine down alongside the Kennebec was speaking, and my ears were assaulted by the manner in which he pronounced the word *Bath*. He sort of spat it out like a small explosion; it sounded like the blat of a sick sheep—*Ba-a-th*.

But to get on with his tale. It was the morning of the

Fourth of July, he said, and there was a fair fresh breeze blowing up off the Kennebec. He was looking for a newsstand, wanted to get the papers and see how the Russians was getting along changing the palace guard. Well, he finally fetched up in a stationery shop, where there was a tall, sleepy-looking feller tending store. He got himself a Boston paper and was reading the headlines to satisfy himself that that was the paper he wanted, when this sleepy-looking feller come up and he says:

"Was you aimin' ter buy that paper?"

"Why?"

"Well, some aims to and some aims not to, an' I jest thought I'd find out which 't'was.

So my friend gave him the change and then he said: "Seems like them Russians can't keep the peace amongst themselves nohow."

"Let alone with anybody else," says this character.

"He warn't the only character that morning in *Ba-a-th*"— my friend continued his story. "My next port of call was a grocery. Looking fer soapflakes for my missus, and I got me into a dingy-looking hole that was half down cellar. Only there didn't seem to be nobody anywheres round. So I bangs on the counter. Then pretty soon she come down.

"I never did see such a woman. She had iron-gray hair and mad black eyes that was just snapping and a face like an outcropping of granite in a pasture. And, man dear, was she loaded fer bear? She was acussing like a steam engine puffing—about that goddamned son-of-a-bitch of a good fer nuthin', worthless bastard of a husband of hers that was supposed to be tending store like she told him to, and instead of that he was out wandering all over the streets of *Ba-a-th*.

"Well, pretty soon in come a quiet little feller. Must have been her husband because she went off muttering like a thunder gust passing to leeward, and then I got my soapflakes off of him. Now, that there woman, she never paid me one mite of heed. She just kept cussing her husband and he was real soft-spoken. I suppose that's the way they do business in *Ba-a-th.*

"But that ain't all. Now you hear this. When I was going down along the Kennebec I drops into a service station and while the feller is filling me up, I says to him: "How's business, Bub?'

" 'Rotten,' he says. 'And what's more, I like it. Seems like it ain't been so peaceful round here as 'tis today since before the last war.'

"Now I tell ye, this *Ba-a-th,* Maine's quite a place for characters."

And that afternoon my friend caught up with another one. We were all having cocktails, a large party, when the telephone rang. My friend went to answer it, and when after a bit he came back, you could see that he was bursting with something.

"Come on Tom, boy, let's have it."

"Well, this character on the other end of the phone, he says to me, is this 304, and I says no—it's 403.

" 'God,' says this feller, 'arse end to on the telephone.' "

Down here, off the mouth of the Kennebec is where you encounter fog—real fog. Here are to be heard such tales as that of the lightkeeper on Seguin Island who shot a moose last fall as he came out of the surf after swimming out through the fog, coming to the call of the foghorn. "Thick o' fog" is the phrase you hear, unless you are greeted thus:

"Nice and fog-*gay,* ain't it? Yes, sir, it's pretty thick today, but this ain't a patch on what 't'was last week. Why last Monday I hired a Frenchman to shingle my barn and come noontime, when I went up to fetch him fer dinner, I couldn't see the feller fer shucks. I could hear his hammer tapping and so I folleyed out long the ridgepole. And, by God, that little feller had shingled hisself forty feet right out in-th'-fog."

. . .

This fellow would always pair this yarn off with one about death or a coffin—like this:

It seems they were putting a new road through a small town way up in Waldo County, and as luck would have it, the thing knocked off the corner of the town graveyard. First thing the fellow running the bulldozer knows, a coffin has come adrift and is setting with the lid askew right out in front of his blade. Well, the name plate on it was the same as the storekeeper's, and so they sent for him to come up and identify the remains. It was his grandmother, and afterwards somebody asks him:

"Well, Enoch, how'd she look?"

"Not too rugged," says Enoch.

Then, if this yarn takes in real good style, he is ready with another, about the resurrection:

They was having a prayer meeting and there was a man had come all the way from Woonsocket to preach. He was a real spellbinder, full of fire and brimstone, and he got them all shook up. When he came to the end of his preaching, he give the call to hit the sawdust trail. He swings his arm out round in front of him and he says:

"All them that's heeded the call o' the Lord and expects to go to heaven, rise up."

And they all riz up, saving one lone man in the front row right down under the pulpit. So this preacher, he levels a long bony finger at this feller and he says:

"Here's a man that ain't heeded the call o' the Lord. Ain't you going to tell us, Mister, where you're aiming to go?"

Then this man—he was a little feller—he riz up and let the spellbinder have it.

"I'm aiming," says he, "to stay right here in the State o' Maine."

. . .

In the watershed of the Penobscot there is still another strata in the culture of the State of Maine. This is evidenced by a word often encountered and in good standing along the banks of the Penobscot—a *Kennebecker*. It came about in this fashion. In the early days of lumbering, before the Civil War, an occasion arose for the importation of some lumberers, as they were then called, from over on the Kennebec. These characters appeared in the lumber camps on the West Branch carrying their possessions in carpetbags. The Penobscot boys, for whom a gunnysack sufficed for the purpose, promptly dubbed these gaily colored receptables—Kennebeckers. And from that day to this, any sort of handbag or valise is known in the Penobscot country as a *Kennebecker*.

The hallmark of the humor of the Penobscot man is understatement, often uttered between compressed lips and tinctured with a bit of the grim. It is to be seen in the everyday survivals of the parlance of the logger and the river driver, who spoke of *twitching* logs out of the woods. And when a recalcitrant log *gilpoked* against the bank, they always aimed to *pick* the resultant log jam. In like manner, when logs were *drug* over the tops of those that had wedged into a logan or a bend in the stream, the operation was known as *shingling logs*.

One of the stories current in the Penobscot country touches the adventure of an excessively large woman, long a maiden, who took to husband an excessively small man, so small, it would always be said, he could hide behind a birch sapling. They were dirt poor, could not afford a honeymoon, and the morning after the wedding, the bride, who was a great housekeeper, was seen outside in the yard.

The yard was full of furniture, all stacked around, and she was housecleaning. She was beating rugs and sweeping off the chairs. The dust was flying and she was going it great guns. About this time the town clerk, who had sold them their marriage license the day before, come along. She was

shaking out the blankets and sheets, and he hollers at her:
"What you doing, Amy? You looking for Elmer?"

I well remember one of Allie Ayer's tales. It was a warm
August afternoon up at Passadumkeag. Allie was sitting in
the doorway of his woodshed with his feet crossed, his stubby
fingers laced and clasping his paunch, and he was peering
at me out from under the pulled-down brim of his old battered felt hat. He was talking of the old days on the East
Branch drive.

"In them days the food was terrible. We was right in the
middle of a brook drive up on Trout Brook. A brook drive's
the hardest kind of work. You were out on the drive from
breaking daylight till away past dark. The work never
stopped, never for a minute. There was a stand-by crew all
night watching out for jams, and a man never knowed when
he was going to be hauled out of his bunk to go and pick one.

"And all that company give us to eat was one meal, beans
—and the next meal, codfish. Then beans, then codfish.
Beans and codfish. If they ever was to vary it, they give us
the codfish first and then the beans.

"Well, anyway, this had been going on for days, and the
days was stretching out into weeks when one morning the
cookee dredged up the last bean in the barrel. And from
then on we et codfish, and more codfish, and nothing but
codfish.

"After about five days of this nothing but codfish, my bunk
mate, Old Jake, he rared up like a old hoss and says he's going to quit. So he goes up to the walking boss and he says:

" 'Ed, I want my time. I'm going to quit.'

" 'Why, you can't do that on me, Jake,' says the walking
boss, 'just when I'm short of hands and right at the peak of
this here brook drive. Git your cantdog man, and git back on
the job.'

" 'No sir!' says Jake, 'I'm quitting. It's that there codfish,

Ed. I've et so goddamned much of that goddamned cod-fish, by God, I'm going up to the head of Trout Brook and SPAWN.' "

Of course, Allie added, he didn't do any such thing. He wasn't going to quit. That was just old Jake's way of kicking about the grub, and the walking boss, he got it all right. The very next day they was a whole side of beef come into that camp from Millinocket.

And so it goes. The tales that have been recounted here are limited to but a few locales. Wherever you go in the State of Maine, it will pay you to take a bit of time off and sit down with people, if it's only to pass the time of day, always provided you are the one who does the listening.

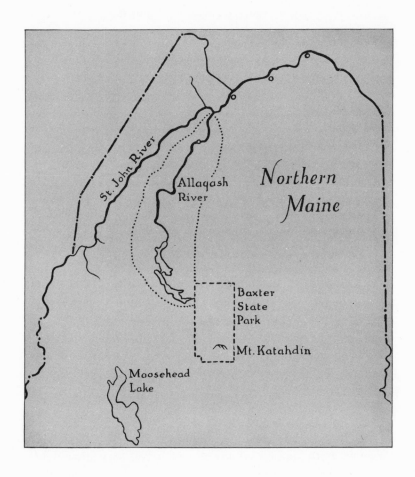

# The Proposed Allagash
# National Riverway

"WHAT IS MOST STRIKING in the Maine wilderness is the continuousness of the forest, with fewer open intervals or glades than you had imagined. Except the few burnt lands, the narrow intervals on the rivers, the bare tops of the high mountains, and the lakes and streams, the forest is uninterrupted. It is even more grim and wild than you had anticipated, a damp and intricate wilderness, in the spring everywhere wet and miry. The aspect of the country, indeed, is universally stern and savage, excepting the distant views of the forest from hills, and the lake prospects, which are mild and civilizing in a degree.

"The lakes are something which you are unprepared for; they lie up so high, exposed to the light, and the forest is diminished to a fine fringe on their edges, with here and there a blue mountain, like amethyst jewels set around some jewel of the first water,—so anterior, so superior, to all the changes that are to take place on their shores, even now civil and refined, and fair as they can ever be. These are not the artificial forests of an English king,—a royal preserve merely. Here prevail no forest laws but those of nature. The aborigines have never been dispossessed, nor nature disforested.

"It is a country full of evergreen trees, of mossy silver birches and watery maples, the ground dotted with insipid small, red berries, and strewn with damp and moss-grown rocks,—a country diversified with innumerable lakes and rapid streams, peopled with trout and various species of *leucisci*, with salmon, shad, and pickerel, and other fishes; the forest resounding at rare intervals with the note of the chickadee, the blue jay, and the woodpecker, the scream of the fish hawk and the eagle, the laugh of the loon, and the whistle of ducks along the solitary stream; at night, with the hooting of owls and howling of wolves; in summer swarming with myriads of black flies and mosquitoes, more formidable than wolves to the white man. Such is the home of the moose, the bear, the caribou, the wolf, the beaver and the Indian."

The words are Thoreau's—written, their context suggests, in the fall of 1846, not long after his ascent of Mt. Ktaadn. The observations and reflections with which he then concluded the account of his excursion to Ktaadn have a singular significance today. He had been reminded by his journey, he said, "how exceedingly new this country still is. You have only to travel for a few days into the interior and back parts even of many of the old States to come to that very America which the Northmen, and Cabot, and Gosnold, and Smith, and Raleigh visited."

The America of his time, he pointed out, was still unsettled and unexplored. "We have advanced by leaps to the Pacific, and left many a lesser Oregon and California unexplored behind us." Then he refers to the city of Bangor, at the head of navigation on the Penobscot for vessels of the largest class, as "a star on the edge of night," and concludes:

"Twelve miles in the rear, twelve miles of railroad, are Orono and the Indian Island, the home of the Penobscot tribe, and then commence the batteau and the canoe, and the military road; and sixty miles above, the country is virtually unmapped and unexplored, and there still waves the virgin forest of the New World."

The changes in the span of more than a century have been considerable. But the essence of what Thoreau saw and so deeply sensed and experienced has survived. The forest of the New World is still there. The Maine woods are still wild. They are still a wilderness.

The native caribou has gone. So has the wolf. The virginity of the timber has long since been despoiled. Settlement has encroached, compacting the woods, but when you reach them, the forest stretches to great distances, mysterious and uninterrupted still.

It is the settlement of the country that particularly strikes the traveler. In 1846, at the confluence of the East and the West Branch, Thoreau found a single house; eleven years later, on coming down the East Branch, he found "quite a village with sawmills and a store." Today, Medway has 1,266 inhabitants. Above there, when ascending the West Branch, Thoreau, who was "particular to give the names of the settlers and the distances"—such information being "of no little consequence to those who may have occasion to travel this way"—had recorded only four houses. The last of these was "old Fowlers" on the carry between Millinocket Stream and Quakish Lake. This was used to portage around the Grand Falls on the West Branch. Today it is the site of the paper-mill town of Millinocket.

The other significant thing today is the fundamental and radical change in the access to this wild country of mountains and forest, lakes and streams. On his last excursion in the Maine woods in 1857, Thoreau made a circuit of Ktaadn —"to the Allagash Lakes, by way of Moosehead and return by the East Branch." In so doing, he carried across the height of land between the watersheds of the Penobscot and the Allagash on Mud Pond Carry. This had been the traditional route of the Indian. Sixty-five years later, when I first made the famed river trip down the Allagash, this same route was still the only feasible one into these wild and remote waters. Then, in 1940, it is significant that when I again visited the headwaters of the Allagash, it was possible to drive from Greenville around the west shore of Moosehead Lake and through the woods, finally to put our canoe in the waters of Caucomgomac Lake, in order then to paddle and portage over into Little Allagash Lake and thence down into Chamberlain.

Now, look what can be done today. A road runs into Telos Lake. Another road connects Churchill Lake with the outside world. And farther down the course of the Allagash River, a third road gives access to the thoroughfare connecting Long Lake and Umsaskis Lake. A fourth ascends the west bank of the river for a considerable distance from its mouth. These roads, which are private roads constructed by the paper companies, are by their permission open to the public. Then also there is the access by air; floatplanes land on the lakes in all seasons, bringing in hunters and fishermen.

What are the consequences? Simply these. Today in these once remote fastnesses, the roar of the motor competes with the liquid notes of the whitethroat, the lonely ululations of the loon, the sharp scream of the fish hawk, and the shrill snort of the deer. Cottages and cabins are beginning to dot the shores of this unique wilderness waterway. And then there are the sporting camps, several of which are now scattered here and there on its wooded shores.

The trend is unmistakable. If it is continued, it will result in the commercialization of this wilderness waterway, and its transformation into a resort area. This would mean its irretrievable loss. Moreover, the destruction of the Allagash has been threatened in yet another way. There is the risk that it will be, in the vernacular of the Maine woods, "flowed out." A dam for public power purposes, proposed to be erected at the Rankin Rapids just above the mouth of the river, would transform it from Churchill Lake on down into another lake. This danger looms at every session of the Maine Legislature in the form of bills introduced on behalf of private power interests to authorize the construction of similar dams.

The suggestion of the Rankin Rapids dam was made by an International Joint Commission appointed to restudy the feasibility of the tidal power project in Passamaquoddy Bay. The dam was conceived as a necessary complement to the harnessing of the tides. The report of the Commission in April 1961 was adverse to the project, and in May, President Kennedy requested the Secretary of the Interior to review it. Concurrent with these developments, the Department of the

Interior released a pamphlet outlining a plan for a proposed Allagash national recreation area, the publication of which had been financed by private funds.

The conjunction of these events projected the fate of the Allagash into a wide forum as a problem of national concern. During the next two years, public discussion and official investigation were concurrent. Then, in July 1963, coincident with the report of the Secretary of the Interior to President Kennedy on the Passamaquoddy project, the Department issued its report on the proposed Allagash National Riverway and recommended its creation by an act of Congress. Meanwhile, the Legislature of Maine declared it to be the policy of the state "to provide for the preservation of the natural beauty and wilderness character of the Allagash River Watercourse while retaining the natural economic resources of the area." There was created an Allagash River Authority, which is charged with certain responsibilities toward that end. Cutting across this, of course, are the various proposals that are urged at each session of the Legislature on behalf of private power projects.

At this writing, that is where the matter stands. That the Allagash should remain a wild, free-running stream, nobody disputes save the private power people. This is the consensus. Disagreement arises when you approach the question of how this is to be achieved, or more specifically, on who is to call the turns with respect to its future use. Shall it be the owners of the land, or the State of Maine, or the Nation? This is a controversial political issue and, as the reader may well surmise, a very hot one.

The owners are a compact group. Upwards of eighty percent of the land involved in the national proposal is owned by three families and two large paper companies, the Great Northern Paper Company and the International Paper Company. On their behalf it is stoutly asserted, and plausibly maintained, that they have been providing the public with adequate recreational facilities in this neck of the Maine woods ever since the day Mr. Thoreau went through it in a birch. And, as they say in Maine, they purpose to go right on doing so.

It is ironic that their long-standing policy of allowing the public access, now that their roads have rendered access so simple, is exactly what has given rise to the present issue. Moreover, when there is coupled with this the standing practice of leasing sites on the lakes and streams for private cottages and commercial sporting camps, it is difficult, for this writer at any rate, to foresee any ultimate result other than the transformation of the famed Allagash waterway into a resort area—which God forbid.

The act creating the Allagash River Authority for the State of Maine contemplates the making of a survey of the region, the formulation of a program of land preservation, and the development of a plan for its use and administration as a conservation area. The Authority was directed to seek and present to the next Legislature, in 1965, agreements between the landowners and the state in furtherance of these ends. The officials charged with the responsibility of the Authority are the Forest Commissioner, the Director of State Parks, the Commissioner of Inland Fisheries and Game, the Director of the School of Forestry at the University of Maine, and the Attorney General, who is chairman.

There the matter rests. As yet no inkling of the state program has been made public, and no report is anticipated until the end of 1964. Until the particulars of whatever plan is proposed on behalf of the State of Maine become known, it would seem to be premature to take a final position.

The recommendations for Congressional action made by the Secretary of the Interior are a two-pronged affair. In the first place, in his report on the Passamaquoddy Tidal Project the Secretary recommended, in respect of the power development on the upper St. John, that instead of a dam on the

Allagash at the Rankin Rapids, one should be constructed on the St. John River upstream from its confluence with the Allagash, thereby preserving "in its entirety the free flowing nature of the Allagash River."

What is envisaged for preservation as the Riverway is this. First, starting with Telos, there is the chain of four connected lakes that at the foot of Churchill empty into the Allagash, and then the course of the river to below Allagash Falls. In addition, there would be included the lakes, ponds, and streams that are the essential tributary waters of the river—three lakes and several streams on the west, some eighteen-odd on the east, and the Mud Pond to the south. These tributary waters are essential not only for their water but because they provide spawning beds and natural nurseries for *Salvelinus fontinalis* and *Cristivomer namaycush*— the familiar squaretail, or brook trout, and the togue or lake trout—and in some instances furnish excellent habitat for waterfowl. All of these waters would be bounded on their shores by an inviolable strip of woods ranging in width from not less than four hundred feet to half a mile. Beyond these limits, there is contemplated the negotiation of scenic easements of half a mile in depth for an agreed fee. These would permit such use of the land, which means lumbering, as would not mar the scenic beauty of the forest as viewed from the water.

How would these thus protected wild waters be used? How managed? The intention is to confine their use primarily to canoemen, who with pole and paddle will seek to travel on these waters as the Indian once did, and as the woodsmen and the sportsmen of the past have done. Also contemplated is the fishing, hunting, and cruising the woods that have always been naturally associated with the traditional river trip in the Maine woods. The administration of the area would be entrusted by the Department of the Interior to the National Park Service. And it is devoutly to be hoped that experienced woodsmen of the State of Maine would be employed, and that there would be cooperation in full measure with the long-established professional public services of the state.

These aims and methods will involve of necessity certain exclusions—notably the motorboat, the airplane, and the outboard motor. My own view is that these should not be permitted within the area, even for administrative purposes. Keep it wild, for God's sake, keep it wild. Also involved would be the liquidation immediately of all commercial camps and activities, the termination of any flowage rights within the area, and the removal ultimately of any private camps and cottages. The blocking and abandonment of all roads within and into the area is contemplated, with three exceptions. These are the roads that lead to Telos Lake, to the Umsaskis-Long Lake thoroughfare, and to Allagash Falls. There canoes, equipment, and supplies could be procured, preferably outside the area. And finally it is significant that, if overnight accommodations prove necessary, these likewise are to be provided outside the limits of the Riverway.

Such in essence is the proposed plan for the Allagash National Riverway.

Would Mr. Thoreau have approved? Let his own words, written on his return from his excursion "a-moose-hunting" on the West Branch, give his answer:

"The kings of England formerly had their forests 'to hold the king's game,' for sport or food, sometimes destroying villages to create or extend them; and I think that they were impelled by a true instinct. Why should not we, who have renounced the king's authority, have our national preserves, where no villages need be destroyed, in which the bear and panther and some even of the hunter race, may still exist, and not be 'civilized off the face of the earth,'—our forests, not to hold the king's game merely, but to hold and preserve the king himself also, the lord of creation—not for idle sport or food, but for inspiration and our own true recreation? Or shall we, like the villeins, grub them all up, poaching on our own national domains?"

Once the plan of the Maine Allagash River Authority is published and its particulars become known, this issue should be ripe for decision. It is an issue of great significance nationally as well as locally. For just as the act authorizing the creation of the Cape Cod National Seashore has set a valuable precedent for the preservation of the nation's beaches on both coasts and in the Gulf, so likewise an act creating the Allagash National Riverway, or the implementation of an adequate State of Maine plan, may well be the bellwether for the similar preservation of the watersheds of still free-flowing streams in other parts of the country. Such opportunities the nation will miss at its peril—at the dangerous risk of not having adequate recreational resources for the fast-growing urban multitudes that will be the inevitable earmark of the future.

Of great significance in the Maine scene is the fact that around Telos Lake the southern end of the proposed Riverway would border on the westerly bound of Baxter State Park. This great wooded and mountainous area, which includes Mt. Ktaadn and now comprises over two hundred thousand acres, is one of the glories of the State of Maine—the generous gift within the span of a generation of a former governor, an imaginative, farsighted man, the Honorable Percival P. Baxter. Significant, too, are the words in which the purpose of this idealistic public trust is stated:

"Forever to be held by the State of Maine in trust for public park, public forest, public recreational purposes, and scientific forestry, the same also forever shall be held in its natural wild state and except for a small area forever shall be held as a sanctuary for wild beasts and birds."

Baxter State Park has been well described by Stewart L.

Udall in his book *The Quiet Crisis* as "the most majestic state park in the nation."

There are other public parks in the state. The federal government maintains nearly one hundred thousand acres in three widely separate locations—the Acadia National Park in the environs of Mt. Desert, the Moosehorn National Wildlife Refuge down east in Washington County, and over on the western edge of the state, the White Mountain National Forest, which extends for several miles into the depth of Oxford County. In addition to the magnificent wild area of Ktaadn, the state also has about eleven thousand acres in some twenty-two scattered locations comprising both parks and historic sites, thirteen in the interior and nine on the coast.

This system is capable of great expansion. The State of Maine, certainly more than any other New England state and perhaps more than any other state on the Atlantic seaboard, stands to profit from the swiftly expanding need for areas devoted to public recreation. Maine is abundantly wealthy in wild woodlands and lakes, streams and ponds, in addition to a long serrated coastline. With the passage by the Congress of the pending Land and Water Conservation Fund Act, which provides for matched funds for the acquisition of land and water areas for public recreation, a great opportunity for expansion will come into existence. It is to be hoped that the state, under the guidance and leadership of its excellent Park Commission, will take full advantage of it.

Considerable groundwork has already been done. In 1954 the National Park Service, with the aid of private funds, undertook an intensive survey of the three great coastlines of the nation—the Atlantic, the Pacific, and the Gulf Coast—in order to determine what areas should be conserved not only for public recreation but as historical or natural sanctuaries. This survey paved the way for the creation of the Cape Cod

National Seashore as well as for the preservation of the Point Reyes area in California.

On the coast of Maine two areas were judged to deserve the highest priority for acquisition and conservation by a public agency. One of these is Crescent Beach, which fronts the ocean on what has been referred to in these pages as the Cape Shore. The other, identified in the survey as the Popham–St. John area, includes the easterly end of Small Point Beach, which I describe in the chapter of that name.

In any discussion of public recreation it is well to keep in mind the dual meaning of the word *recreation*. Indeed, it may be said to have a primary and a secondary meaning, a higher and a lower connotation. As ordinarily used, the verb *recreate* and the noun *recreation* are best fitted by the dictionary meaning—to refresh or be refreshed after wearying toil or anxiety. In this sense, *recreation* encompasses all the various diversionary activities of a vacation away and aside from a man's calling.

But the word has a far deeper meaning in a much higher context. And it is only when you introduce a hyphen into it, thus—*re-create* and *re-creation*—that its true and higher meaning comes to the fore and is restored to its rightful primacy. For the word derives from the Latin *creare*—to create —and when it is prefixed by *re,* it means "to create anew." This is its primary meaning.

Hence, in the context of man's relation to his ecology, the act of recreation is a creative one.

When with pole and paddle, canoe and gear, I set forth to go down the Allagash, or when barefoot I walk the sands of Small Point Beach following, between the dunes and the sea, the escalloped lines of the eternal tides, there is always and ever anew a re-creation of myself and of my relation to the universe. This creative experience is not a thing peculiar to me; it is common to all mankind. But in the exposure of an American to the wilderness, the wilderness of his native land, there *is* something unique. This is the truly precious part of our American heritage—our vanishing wildness and wilderness—and segments of it should be preserved, no matter what the cost. For, in large measure, exposure to it is what has made Americans what they are.

In this context, the significance of the Allagash country and of the easterly end of Small Point Beach is their relative inaccessibility. The former is barred, aside from the recent breakthrough of bulldozed roads, by mountains and forest; the other is encompassed by a granite mountain, by marshes and two salt streams. It is this that makes their preservation *in their natural state* at once so desirable and so feasible.

The projection of existing trends by competent authority leads to the forecast that within a few short years the six-hundred-mile stretch of the Atlantic seaboard from the western end of the coast of Maine to the mouth of the Potomac will be a long, connected urban and suburban area, and that it will contain a fifth of the population of the country. The need for the preservation of areas of wildness and wilderness is imperative. For with every snort of the ubiquitous bulldozer, the tocsin of the destruction of our countryside is sounding, and the tide of time is running out.

# A NOTE ON THE TYPE

THE TEXT of this book was set in a typeface called *Primer,* designed by RUDOLPH RUZICKA for the Mergenthaler Linotype Company and first made available in 1949. Primer, a modified modern face based on Century broadface was designed with a view to greatest legibility in the use of today's methods of composition and printing.

Primer is Ruzicka's third typeface. In 1940 he designed Fairfield, and in 1947 Fairfield Medium, both for the Mergenthaler Linotype Company.

Ruzicka was born in Bohemia in 1883 and came to the United States at the age of eleven. He attended public schools in Chicago and later the Chicago Art Institute. During his long career he has been a wood engraver, etcher, cartographer, and book designer. For many years he was associated with Daniel Berkeley Updike and produced the annual keepsakes for The Merrymount Press from 1911 until 1941.

Ruzicka has been honored by many distinguished organizations, and in 1936 he was awarded the gold medal of the American Institute of Graphic Arts. From his home in New Hampshire Ruzicka continues to be active in the graphic arts.

*Composition and binding by H. Wolff, New York*
*Offset Lithography by*
*Murray Printing Co., Forge Village, Mass.*
*Typography and binding design by*
HERBERT H. JOHNSON